MEDITATION AND THE CLASSROOM

SUNY SERIES IN RELIGIOUS STUDIES
Harold Coward, editor

Meditation
and the
Classroom

CONTEMPLATIVE PEDAGOGY
FOR RELIGIOUS STUDIES

Edited by
Judith Simmer-Brown
and
Fran Grace

Cover photo courtesy of iStockphoto.com/Dean Mitchell Photography

Published by State University of New York Press, Albany

©2011 State University of New York Press

For information, contact State University of New York Press, Albany, NY
www.sunypress.edu

Production by Diane Ganeles
Marketing by Michael Campochiaro

Library of Congress Cataloging-in-Publication Data

Meditation and the classroom : contemplative pedagogy for religious studies / edited by
Judith Simmer-Brown and Fran Grace.
    p. cm. — (SUNY series in religious studies)
Includes bibliographical references and index.
ISBN 978-1-4384-3787-3 (hc. : alk. paper)
ISBN 978-1-4384-3788-0 (pbk. : alk. paper)
1. Meditation—Study and teaching. 2. Religion—Study and teaching. I. Simmer-
Brown, Judith. II. Grace, Fran.
BL627.M397 2011
204'.35—dc22

                                                          2011004018

                    10 9 8 7 6 5 4 3 2 1

CONTENTS

VI.
CONCLUSION: DOES IT WORK? EVALUATIONS FROM OUR STUDENTS

Acknowledgments

JUDITH SIMMER-BROWN: It has long been an irony that books appear to be authored by individuals, when every single one, whether an edited collection such as this or an independent project, is the result of interdependence. David Bohm calls it "the implicate order" that is always dynamic and unfolding. I have had the good fortune to be part of a community of collaborators in practice, education, and life, and continue to grow and change as a result of their authentic presence, kindness, and constantly incisive feedback. Thanks to all of them, especially Richard Brown, my husband, colleague, and best friend; in addition, I have received invaluable assistance in this project from Naropa colleagues Tom Coburn, Susan Burggraf, Gaylon Ferguson, Dale Asrael, Reed Bye, Barbara Dilley, Lee Worley, Mark Miller, Zoe Avstreih, and my graduate assistant, T. J. DeZauche. Sakyong Mipham, Rinpoche, and his father, Chögyam Trungpa, Rinpoche, have never swayed from the conviction that we can build a diverse, contemplative, enlightened society when we have transformed our education to affirm the basic goodness of every person; their inspiration sustains me daily.

FRAN GRACE: In her contemplative masterpiece, St. Teresa of Avila advises: "Do that which best stirs you to love" (*Interior Castle* 4.1.7, trans. E. Allison Peers). I am blessed to do what I love with people I love. Deep and abiding gratitude goes, first of all, to my present and former students for their courage, inspiration, and affection. May this book honor you and your insights through meditation. Thanks also are due to my University of Redlands colleagues whose support has energized and expanded me in ways too numerous to name but hopefully discernible to you: Bill Huntley, Emily Culpepper, Julius Bailey, Karen Derris, Lillian Larsen, John Walsh, Lorenzo Garbo, Nancy Carrick, and Barbara Morris. For nurturance of an inner sanctum in the midst of day-to-day demands, thanks to Donna L. Robinson. To Dr. David R. and Susan Hawkins, gratitude beyond words.

INTRODUCTION

JUDITH SIMMER-BROWN AND FRAN GRACE

BEGINNING WITH THE END

We begin this book by telling you how it ends. The final section gives detailed reflections from our students about their experience with "meditation in the classroom." Students certify that meditation benefits them keenly, both in their academic work and as a lifelong skill. Their learning assessments through the years have confirmed over and over again that meditation refines the mind and hones the heart. As a teaching method, we know it works.

Yet, we also know that the prospect of meditation in the classroom produces concern for some educators who fear that contemplative methods may be intrusive and coercive to students at worst, or simply a waste of time at best. A book like this must speak to the cautions of our colleagues, even as it must remain true to the delight of our students. Certainly, we are well versed in the concerns raised against the use of meditation in the classroom, because we have had to resolve such questions within our own minds. This collection of essays represents a culmination of pedagogical self-examination and conversations among us that, in the case of some contributors, span nearly three decades.

This book is the first of its kind as a resource on meditation in the college classroom. Although meditation, mindfulness, and contemplative practices boast a pervasive presence in our culture, and although the prevailing literature on liberal education emphasizes the importance of the inner life, there has been little academic leadership to guide such ventures into the interior.

The twenty-five contributors to this book have risen to the challenges of articulation, reflection, and praxis. While in agreement as to the value of meditation in the classroom, our pedagogical practices and personal worldviews offer an enlightening diversity. We come from a variety of institutional contexts, including state universities, private liberal arts institutions, and traditional church-related colleges. Some of the authors have been using contemplative pedagogy for decades, and some for little more than a year. Many of the authors cultivate a contemplative lifestyle, and for some, this self-cultivation takes place in the context of a religious tradition or spiritual community. For others, there is no specific religious identity or spiritual practice. We, as the two editors of this volume, exemplify the book's diversity.

Judith has been a visionary voice in the nation-wide contemplative education movement for the last three decades from her institutional base at Naropa University, a nonsectarian, Buddhist-inspired private college and graduate school. She has been a major contributor to the articulation of an ethic of pluralism for interreligious dialogue in the classroom.[1] She is one of the team leaders with the Center for the Advancement of Contemplative Education (CACE) at Naropa. In 2007, she designed and directed, with a group of her academic colleagues, Naropa's first annual seminar on contemplative teaching for university faculty from diverse disciplines across the country. Judith's training and work as a scholar-practitioner align principally with Indo-Tibetan Buddhism. She is on the steering committee of the Buddhist Critical-Constructive Reflection Group in the American Academy of Religion, and she served for a decade on the board of the Society for Buddhist-Christian Studies.

Fran is a mid-career scholar-practitioner in a secular university community. In 2004, she underwent a profound inner shift that led her to develop contemplative pedagogies after a decade of fairly traditional teaching. In 2007, her university opened its Meditation Room, a spacious classroom equipped with meditation cushions and yoga mats, and she currently teaches all of her classes in this space dedicated for interior learning. Although her original training as a scholar and practitioner took place within the Christian tradition, she is now more integrative than tradition specific in her contemplative approach and research. She has served as a co-chair of the Teaching Religion section within the American Academy of Religion and as a workshop facilitator for the Wabash Center for Teaching and Learning in Theology and Religion.

As the reader will see, there is no single contemplative pedagogy and no single prototype of the contemplative professor. With such a wide range of institutional settings and individual commitments expressed in this book, how could there be a single pedagogical way? But, as contributors, we do agree on one thing: there is a singular place for meditation in the classroom.

We came to this conclusion cautiously. Although familiar with the benefits of meditation through our own practice and studies of recent scientific research, we needed to ask whether the benefits of meditation were directly relevant to the students' development as "liberal artists." For, as we know, there are many beneficial human explorations that have no place in a classroom. Our years of collecting and analyzing qualitative data from contemplative methods have brought us to the conclusion that meditation is not only a beneficial human endeavor, but also a fulfillment of the aims and purposes of liberal education.

INTERIORITY AND LIBERAL EDUCATION

In 2007, the Association of American Colleges and Universities (AAC&U) published *College Learning for the New Global Century*, a comprehensive analysis of higher education that outlines "Essential Learning Outcomes" such as "inquiry and analysis," "critical and creative thinking," "personal and social responsibility," "ethical reasoning and action," and the "foundation and skills for lifelong learning."[2] These current learning outcomes are congruent with earlier documents. For example, *The Great Conversation: The Substance of a Liberal Education* (1952) proposed that liberal education aimed to foster "excellence, both private and public," and to "train the mind."[3]

At the heart of such documents is the importance of interior accomplishments as an outcome of liberal education. The *College Learning for the New Global Century* authors propose that it is precisely the inner learning that distinguishes "liberal" education from "instrumental" education:

> Throughout history, liberal education—especially the arts and humanities—has been a constant resource not just for civic life but for the inner life of self-discovery, values, moral inspiration, spiritual quests and solace, and the deep pleasures of encountering beauty, insight, and expressive power. Ultimately, it is this dimension—serious engagement with questions of values, principles, and larger meanings—that marks the difference between instrumental learning and liberal learning.[4]

As to specific interior qualities that befit a "liberal artist," the recent AAC&U document mentions "inner fortitude, self-knowledge, and personal renewal," and it underscores "empathy, the ability to care about and even identify with perspectives and circumstances other than one's own." Ultimately, the AAC&U proposes a "liberating" college education.[5] Throughout human history, contemplative process has been valued as one of the foremost means of liberation. Why is that?

First-person methodologies such as meditation train students to a subtle mastery of mind. For this reason, such methodologies certainly appear to fulfill the Socratic reflection that "The unexamined life is not worth living." What does "the examined life" entail? Martha Nussbaum suggests that self-examination sparks the liberation of mind that makes possible a "cultivation of humanity":

When we ask about the relationship of a liberal education to citizenship, we are asking a question with a long history in the Western philosophical tradition. We are drawing on Socrates' concept of "the examined life," on Aristotle's notions of reflective citizenship, and above all on Greek and Roman Stoic notions of an education that is "liberal" in that it liberates the mind from bondage of habit and custom, producing people who can function with sensitivity and alertness as citizens of the whole world. This is what Seneca means by the cultivation of humanity.[6]

Although not all of our contributors use meditation *per se* in the classroom, they have developed a range of contemplative teaching methods that fulfill the classical aims of liberal education. Each professor's contemplative pedagogy is based on his or her particular institutional setting, student population, personal background, and subject matter.

MEDITATION AND CONTEMPLATIVE EDUCATION

Since the 1990s, as professors across the spectrum of academic disciplines are exploring ways of integrating meditation into their course curricula, a movement called "contemplative education" has become increasingly popular in American universities.[7] The American Council of Learned Societies (ACLS), in partnership with the Fetzer Institute, has awarded over one hundred Contemplative Practice and Teaching Fellowships during the last decade. These Fellows have designed and implemented contemplative-based courses in literature, religious studies, art, music, math, environmental studies, and history, in over eighty different institutions. Fellowships have also been granted to institutions for the establishment of programs in contemplative studies.

Publications about contemplative education have appeared in the *Chronicle of Higher Education*, the *Teacher's College Record*, the *New York Times* (November 7, 2007), and most recently (December 3, 2007) in the national higher education online journal, *InsideHigherEd.Com*, with an article that featured meditative spaces on college campuses. The *Los Angeles Times* (May 5, 2007) described what appears to be a nationwide "trend" on college and university campuses: the establishment of meditation centers, contemplative areas, interfaith and interreligious centers, outdoor labyrinths, and special landscaping for meditation gardens.[8]

Academic initiatives like the Center for Contemplative Mind in Society are fostering the teaching of contemplative practice in the college classroom under the leadership of Arthur Zajonc (2006), physicist from Amherst, the academic program director. Ed Sarath (2006), professor of jazz from the University of Michigan, directs the Program in Creativity and Consciousness Studies at the

University of Michigan. In its thirty-five year history, Naropa University has developed contemplative education as the foundation across its curriculum, in all academic disciplines.[9] Religious studies has begun to develop other programs as well: Harold Roth (2006), a professor in Chinese religions, directs the Contemplative Studies Initiative at Brown, and the University of Redlands Department of Religious Studies has developed a core of contemplative courses and opened a meditation/contemplative classroom in 2007.[10] Rice University boasts an active core of faculty with a contemplative orientation to their courses and teaching. Emory University has just initiated a Contemplative Studies program as a collaboration between the medical school and the graduate Religious Studies department. These institutional initiatives led to a series of sessions and conversations on contemplative pedagogy at the annual meeting of the American Academy of Religion (2006–2008), sponsored by the Teaching Religion section. Outside the academy, the Garrison Institute and The Forge are developing initiatives to nurture contemplative pedagogy in education.

These initiatives have grown from the recognition of a central paradox in our academic teaching: liberal arts higher education, founded in part to promote enrichment of the inner lives of faculty and students, has lost the purpose and will to do so. Scientific studies are demonstrating the peril of neglecting the inner life and the promise of meditative disciplines to enhance it. Neurological research has expanded our understanding of the mind beyond previous views of merely discursive or logical functions.[11] Scientific studies of contemplatives have demonstrated that the meditative mind achieves states of concentration, attention, awareness, creativity, happiness, well-being, and compassion for others more frequently and more powerfully than the noncontemplative mind.[12] Alongside such neurological findings are multiple studies in the clinical applications of meditation, demonstrating its salutary effect on physical and emotional disturbances such as cancer, psoriasis, depression, and obsessive-compulsive disorders.[13]

Current university studies are exploring how meditation might cultivate human flourishing and happiness through inner balance beyond the physiological realm.[14] For example, a study at the University of Kentucky found that students who did a forty-minute meditation showed more enhanced brain functioning than students who spent the forty minutes taking a nap, reading, talking to friends, or watching television. The meditation period appeared to refresh the mind in a unique way.[15] The results from university research so far suggest strongly that a person's inner life, including subtle states of mental awareness, has a penetrating effect on his or her quality of life and contribution to the human collective.

Yet, despite these advances in the world of laboratories and clinical settings, many university professors have so far been hesitant to openly acknowledge the "inner lives" of students. Traditional pedagogical methods across the disciplines address the student as if only one inner quality—discursive rationality—were present. University educators have focused on enabling students to learn the content of this or that idea/theory/history/doctrine and have assumed that they will learn how to process it interiorly, in their own lives, on their own. We some-how take for granted that students already know how their own minds work, so we do not teach them *how* to think, reflect, and attend—only *what* to think. Religious studies professors even ignore pedagogical applications of centuries of contemplative literature from the world's religions mapping highly sophisticated portraits of mental and inner life.

Conventional teaching aims, almost solely, at requiring students to "think *about*" rather than "know from *within*." Brown University professor of East Asian Religions Harold Roth comments on the paradox of scientific and techno-logical mastery that lacks inner self-mastery:

> We can use our technology of the outer world to treat previously incur-able diseases, but our mastery of the "technology" of the inner world is so rudimentary that we can barely contain the passions that lead us to destroy the very human life that we, paradoxically, struggle so hard to preserve. . . . We have never known more about how the mind works, yet our ability to apply this knowledge to our own experience has not been correspondingly developed.[16]

We professors notice that only a few students enter college in command of their own inner world. Few seem to know how to cultivate the mind for intellectual pursuit, aesthetic appreciation, or ethical development. Their mental landscapes can seem to storm with uncontrollable anxiety, fear, self-concern, a desire for approval, and sometimes immobilizing despair. They can be lost in random dis-cursive thoughts as well, not able to think clearly about the matters at hand. Par-adoxically, the mind can appear to be their worst enemy in the learning endeavor. Many professors testify that even intelligent and talented students are sometimes hampered in their learning by test anxiety, self-consciousness in the classroom, jumbled discursivity, and personal emotional problems. In a 2007 survey, 41.5 percent of college juniors reported that they "frequently" feel that their lives are "filled with stress and anxiety."[17] Undoubtedly, such interior tur-moil impedes intellectual success and overall well-being.

When students learn meditation or contemplative process, they are learning that it is possible to release repetitive emotional and conceptual patterns and tune into the subtle potential of the mind. In this way, they learn to refine the mind so that it can actually be of service to learning and life-meaning rather than a distracting impediment. Some of them experience freedom from test anx-iety, depression, rigid judgmental thinking, and eating disorders for the first time. They speak of a sense of empowerment in meditation when they realize that they do not have to be victims of the distractive irrelevancies and repetitive negativities of the mind. They attest that this confidence enhances all areas of life, from their college learning, to interrelational maturity, and to a deeper appreciation of nature and, indeed, life itself.

Through the contemplative approach, students can learn to experience not only *which* thoughts they have, but the very nature of the thought process itself. They can see, not only *which* emotions arise, but the very nature of the emotional process. Instead of being tossed in the "waves" of thoughts and emotions, they can develop the inner discipline of riding "the crest of the wave" by attending to the precise moment at hand and discover the clarity and openness of the mind itself. Contemplative methods such as meditation facilitate the interior accomplishments of self-knowledge and self-mastery.

Self-knowledge and self-mastery are at the root of the liberal arts dictum "know thyself." As Diana Chapman Walsh, president of Wellesley College, wrote in 2005: "Moral citizenship arises out of an inner core of integrity. . . . The liberal arts disciplines instill in students humility, awareness of the limits of their knowledge, eagerness to hear responsible critique, appreciation that the first and most difficult obligation of a citizen is the Socratic injunction to 'know thyself.'"[18] Meditation and contemplative practice have, for centuries, been recognized as an "inner science" for self-knowledge that makes accurate knowledge of the outer world possible.

Indeed, the much-discussed "critical thinking" may be possible only when scholars submit themselves to the rigor of self-examination first. Quantum physicist David Bohm saw the interrelation between self-inquiry and critical thinking in the sciences. He strongly recommended the practice of meditation for the scientist to clean the mirror of the mind so that it might reflect an accurate image of the world and discern the right measurements with which to investigate it. The fragmented, self-seeking mind designs a skewed measurement, and a skewed measurement results in a distorted outcome. He recommended "techniques of meditation that lead the whole process of mental operation nonverbally to the sort of quiet state of orderly and smooth flow needed to end fragmentation both in the actual process of thought and in its content."[19]

Bohm linked the inner mental harmony of the scientist with an outer harmony of the investigated world. There is a porous interconnectivity between the inner and outer worlds. In fact, scientists, educators, social reformers, and religious leaders alike have reiterated something akin to this remark from the Fourteenth Dalai Lama, Tenzin Gyatso: "If there is no peace in one's mind, there can be no peace in one's approach to others, and thus no peaceful relations between individuals or between nations." As the keynote speaker at Emory University's conference Educating the Heart and Mind (October 2007), the Dalai Lama repeated this emphasis on inner education: "Inner disarmament first, then outer disarmament."[20] The roots of social violence and fragmentation exist within all of us, he explained. Therefore, we are not likely to achieve world peace without inner peace, nor outer disarmament without inner disarmament. Rigorous interior examination such as that learned in contemplative process can facilitate a self-chosen "disarmament" of anger, craving, hatred, biases, and pride, all of which prevent students from being aware of their connection to others and the world. Self-knowledge then becomes a solid foundation for self-transcendence and a sustainable life of service to local and global communities.

MEDITATION IN THE RELIGIOUS STUDIES CLASSROOM

Despite the call for interior cultivation as a goal of liberal arts education, religious studies has been slow to accept contemplative methods. University religious studies departments have particular challenges in the implementation of contemplative pedagogies, and yet, we would suggest, a particular urgency to do so. In the 1960s and 1970s, religious studies departments charted a course to become legitimate academic departments at public universities, freeing themselves from the often apologetic stance of church-affiliated private colleges and divinity schools at major universities. This process of legitimization required the honing of objective distance and the clarification of specific academic methodologies in working with religious phenomena.

But while religious studies has succeeded in establishing itself as a legitimate academic discipline in higher education, it has often exaggerated scholarly objectivity at the expense of personal meaning, subjectivity, and empirical self-knowledge in the study of religion. Perhaps in our vigilance to apply a hermeneutics of suspicion, we overlooked the possibility of a "hermeneutics of hunger" that would affirm people's hunger for dignity and community, acknowledging that they often find it in religion, spirituality, or contemplative practice.[21]

College students seem to have this hunger, yet it appears to go mostly unsatisfied. Recent analysis of data related to introductory courses in religious studies in the United States postulates a "Great Divide" between the objective, content-based goals of professors and the subjective meaning-based goals of their students.[22] The students want to pursue interior learning. According to the national survey of college students conducted by the UCLA Higher Education Research Institute, college students have high levels of interest in spiritual, religious, and existential matters. A majority of entering students expected their college education to develop their "self-understanding" and be supportive of their inquiries into the "meaning and purpose of life." They also expressed the desire to become "more loving and compassionate people." However, the students' expectations were largely not met.[23]

While pioneers in contemporary religious studies methodology, such as Wilfred Cantwell Smith, Mircea Eliade, and Ninian Smart, valued the personal dimension of religious phenomena in human culture, subsequent influences from allied academic disciplines introduced increasingly objectivist scholarly methods from the social sciences. Previous emphasis upon "participatory"[24] study, or of "tradition" and "faith,"[25] coming from the first generation of religious studies scholars gave way to a reductive tendency to approach religion solely as a construct of social factors, understood through critical examination and deconstruction alone. Many contemporary religious studies scholars now write about religious phenomena from a scientific distance that sometimes appears contemptuous of religiousness, spirituality, or any living phenomena of religion.[26]

While this may be a healthy trend in any truly academic field, this view now often dominates our departments and academic meetings, squelching creativity in participatory pedagogy or conversation about meaning. Contemplative pedagogy has tremendous potential to enliven the religious studies classroom and to deepen the learning that takes place there. With proper introduction and context, meditation and contemplation are content-appropriate activities that model religious experience and intuitive knowing described or expressed in our curricula. Students who yearn for relevant exposure to issues of the inner life welcome the opportunity to develop different ways of knowing in the religious studies classroom, and appreciate the nonproselytizing atmosphere of the university as a way to explore this. When this is balanced with appreciation for issues of pluralism, critical perspective, and dialogue between traditions, students learn life skills that will benefit them for years to come.

From a wider perspective, it is essential that the academic discipline of religious studies provides leadership in contemplative pedagogy. With the growing diversity of religious America, it is commonly acknowledged that the formerly WASP establishment has come undone, and individuals in every sphere of public life are becoming more explicit with their religious convictions, as indicated in recent political campaigns. At the same time, evangelical campus ministries have vociferously proselytized and pressed an agenda on college students. As many more of our faculty colleagues come out of the closet, albeit tentatively, to engage issues of religious identity, they are unsure how to do so. How are we to address religious identity and spiritual inquiry in the classroom without falling into extremes? Can we move from fearful retreat to responsible engagement? Religion and spirituality have become such powerful and manifest forces in civil society and in education that we in religious studies must do more than ruminate—we must participate and educate. We see this book as a first step toward addressing contemplative education from its disciplinary foundation in religious studies.

The growing popularity of contemplative process and meditation spaces in educational settings is exciting but comes with the risks of cultural appropriation, shallow faculty preparation, and hidden motivations to proselytize. Therefore, we see the clear need for a resource that grounds contemplative pedagogy in its home discipline of religious studies where responsible methodologies can be critically fleshed out in a refereed academic discourse that has a long and rich history among scholars and practitioners of contemplative traditions. This book is a seasoned yet innovative response to the searching question posed by leaders in higher education who know that interior education is a crucial goal but do not know how to effectuate it:

> How do we prepare students to cultivate their own inner resources of spirit and moral courage?
>
> How do we enable them to engage moral and social dilemmas with clarity about their own values . . . ?
>
> And, how, without proselytizing, do we foster students' own development of character, conscience, and examined values?
>
> —Association of American Colleges and Universities, 2007[27]

OVERVIEW OF THE BOOK

The book opens with essays from senior scholars within religious studies who have been at the forefront of contemplative education and contemplative studies initiatives. Tom Coburn and Bob Thurman describe particularly potent contemplative practices and meditative moments, which they situate historically in Western culture and South and Central Asian spiritual traditions. Given its power to bring about liberation from suffering and to catalyze noetic breakthroughs, they view contemplative insight as "inevitable" and "necessary" features of liberal education. Whereas Thurman (and many of the book's contributors) see religious studies departments as the appropriate auspices under which "to restore to the curriculum the resources of the world's great spiritual traditions for self-exploration, self-cultivation, self-liberation, and self-integration," Harold Roth proposes that contemplative knowledge will thrive in the academic realm only if it is sustained by collaborative and interdisciplinary faculty and kept outside of religious studies departments, because of their problematic "Eurocentric" biases. Laurie Patton speaks further to collaborative synergies that can coalesce to support contemplative curricula. With an eye to administrative priorities, she emphasizes the pragmatic benefits of an alliance between religious studies and the sciences.

Although the book opens with the larger conversation about the place of contemplative study in relation to higher education, institutional initiatives, and department programs, it moves in section 2 to the inner journeys that have made those conversations possible. Without professors who have awakened to the potency of meditation, who would be interested in such initiatives? Taking the inward-outward journey of the Labyrinth as a metaphor for her development as a professor, Fran Grace describes the inner evolution that came to express itself in three major pedagogical shifts, from content-based (third-person) to context-based (second-person) to contemplative-based (first-person) teaching. Chris Bache offers examples from decades of teaching that illumine his vision of the classroom as a "field of collective consciousness" in which the inner world of the professor is inevitably in sync with the inner worlds of students. If that collective dynamic truly happens, then professors become responsible for our inner state and for sustaining a classroom environment that attunes to coherence and attentiveness. Richard Brown, a longtime trainer of contemplative teachers, helps us with that challenge by providing concrete methods to facilitate a contemplative environment in the classroom and in oneself as the teacher. Drawing on several years as a workshop leader and meditation teacher outside of academe, John Makransky offers practical assistance to educators in need of tools to cultivate a human life that is sustainable from the inside-out. Louis Komjathy shares how his study and practice of Daoism inform his pedagogical work with students. In a disclosure that likely many of the authors and perhaps the readers will resonate with, he speaks of the allure of his meditation "hut" and the difficulty of coming out of it into the conventional academic world of discursive debate, multitasking, and institutional politics.

Section 3 deals with critical issues in contemplative teaching, questions that may arise in religious studies about our approaches, motivations, and the overall effect on our students. Judith Simmer-Brown proposes ethical standards for contemplative teaching, drawing from decades of conversation among academic colleagues both within and outside of Naropa University. Sid Brown explores the challenging dynamics of the inner motivations of the professor and the responses of students. In contrast to the many studies of meditation that emphasize the health and well-being aspects, researcher Tobin Hart brings what he calls the "neuro-phenomenology" of contemplation and meditation to bear on the learning process itself. How does meditation benefit learning? While the focus of the book is the religious studies classroom, we drew from three contemplative teachers in other fields who had special perspectives designed to enrich our religious studies teaching: history (Wu), psychology (Hart), and education (Richard Brown).

Our next two sections give case studies of what religious studies faculty are actually doing in the classroom. Section 4 introduces concrete examples of courses within religious studies departments that integrate meditation and contemplative pedagogy into learning. They demonstrate how to incorporate content-appropriate assignments while giving students choices in how to participate without a sense of coercion. They also model methods such as bringing in guest teachers, conducting reflective discussion, and engaging in contemplative fieldwork. Section 5 gives specific class exercises and activities that address course content in areas such as body awareness, ecology, and the arts. One chapter addresses meditation methods in online teaching, while another addresses contemplative evaluation methods.

The final section of the book returns to the point at which we began—students' experience. These two chapters draw from student anecdotal report about their experiences in contemplative learning, addressing their general outcomes as well as their emotional development, their focus and commitment to their studies, their personal discoveries, and their experience in service learning environments. Comprehensive quantitative studies in meditation and learning have yet to be completed, but these student reports indicate the importance of deeper measures of student outcomes.

A note of clarification: the word "meditation" has a variety of meanings in this book, depending upon the context. Generally speaking, we can say it means a conscious and gentle focusing of the mind on an object such as the breath or a phrase or sound, and the continuous return of attention back to that object again and again. The object is a neutral one, but can be varied, depending upon the context—it is not inherently "religious" in any way. This cultivation is sometimes called "mindfulness," and refers to the ability to remain present with this focus of attention, at first in a formal session of practice and eventually in varied and distracting environments that are more challenging. The word "meditation" also is applied to the development of insight or awareness that may arise from such cultivation of attention.

In our chapters, we also speak of "contemplation" and the "contemplative," though these terms are used generically, meaning application of meditation methods to learning pedagogies where no meditation *per se* is taught. Generally speaking, we are pointing to interiority or personal reflection, which are first-person methods of investigation. For the purposes of this book, we are using the terms "meditation," "mindfulness," "awareness," and "contemplation" interchangeably, and not in the more technical ways the terms are used in specific religious traditions.[28] Each of them is often paired with the words "practice" or "pedagogy," demonstrating that these methods are properly considered praxis in our educational endeavors.

The book you hold in your hands invites you into an important conversation. This conversation about contemplative teaching and higher education has been going on most recently for three decades, and we hope it will continue long after us. It is like a flowing river and we put in our raft at different points along its course. This "river" of conversation is wide enough to hold many different viewpoints, as you will see from the range in this book. Each of us speaks from the place to which our "raft" of life experience has carried us, even as we are aware that the raft is neither the river nor the shore. This book is not the final destination but a mindful stop in the conversation to take stock of how far we have traveled and how much farther there is to go. Thank you for joining us at this momentous juncture.

NOTES

1. Judith Simmer-Brown, "Commitment and Openness: A Contemplative Approach to Pluralism," *The Heart of Learning*, ed. Steven Glazer (New York: Tarcher/Putnam, 1999), 97–112.
2. *College Learning for the New Global Century* (Washington, DC: Association of American Colleges and Universities, 2007), 3.
3. *The Great Conversation: The Substance of a Liberal Education*, Vol. I, Great Books of the Western World (Chicago: Encyclopedia Britannica, 1952), 3, 26.
4. *College Learning for the New Global Century*, 22.
5. Ibid., 23, 6.
6. Martha Nussbaum, *Cultivating Humanity: A Classical Defense of Reform in Liberal Education* (Cambridge: Harvard University Press, 1997), 8.
7. To our knowledge, this is the first book on meditation in higher education. However, there are important related works from higher education experts that highlight the learning benefits of contemplative practices: Laura I. Rendon, *Sentipensante (Sensing/Thinking) Pedagogy* (Sterling: Stylus, 2009); John P. Miller, *The Holistic Curriculum*, second edition (Toronto: University of Toronto Press, 2007).
8. John Gravois, "Meditate on It: Can Adding Contemplation to the Classroom Lead Students to More Eureka Moments?," *Chronicle of Higher Education* (October 21 2005); Angie Green, "A Space Where Students Can Nurture Their Minds, Spirits," *Los Angeles Times* (5 May 2007), B2; Elizabeth Redden, "Meditative Spaces," *insidehighered.com* (3 December 2007): www.insidehighered.com/news/2007/12/03/meditation.
9. See www.naropa.edu/cace.
10. See www.brown.edu/Faculty/Contemplative_Studies_Initiative/; http://www.redlands.edu/4875.asp.
11. B. Alan Wallace, *Contemplative Science: Where Buddhism and Neuroscience Converge* (New York: Columbia University Press, 2007).
12. See Michael Murphy, Steven Donovan, and Eugene Taylor, *The Physical and Psychological Effects of Meditation: A Review of Contemplative Research 1991–1996*, 2nd ed. (Petaluma: Institute of Noetic Sciences, 1997); A. Lutz et al., "Long-term Meditators Self-induce High Amplitude Gamma Synchrony during Mental Practice," *Proceedings of the National Academy of Sciences* (2004), 101: 16369–73; Sarah Lazar et al., "Functional Brain Mapping of the Relaxation Response and Meditation," *NeuroReport* (15 May 2000): 1–5; Arthur Zajonc et al., *The New Physics and Cosmology Dialogues with the Dalai Lama* (New York: Oxford University Press, 2004); Richard Davidson and Anne Harrington, *Visions of Compassion: Western Scientists and Tibetan Buddhists Examine Human Nature* (OUP, 2001); B. Alan

Wallace, *Attention Revolution: Unlocking the Power of the Focused Mind* (Boston: Wisdom Publications, 2006).

13. Sharon Begley, *Train Your Mind, Change Your Brain* (New York: Ballantine Books, 2007), offers a cogent summary of the studies related to substantial enhancement of physical and mental health through the alleviation of problems such as depression, eating disorders, OCD, and PTSD. See also: "The Science and Clinical Applications of Meditation," Washington, D.C., 2005, hosted by the Johns Hopkins School of Medicine, Georgetown University, and the Mind and Life Institute (6-disc DVD).

14. See the research results from the following projects: Santa Barbara Institute www.sbinstitute.com; Stanford University's Carstenson Life-Span Development Lab www.psych.stanford.edu/%7Elifespan/; University of California at Davis's Center for Mind and Brain www.mindbrain@ucdavis.edu; and University of California Los Angeles's Mindful Awareness Research Center www.marc.ucla.edu/.

15. Bruce O'Hara, research presented at Society for Neuroscience, Annual Meeting, Washington, D.C., 2005, reported in Alison Motluk, "Meditation Builds Up the Brain," *New Scientist* (15 November 2005).

16. Harold D. Roth, "Contemplative Studies: Prospects for a New Field," *Teachers College Record* 108, no. 9 (September 2006): 1787.

17. Based on the Higher Education Research Institute survey, reported by Elizabeth Redden, "More Spiritual, But Not in Church," *Inside Higher Ed.Com* (18 December 2007).

18. www.collegenews.org/x3716.xml

19. David Bohm, *Wholeness and the Implicate Order* (New York: Routledge and Kegan Paul, 1980), 25.

20. *My Land, My People: The Original Autobiography of His Holiness the Dalai Lama of Tibet* (New York: Time Warner Books, 1997), 28. For a report on the Emory University speech: en.epochtimes.com/news/7-10-26/61212. html.

21. Dorothee Soelle, *Silent Cry: Mysticism and Resistance* (Minneapolis: Fortress Press, 2001), 48–51.

22. Barbara E. Walvoord, *Teaching and Learning in the College Introductory Religion Courses* (Oxford: Blackwell Publishing, 2008).

23. Higher Education Research Institute (HERI), *The Spiritual Life of College Students: A National Study of College Students' Search for Meaning and Purpose: Executive Summary* (Los Angeles: University of California, Los Angeles, 2005); Elizabeth Redden, "More Spiritual, But Not in Church," *Inside Higher Ed.Com* (18 December 2007), under http://www.insidehighered. com (accessed 15 March 2009). For a range of viewpoints on the HERI data from Academy of American Religion members, see the special issue,

"Spirituality in Higher Education: Problems, Practices, and Programs," *Religion and Education* (Summer 2009).

24. This term is used by Ninian Smart to describe how the scholar of religion can participate in order to more deeply understand religious phenomena. Ninian Smart, "Beyond Ideology: Religion and the Future of Western Civilization," lectures delivered at the University of Edinburgh, 1978–1980 (San Francisco: Harper & Row, 1981), 47. For a recent revisioning, see Jorge Ferrer and Jacob Sherman, *The Participatory Turn: Spirituality, Mysticism, Religious Studies* (Albany: State University of New York Press, 2008); Christopher M. Bache, *The Living Classroom: Teaching and the Collective Consciousness* (Albany: State University of New York Press, 2008).

25. Smith spoke of faith as "inner religious experience or involvement of a particular person" rather than a classification, emphasizing that religion is about the particulars of human life in a larger context of history and culture. Wilfred Cantwell Smith, *The Meaning and End of Religion* (Minneapolis: Fortress Press, 1991), 187.

26. Examples of these views are found in Russell T. McCutcheon, *Critics Not Caretakers: Redescribing the Public Study of Religion* (Albany: State University of New York Press, 2001).

27. *College Learning for the New Global Century*, 23.

28. For example, in Buddhist traditions, meditation (*bhavana*) relates to this cultivation of one-pointed mind (*shamatha*) that develops insight (*vipashyana*), while contemplation (*cintamayi-prajna*) refers to sacred reading; in Christian traditions, meditation refers to sacred reading practices such as *lectio divina*, while contemplation refers to more formless practices of prayer and reflection.

I

WHY CONTEMPLATIVE PEDAGOGY?

The Religious Studies Dialogue

1

THE CONVERGENCE OF LIBERAL EDUCATION AND CONTEMPLATIVE EDUCATION—INEVITABLE?

THOMAS B. COBURN

Each fall it has been my privilege to address newly matriculating students at Naropa University on the topic "Introduction to Contemplative Education." This is the counterpart to the kind of orientation talk on liberal education that students hear from countless college presidents across the country, passed through the lens of Naropa's signature activity of contemplative education. This kind of education is described by the university's mission statement as "Buddhist-inspired, ecumenical, and non-sectarian." It is also my effort to speak synoptically about a kind of education that enrolls 1,100 students, two-thirds of them graduate students, spread across eleven undergraduate majors and a dozen graduate departments. The fact that Naropa is the first choice of over 90 percent of the entering students indicates that, even before matriculation, they have discerned a personal resonance with the university's mission. But precisely because this resonance is so deeply personal, and because these students will be scattered across a range of departments, my introductory talk is an attempt to identify what I think will be commonalities in their experience and to connect that experience with the more conventional kind of liberal education with which most of them are already at least partially familiar. The talk is based not only on my own experience of and at Naropa University, but also on my training as a historian of religion and thirty years of teaching in a variety of settings.

In this essay I want to maintain the rhetorical flavor of that oral presentation, while adapting it to the written word. I invite you to read it with your ear, as well as your eye, and to test its descriptions of teaching and learning against your own experience. My own sense is that contemplative education is an extrapolation from more conventional education and that any subject matter, including religious studies, can be taught contemplatively. But, as the history of the academy over the past several centuries and of the discipline of religious studies over the past decades shows, it is also possible to suppress that contemplative potential. In what follows, I want to identify some factors that can liberate that potential and that raise the question of whether we are headed toward an inevitable convergence of contemplative and liberal education.

I

I begin here, as we begin every class and every committee meeting, with a bow. I invite you, on completing the first section of this essay, to pause in your reading and to do your own bow. This ritual gesture was created by Naropa's founder, Chögyam Trungpa, Rinpoche, and it provides a ritual framing for our interactions, first anticipating the interactions to come, and then bringing them to closure. The bow has three parts: first, sitting erect, feet flat on the floor, hands on upper thighs. We lower our eyes and gently say good-bye to wherever our thoughts and emotions have been taking us, bidding farewell to the multitasking that so pervades our lives. Second, we feel ourselves fully present, attending to this particular place, gently aware of the people to our right and left, to the floor beneath and the ceiling above. Then, third, we bow from the waist, offering ourselves to those who are gathered with us (or, in the present case, to the text we are reading), acknowledging that we have agreed to be present to and for one another, constituting a little community for the duration of our time together.

II

The bow is a very simple, somatic introduction to "contemplative education," Naropa's core institutional activity. Because it is an action, it is immediately intelligible—to Buddhists and non-Buddhists, to the spiritually inclined and secularists, and to all ages, including my three-year-old grandson. In light of the deeply personal nature of contemplative education, definitions are elusive, so let me capture its spirit with some examples. An analogy would be to think of contemplative education as a three-dimensional sculpture whose vitality eludes a single photograph. But in walking around the sculpture, a sense of its three-dimensionality and dynamism becomes apparent. Here are six quick snapshots of contemplative education from different angles.

First, contemplative education sits at the historical confluence of two rivers, one flowing out of Asia, the other out of the eastern Mediterranean. The former has its headwaters in the contemplative traditions of South and East Asia, particularly in the experience of the Buddha, an experience that launched the world's first missionary activity. These traditions spread far beyond their origins and have increasingly become part of European and American life. The other river has its headwaters at about the same time in Greece, in the classical liberal arts tradition. This tradition, too, has had a missionary quality and spread far beyond its homeland, becoming, in particular, the basis for most colleges in America. The confluence of Asian and Western rivers now under way in American higher education has historical roots, but no exact precedent. In the context of global history, this has never happened before.

A second snapshot. All colleges in the country aspire to cultivate in their students the fundamental liberal arts skills of reading, writing, and speaking. But very few address the reverse side of speaking, that is, listening—listening to heart as well as head, and listening to the other individual or group, quietly, patiently, letting them have their voice uninterrupted, without trying to straighten them out. Contemplative education adds to the familiar list of liberal arts skills the skill of listening. Developing this runs counter to what Deborah Tannen has so aptly called *The Argument Culture*.[1] Listening entails real discipline, directed inwardly toward oneself and outwardly toward others. In a world where the facts of diversity and difference are so often contentious, and when the college-going population is becoming so much more diverse, the deep, disciplined, nonjudgmental listening that is part of contemplative education offers a glimmer of what it might mean actually to *celebrate* the differences that so often divide us, rather than seeing them as sources of conflict.[2]

A third snapshot. While contemplative education is partly a function of the confluence of rivers, it also has roots deep in the American heritage. The great psychologist and educator William James claimed nearly a century ago: "The faculty of voluntarily bringing back a wandering attention, over and over again, is the very root of judgment, character, and will. . . . An education which should improve this faculty would be *the* education *par excellence*."[3] More recently and in a similar vein, the German philosopher Ludwig Wittgenstein has reflected on awareness of the present moment: "Death is not an event in life: we do not live to experience death. If we take eternity to mean not infinite temporal duration but timelessness, then eternal life belongs to those who live in the present."[4]

Another snapshot, this one the famous aphorism from Mahatma Gandhi: "Be the change you want to see in the world." In other words, do not just talk about how to make the world better. Model it in your own life. Robert Bellah captures the vision of contemplative education wonderfully when he says: "Revolutionaries who do not in their own lives embody the future cannot bring it."[5]

A fifth snapshot. By training I am a historian of religion, and I know that contemplatives, in all traditions and throughout history, have tended to live their lives along a spectrum. At one end are the recluses, those who withdraw from the world to live in seclusion: one thinks of the yogi living in a mountain cave. At the other end are the activists, those who are engaged in the struggle for peace, justice, and social equity. One thinks of Martin Luther King, Thich Nhat Hanh, Mahatma Gandhi, Dorothy Day, and countless others, all deeply contemplative and all deeply engaged in transforming the world. Teaching contemplative education requires that we introduce our students to this broad range of possibility, so they can decide for themselves how they would like to bring their contemplative lives to bear on the world, recognizing that, if they are like the rest of us, that choice will vary over the course of time. Contemplative education thus involves rescuing the concept—and the reality—of contemplation from the misconception that it is done only in solitude, by withdrawing from the world. Once one gets beyond the stereotype that the contemplative life requires disengagement from the world, one sees contemplative activists everywhere.

A final snapshot suggests that contemplative education occupies the "in-between" space. This is obvious in the contemplative emphasis on the present moment, situated between past and present. But contemplative space also exists in other liminal spaces and moments: between student and teacher, between head and heart, between intellect and intuition, between east and west, between in-breath and out-breath, and so on. Wherever we find polarities, contrasts, dualities, antagonisms, contemplative space is the place in between. It defies our inclination to take sides. It wants to hold together both poles of every polarity, hovering happily, mysteriously, beckoningly between them. It honors all differences, but with the spirit of nondualism.

III

Let me now suggest how the dynamics of conventional learning point suggestively in a contemplative direction, against the backdrop of two well-known research findings about how learning occurs.

We now know, first, that learning occurs optimally, for all organisms, under conditions of moderate discomfort, when the organism is extended beyond its comfort zone. The challenge for teachers is to create imaginative activities in the broad middle ground—the in-between space—between boredom, on the one hand, and terror, on the other. A skilled teacher opens up this space in a way that is also beyond his or her own comfort zone, so that the teacher, too, is engaged in the edgy, challenging space where learning occurs optimally.

The second research finding is that the single most important variable in learning is for the teacher to catch the student or students at the "teachable moment." This occurs when the individual or the group is ready to break out of established patterns of thought and become profoundly open to new possibilities—when he, she, or they are living, if only for a moment, beyond the comfort zone.

In my experience, we find ourselves in teachable moments by one of two routes. Sometimes it is possible for a teacher deliberately to create the conditions for them, through a sequence of assignments or developing a particular line of thought, building momentum so that students gradually find themselves on new terrain and can say, "Aha, so that's how it works!" The fact that good teachers can, in disciplined and orderly fashion, intentionally craft some teachable moments is what makes teaching part science.

But there is another route to those wondrous breakthroughs to new understanding, and it is here that good teaching is not science, but art. These occur when an individual student or a classroom suddenly finds itself, through the complex, mysterious dynamics of individual or group development, beyond its comfort zone and broken open, ready for the word or act that will move it to a new level of understanding. The teacher has to recognize such moments in a split second, as they occur in the midst of classroom discussion or in a private conversation. From a teacher's perspective, there is nothing more exhilarating than recognizing a teachable moment, rising to the opportunity, and literally seeing the individual or the group ascend to a new level of insight and maturity. Conversely, there is no worse experience than recognizing, usually in retrospect, that there was a golden opportunity of a teachable moment staring me in the face and I lacked the wit to recognize it. Occasions like this tempt me to go home, crawl under the bed, and say, "Well, at least my mother loves me. . ." But it is also those same failures that help us as teachers to get better over time.

Good teachers, then, recognize the two paths to teachable moments—one shaping the moments intentionally, the other recognizing them as they occur in the present moment—and they spend their lives developing as scientists, and as artists, in the craft of teaching.

All of us who have spent extended time in the classroom, I suspect, have mused upon the real source for these moments of insight, whether laboriously crafted or serendipitously emerging. We ruminate beyond the realm of the course syllabus, or specific assignments, or particular pedagogical techniques. Here we are on the cusp of recognizing the contemplative potential in all learning, and in all teaching. Here contemplative experience, as variously manifested in and out of the world's spiritual traditions, has great potential to illuminate our mundane experience as teachers and to raise the possibility of a convergence between liberal and contemplative learning.

The Upanishads, for instance, those haunting, mystical Sanskritic intuitions from classical India, describe the inner resource from which all learning and all insight derives this way: *Purnam adah purnam idam / purnat purnam udácyate / purnasya purnam adáya / purnam eva sísyate.* "It is infinitely complete in every way. Whatever comes forth from it is complete in just the same way. It is never diminished, no matter how much or what comes forth from it."[6]

Let us explore this further via two provocative phrases from the meditation teacher/scholar who founded Naropa University, Chögyam Trungpa, Rinpoche. At the heart of these phrases lies a paradox. On the one hand, there is Trungpa's provocative claim that the arrival of "chaos should be greeted as extremely good news."[7] On the other, there is his assertion that "'Contemplative' . . . means being with a discipline fully and thoroughly, as a hungry man eats food or a thirsty man drinks water. . . . Naropa . . . needs an emphasis on discipline. . . . Education [here] could be a powerful one, a tough one that imposes discipline on the student."[8] How does one hold these together, the insistence on discipline, on the one hand, and the celebration of chaos, on the other?

An answer to this question lies in realizing that contemplative education, like liberal education, is *both* about cultivating great discipline *and* about celebrating the great chaos that inevitably and serendipitously erupts and shatters one's discipline, one's ego. Education of all sorts is a "both/and" enterprise, not an exclusionary "either/or" one. If we miss the discipline, we miss half the enterprise. And if we miss the occasional chaos, we miss the other half.

Evidence in support of this realization lies in the lives of contemplatives and mystics themselves. For over thirty years now I have taught a course called Mystical Experience, East and West, based on primary source readings from around the globe and throughout the centuries. It quickly becomes apparent to students that there is a paradox woven into contemplative or mystical life. On the one hand, the discipline of the contemplative path is second to none—including that of modern-day athletes and artists—in the discipline required. Discipline—orderly, sustained, patterned restraint—is woven into contemplative life. On the other hand, many contemplatives know the experience of an uninvited transformation of consciousness for which they can claim no responsibility, and absolutely no agency. Something literally "comes over them."

The former pole of the paradox is found in such training manuals as the *Yoga Sutras*, the cornerstone for much of the religious practice of South Asia. The second *sutra* reads: "Yoga is the restraint of mental modifications," on which a modern editor comments: "The special feature of the Yoga system is its practical discipline, by which the suppression of mental states is brought about through the practice of spiritual exercises and the conquest of desire."[9] The well-known Buddhist practice of *vipassana* and *shamatha* meditation also exemplifies this style.[10] The literature of contemplative life is filled with examples of disciplined exertion.

The other pole of contemplative life, where discipline seems utterly absent and the mystic is taken over by an unanticipated and overwhelming presence, is captured in R. M. Bucke's famous experience:

I was in a state of quiet, almost passive enjoyment. . . . letting ideas, images, and emotions flow . . . through my mind. All at once, without warning of any kind, I found myself wrapped in a flame-colored cloud. . . . I thought of . . . an immense conflagration somewhere close by . . . [and then] knew that the fire was within myself. Directly afterward there came upon me . . . a sense of immense joyousness . . . immediately followed by an intellectual illumination impossible to describe. . . . I saw that the universe is not composed of dead matter, but is . . . a living Presence; . . . that I possessed eternal life . . . ; . . . that all men are immortal; that . . . all things work together for the good of each and all; that the foundation principle of . . . all the worlds . . . is what we call love, and that the happiness of each and all is in the long run absolutely certain. The vision lasted a few seconds and was gone; but the memory of it and the sense of the reality of it has remained during the quarter of a century which has since elapsed. I know that what the vision showed was true. I had attained to a point of view from which I saw that it must be true. That view, that conviction, I may say that consciousness has never, even during periods of the deepest depression, been lost.[11]

This paradox of contemplative life—of transformation sometimes coming through extraordinary discipline, and sometimes as an unwarranted gift—is nicely captured by Alan Watts, when he says that there are two ways to the planets. One is to build a missile to distant parts, at great expense and with much labor. The other is to look down and to realize that a planet lies under our feet.[12]

IV

There thus appears to be at least a structural parallel between liberal education and contemplative education. Learning in both contexts requires effort and exertion beyond the comfort zone for anyone who would learn and grow. While disciplined endeavor is no guarantee that one will progress in knowledge of either the external world or the internal, the experience of countless students is that it certainly helps. In most cases discipline is a prerequisite for the growth one is seeking. But sometimes teachable moments come upon student and teacher without warning, unbidden, a gift from a mysterious somewhere. In this respect, they seem to resemble the transformative mystical experiences that arrive uninvited, out of the blue. The structure of learning in all contexts appears to be a dialectic between disciplined order, on the one hand, and explosive, even chaotic insight, on the other. The moral, for both students and teachers, is to pay rapt attention to the discipline side of the equation, to the need for order and accountability, for this is the way much learning occurs, as we craft teachable moments together. But we also need to have our radar out for those serendipitous occasions, those eruptions of chaos, for they are the other half of the equation of learning, both conventionally and contemplatively. As with other forms of learning, contemplative education is part science, part art, and we need to be open to transformation via both paths.

This structural convergence between liberal learning and contemplative education invites us to think further about how the former might open out into the latter. The answer, I believe, lies not in any difference of subject matter, particularly if my claim that any subject matter can be taught contemplatively is correct. Rather, it lies in the nature of the teacher. I cannot pursue this in detail here, but I note that contemplative traditions around the globe have affirmed that the key to deepening a student's inner life is studying with someone who already has that firsthand, inner, experiential knowledge. It is no surprise that this historical evidence coincides with the fundamental message emerging from Parker Palmer's powerful, revolutionary work in training teachers at all levels and in all subject matters: "You teach who you are."[13] In the years ahead, a teacher who her- or himself has a rich inner life will likely prove to be the single most important factor in moving conventional liberal education in a contemplative direction.

V

Let me conclude by proposing a geometric image for thinking about contemplative education. Plato called the circle the perfect shape, each point on the circumference equidistant from its center. The mathematicians of his day aspired to make sense of the solar system using the circle as a model. This is indeed possible, but the equations required to describe planetary motion as circular are frightfully complex. Two thousand years later, astronomers found that everything becomes both simpler and more elegant by assuming that planets move in elliptical orbits with varying speeds.[14]

Similarly, I suggest, there is no single center for contemplative education, or if one thinks one has found it, it will be limited, just as Plato's circular model for the solar system was. The ellipse with its two foci provides something more dynamic and alive, something that captures the dialectic between: east and west, teacher and student, teachable moments that are carefully crafted and those that arrive unexpectedly, discipline and the shattering of discipline in chaos, strenuous effort and the unsought arrival of insight, outer world and inner world, inbreath and out-breath, intellect and emotion, body and mind, the arts and the sciences, and so on. The heart of contemplative education is a creative tension, a dialectical back and forth, always vibrant in the in-between space, with no simple, single core.

That, of course, is what we should expect, for the external world in which we live our daily lives—the world of conventional liberal education—is indeed the world of contrasts and polarities, light and dark, good and bad, the world of dualism, where we distinguish between subject and object, between self and other. But the ellipse is also a kind of mystery, what Zen Buddhists call a *koan*, a finger pointing at the moon, pointing at the spaceless world between all antinomies and outside the boundary of the ellipse, where words fail, where all distinctions dissolve in what Buddhists call *shunyata*, "the Void," "emptiness," or "the great unborn," what others have called Godhead, the nameless Tao, the Great Mother, and so on. The convergence of liberal and contemplative education depends on the cultivation of the in-between space and this broader horizon that are implicit in *all* forms of education.

NOTES

1. Deborah Tannen, *The Argument Culture* (New York: Random House, 1999). See also Carol Trosset's documentation that when college students call for more discussion in the classroom, they mean "the opportunity to persuade others of the rightness of my views," rather than "listening to others, so that I might change my mind." Carol Trosset, "Obstacles to Open Discussion and Critical Thinking," *Change* 30, no. 5 (Sept./Oct. 1998): 44–50.

2. The most powerful argument I have seen for linking diversity education and contemplative education is made in Laura I. Rendon, *Sentipensante (Sensing/Thinking) Pedagogy: Educating for Wholeness, Social Justice and Liberation* (Sterling: Stylus Press, 2009).

3. William James, *The Principles of Psychology* (New York: Dover, 1950), I, 424.

4. Ludwig Wittgenstein, *Tractatus Logico-Philosophicus*, trans. D. F. Pears and B. F. McGuinness (London: Routledge and Kegan Paul, 1961), 6.4311.

5. I know of no published source for this quotation, which I first saw on a plaque forty years ago and which has stayed with me ever since.

6. Isa Upanishad, invocation. My translation.

7. "Working with Emotions," in *The Collected Works of Chögyam Trungpa*, ed. Carolyn Gimian (Boston: Shambhala, 2003), III, 232.

8. Naropa faculty meeting notes, 1975, unpublished.

9. Sarvepalli Radhakrishnan and Charles A. Moore (eds.), *A Sourcebook in Indian Philosophy* (Princeton: Princeton University Press, 1957), 454, 453.

10. See Henepola Gunaratana, *Mindfulness in Plain English* (Boston: Wisdom Publications, 1993). On the larger question of the relation between intellectual learning and mindfulness training, see Ellen Langer, *The Power of Mindful Leaning* (Reading, MA: Addison-Wesley, 1997).

11. Quoted in William James, *The Varieties of Religious Experience* (New York: Penguin Books, 1982), 399.

12. Alan Watts, *Behold the Spirit: A Study in the Necessity of Mystical Religion* (New York: Vintage Books, 1972), 72.

13. See Parker Palmer, *The Courage to Teach: Exploring the Inner Landscape of a Teacher's Life* (San Francisco: Jossey-Bass, 1998); and http://www.couragerenewal.org, website of the Center for Courage and Renewal. I also note the emphasis placed by the two major agents of training contemplative teachers—the Center for Contemplative Mind in Society and Naropa University—on the importance of deepening the inner life of teachers. See http://www.contemplativemind.org/, and http://www.naropa.edu.

14. I have explored the heuristic utility of the ellipse elsewhere, in "Asia in the Undergraduate Curriculum," in *Asia in the Undergraduate Curriculum*, ed. Suzanne Wilson Barnett and Van Jay Simons (Armonk, NY, and London: M. E. Sharpe, 2000), 3–22; and in "Secularism and Spirituality in Today's Academy: A Heuristic Model," *Liberal Education* 91, no. 3 (Summer/Fall 2005): 58–61.

2

MEDITATION AND EDUCATION

India, Tibet, and Modern America

ROBERT A. F. THURMAN

What is "meditation"? What is "contemplative mind"? When we feel we've lost it, need more of it, can improve our health with it, what is this "it"? How did it get lost in the West and the modern world? Who has been for it, who against it?

It is fair to say that classical Indian civilization incorporated the contemplative far more than any other, then or now. The contemplative marked that civilization in every way. It caused that civilization to develop unparalleled "inner sciences," as they are often called, which were shared among the various religions. The Buddhist inner sciences were the most broadly developed because their monastic institutions of higher learning were the most numerous. We can conveniently use a Buddhist analysis of meditation and contemplative mind as typical for our general discussion. Meditation translates from the Sanskrit *dhyana, bhavana,* and even *samadhi,* which all designate organizations of the mind-body complex considered different from sensory and intellectual receptive states (as in learning) and intellectual reflective or discursive states, though they include these states sometimes. There are usually said to be two main categories of meditation: *shamatha* (calming) and *vipashyana* (seeing, knowing, or transforming), with both again dividing into critical and creative types.

Calming meditations are deep concentration states, culminating in one-pointed trance, usually devoid of all sensory awareness or mental flow, though also able to entertain with great stability a fixed picture or even a full environment. They produce marked physical effects and equip the mind with fitness

*Reprinted from *Teachers College Record* 108, no. 9 (September 2006):1765–74. Copyright by Teachers College, Columbia University 0161–4681.

and fluency in executing whatever tasks it addresses. When our health researchers note and study effects of meditation, they are almost always referring to calming, one-pointed, thought-free meditation, with or without images. Calming benefits health and empowers the mind but by itself it is not thought to produce in a person either positive or negative evolutionary transformation.

Seeing-through or transforming meditations are also numerous. They range from basic scanning mindfulness meditations, through critically penetrating insight meditations, up to imaginatively creative visualizing meditations. They are considered most important in psychological, intellectual, and spiritual development. They have been studied relatively little but are generally viewed as closely related to reflective states.

Both types of contemplative mind exist in all cultures, even the simplest: naturally, hunters and mothers cultivated the most one-pointed mind-states, and the maker, the shaman and the poet, the most transformative. I think it can be quite misleading to speak of our culture as lacking contemplative mind. When we make that claim, we are rather lamenting the deplorable contemplative states within which the common mind is absorbed. Our minds are absorbed in continuous reverie almost all the time, and when we sleep, we experience a withdrawal from sensory stimuli. Education in any particular culture builds up a worldview, constantly reinforced by symbols and images that are contemplated throughout life. Television, modern culture's peculiar contemplative shrine, supplies a contemplative trance to millions of people, for hours on end, day after day, year in and year out. It is unfortunately a trance in which sensory dissatisfaction is constantly reinforced, anger and violence is imprinted, and confusion and the delusion of materialism is constructed and maintained.

Thus, when we talk about seeking to increase and intensify contemplative mind in our culture, we are actually talking about methods of transferring contemplative energies from one focus to another. We would like for people to develop contemplative states that increase contentment, detachment, tolerance, patience, nonviolence, and compassion, which simultaneously decrease feelings of anger, irritation, and paranoia. We would like them to develop more wisdom, more freedom, and more capacity for responsibility and creativity by seeing through the constructed realities in which our materialist culture has enmeshed us. It is important that we recognize the value choices implicit in our esteem for contemplation. Only by doing so can we understand the opposition that we are encountering, deriving from other value choices.

Commercial interests, with their advertising industry, do not want us to develop contentment and less greed. Military interests in economic, political, ethnic, or nationalist guises do not want us to develop more tolerance, nonviolence, and compassion. And ruling groups in general, in whatever sort of hierarchy, do not want the ruled to become too insightful, too independent, too creative on their own; the danger is that they will become insubordinate, rebellious, and unproductive in their allotted tasks. Therefore, in Asia, contemplative institutions at times received their licenses from the governments by creating a second society—ritually outside the ordinary society—wherein contemplation in the directions we consider positive was encouraged, and by tacitly promising not to interfere too much with the dominant culture's ongoing contemplation of its own necessity. In the community outside the mundane society (*sangha*), calming and insight could be valued, even by the ruling elite, as a sort of safety-valve activity for unsocializable individuals.

The fact is that developing contemplative capacity—either calming or seeing-through—greatly empowers an individual, the combination even more so. Civilizations that suppressed these capacities had reason for wishing to disempower individuals: they tended to be collectivistic and persistent in regimenting their people because of their insecurity with respect to the environment and their neighbors; hence, these civilizations maintained substantial armies.

Though we Euro-Americans like to think of ourselves as primarily individualistic (even when we simultaneously consider too much of that a bad thing), Western societies have tended to suppress individualism over the millennia. Socrates finally was given the hemlock cocktail for corrupting potential soldiers with critical thought, and Sparta was the dominant model, not Athens. Therefore, the kind of humanistic and humanizing contemplative orientation we would like to develop has been systematically suppressed all along.

We must not be surprised if commercial and military influences and conservative ruling groups still active in our society set themselves against any contemplative movement even today. On a more positive note, if the liberal education so essential to a modern democratic society really wants to empower the individuals who must constantly re-create democracy, it needs to incorporate contemplative dimensions in its curriculum. For liberal education to fulfill its responsibility, the teaching of contemplative skills is a necessity, not a luxury.

Our society has entered a quite complicated and ill-understood time, the so-called postindustrial and postmodern age. Democracies are meritocratic in ideal and so are compelled in principle to try to provide each individual with the opportunity and ability to rule the whole. Individuals have the responsibility to make crucial decisions and the technological power to cause immense destruction if they make deluded, greedy, and angry choices. It is the kind of situation in which we oscillate between terminal, doomsday pessimism about our chances of surviving as a species at all and a utopian, optimistic vision about how our society might evolve through an increased use of contemplative practices. I prefer the latter kind of view (while not blinding myself to the dangers of negative outcomes) and remain fully aware that those who think the future hopeless will not support— indeed, will actively oppose—any attempt to create a more contemplative awareness. I personally consider broad-scale individual development of contemplative insight to be necessary for survival.

There are many ways to make our society more contemplative. James Joyce wrote *Finnegan's Wake* to make unthinking embeddedness in words more difficult to maintain. Maharishi Mahesh Yogi from Transcendental Meditation has tried to organize contemplative SWAT teams to travel to trouble spots to send out mass meditation waves to calm groups caught in the flames of fury and violence. Contemplation is taught in thriving Eastern-based centers and various Western monasteries such as Cistercian, Trappist, and Benedictine. In recent times, it has begun to be taught more widely in our educational institutions.

I have chosen the liberal arts and sciences university as the individually liberating institution left over from our Western extrasocial contemplative communities. It has, however, been too much co-opted to empower and train individuals who are destined to serve as the ruling elite of materialist, modern societies. I view the technological media as branching out, however clumsily, from this university complex to enfold the larger society within it. Therefore, if our concern is to heal, enlighten, and empower individuals to live better and create a more humane society by learning how to manage their own contemplative energies, the academic community should become a vital arena within which a more positive future can be determined.

What is the Buddhist approach to contemplation and meditation? How was it used in Buddhist civilizations? How can it be relevant to our modern societies?

The essence of the Buddha's awakened vision of life is that its purpose is evolutionary. Beings naturally seek happiness and can effectively evolve into a condition of perfect happiness through awakening to the reality of the world. The cause of suffering is ignorance, an active misknowing of unreality as if it were reality. The antidote to misknowing is awakening, which leads to superknowing, insight, or wisdom. The human life form is already immensely evolved toward awakening, and the ideal occupation of a human lifetime, therefore, is disciplines and practices that enhance and accelerate evolution toward awakening. Because wisdom is the ultimate cause of awakening, of liberation from ignorance, then these disciplines and practices are educational in the classical sense. One person cannot awaken another. No God can awaken someone. No belief can awaken someone. No meditation can awaken someone. The individual's transformative understanding is the cause of awakening. Realistic beliefs, helpful and skillful others, meditations and practices—all these can help by supporting the process of education. But the realistic understanding that liberates is the individual's own process and attainment.

Therefore, the Buddhist civilizations developed institutions and curricula that empowered individuals. India became the most individualistic of all civilizations after the time of Buddha. Buddhist India was the first to develop cenobitic monasticism, and that monasticism developed into a network of universities with a liberating curriculum. The Buddhist curriculum always cultivated contemplative mind, both for empowerment and for liberating transformation.

The Buddhist tradition should thus be viewed essentially as an educational tradition. In its essence and beginnings, it is not too religious in the usual sense of that word—that is, focused on the transcendent, the sacred, concerned with ultimate realities, warrants of meaning. Its goals are rather liberative and evolutionary. The Buddha broke with the dominant religious system of his world, the powerful religious atmosphere of the Vedic Brahmins. He found it misleading, not liberating, and not necessarily evolutionary in a positive direction. It wrongly submerged the individual in the collectivity, reinforcing the sense of social duty at various levels with ultimate sacred sanctions. It relied on deities; Buddha did not question their existence but thought their powers to be not as believed by the Brahmins. He thought that these deities had mundane powers but not the power to liberate individuals from suffering, or even themselves from their own devastating agonies. And the Vedas enjoined rituals of sacrifice that cause suffering and death to many animals, which turned evolution in a negative rather than a positive direction. The Buddha rejected all this, and set forth the following:

1) Individuals have to take charge of their own evolutionary destiny, not rely on deities or any others;
2) Individuals have to face the fact that all life bound by delusion is inevitably frustrating and ultimately miserable, and hence seek to overcome delusion by cultivating wisdom; and
3) Because positive evolution has no limits, individuals can participate in creating a world of happiness for all instead of the unenlightened world of universal suffering.

I would like to emphasize that in Buddhist and, consequently, Indian thought in general, delusion is the root cause of suffering, and wisdom is the antidote for delusion and thus the root cause of liberation. Wisdom (*prajna*) is not accumulated instrumental knowledge, but is rather a special kind of super-knowing, a knowing by becoming the known, by transcending the subject-object dichotomy. Thus, liberation is achieved not by believing, not by participating in any ceremony or belonging to any group, but by understanding in the deepest possible way. The cultivation of such understanding naturally became the task of the Buddha's teaching and the mission of the Buddhist tradition. Contemplation was an indispensable discipline for deepening and empowering this understanding.

The path to freedom was viewed as having eight branches, eight channels of realism that can gradually overcome the massive unreality generated by instinctual delusion. These eight are called realistic worldview, realistic attitude, realistic speech, realistic action, realistic livelihood, realistic effort, realistic mindfulness, and realistic meditative concentration. These eight are grouped into the Three Spiritual or Higher Educations (*adhishiksha*): the Higher Educations of Justice or Morality, Meditation, and Wisdom. The Buddha found that he was unable to liberate people by the sheer force of his own wisdom or compassion. He could only help them to open their minds to a new understanding of self and world; he was thus forced to channel all his wisdom and compassion into education. So it is that the Buddhist tradition has always focused on spiritual education. The Buddhist monastery was not primarily a place of solitude, but was rather a place of cultivation. Wisdom, the engine of liberation, was cultivated at three levels, by learning, critical reflection, and contemplative penetration. First, one learned the Dharma, and one moved away from one's inherited deluded mind and into the Buddha mind by engaging with the enlightened speech recorded in the *Sutras* and their elucidations. Having understood the teachings at the surface level, one then had to pit one's instinctively deluded mind against the new, inferential, and relatively delicate understanding of the verbal Dharma, and struggle back and forth, cultivating doubt intensely through critical reflection that seeks to delve below the surface to find the deeper meaning. When this process is pursued with great energy and determination, critical reflection becomes penetrative concentration upon the cultivated, doubt-deepened understanding. This concentration draws energy away from instinctual misknowledge and pours it into the liberating insight of transcending wisdom until realistic understanding becomes intuitive and instinctual. Wisdom becoming intuitive, the self realizing its selflessness, and the person enjoying liberation all occur at the same time.

This kind of core curriculum was maintained for more than ten centuries in hundreds of Buddhist monastic universities all over India. Many more developed in most other Asian countries, from Sri Lanka all the way to Japan. India's abundant economic situation, the special gentleness of its gracious ancient culture, and its tolerance of individual liberation were not easily duplicated in other countries where conditions were harsher. After the Indian classical civilization was utterly smashed by the Muslim invasions at the end of the first millennium CE, this curriculum was most faithfully preserved and implemented in the high mountain refuge of Tibet, where so many of the great Indian masters fled. So it is that fragments of the full educational program of the global Buddhist movement have only begun to emerge fully since the opening of Tibet.

What are we doing in liberal arts colleges and universities to provide humanistic education? Can it be furthered by developing a more contemplative orientation on the part of faculty and students?

Within our institutions of higher education, we attempt to liberate critical intellect, emotional stability, aesthetic sensitivity, and moral decency. Supposedly, natural sciences develop intelligence and knowledge of reality, social sciences develop awareness of the social dimension, and humanities provide emotional stability and aesthetic sensitivity and mold a sense of moral decency. Religion was originally driven away from the humanities— its content divided between literature, history, philology, and philosophy— because the scientific study of religion could not proceed effectively as long as it was dominated by a particular religion. This tradition was born of the Renaissance through Enlightenment's impulse toward awakening the full powers of the human. The new notion was that the purpose of human life is to move beyond the worship of a transcendent reality (conceived as a mysterious, all-powerful God) to the understanding of reality, assuming responsibility for the self and the environment, the whole existential situation. Therefore, it is only natural that religion should be regarded with suspicion by the academy. However, without the assistance of religion's deepest disciplines, contemplative and intellectual, the liberal arts and sciences are effectively prevented from becoming liberating arts and sciences. People are informed and certified but not properly prepared to exercise the responsibilities that humanism imposes on the individual. It is not that religion can make this contribution because of the efficacy of one belief or another, or one practice or another (including the practice of meditation). Religions concern themselves with humans' ultimate orientation, with their ultimate aims, and so possess a broad repertoire of arts and disciplines, enabling individuals to integrate their entire being—their physical, ethical, emotional, intellectual, and spiritual elements. Although no particular religion could, or should, dominate the academy again, the moral, psychological, contemplative, and philosophical disciplines embedded within various religions must be made available to faculty and students if education is to go beyond being merely informative and become transformative.

Fortunately, the study of religion in religious studies departments has returned to the humanistic universities, although it labors under the suspicious regard cast upon it by scientists (natural and social) and other humanistic scholars strongly mindful of the prevailing canonization of secularity. Nevertheless, religion departments are able to restore to the curriculum the resources of the world's great spiritual traditions for self-exploration, self-cultivation, self-liberation, and self-integration. However, this must be carried out in an impeccable manner, not only because of the surrounding suspicion but also to ensure pluralism. No one religion can again become normative, its resources dominant, its approach controlling others, so a modern religion department must incorporate courses in all the major traditions.

In this context, we can approach with greater clarity the issue of contemplation within the university. We have seen that contemplation fits in the traditional inner science curriculum at the highest level through the cultivation of wisdom. Therefore, it is virtually indispensable if wisdom is to become fully transformative. The question, then, for academic institutions is not a question of adding a desirable frill to their vast smorgasbord of offerings. Rather, it is a matter of their effectively fulfilling their duty to provide a liberal—that is, a liberating and empowering—education. The ideal pedagogical process is first to learn something really well, using memorization and broad study; then to reflect upon it internally, assisted by energetic debate and discussion with teachers and other students; and finally to meditate upon the first tentative understandings in a sustained and focused way in order to develop insight to a transformative depth.

What are some programs that would help make contemplative practices a normal part of a liberal arts curriculum?

We should recognize that we already do provide contemplative opportunities to our students off campus in that we provide opportunities to study abroad in countries such as India, Thailand, Tibet, Nepal, and Sri Lanka. We are also aware, though institutionally it is an uneasy awareness, that our students join meditation centers and go on retreats offered by all religions (though primarily Eastern-based ones, which have become especially popular in this country). There are also student groups on campus, often fundamentalist ones, that offer opportunities for participation in their rituals, chanting sessions, prayer meetings, and confessional activities of various kinds.

Finally, on the therapeutic or athletic model, there are stress-reduction clinics and yoga and tai chi classes in our physical education departments. The point of reciting these ongoing activities is to remember, before we consider other methods, that we should reinforce those activities that are already performing valuable service.

Other strategies that might be developed include the following:

1) Encouraging the establishment of contemplative centers on campuses such as that proposed at Middlebury College by Steven Rockefeller. Harvard University's Center for the Study of World Religions was set up by its donors with such a purpose in mind, though significantly, its meditation room was eventually turned into a library. Colgate University's Chapel House was set up by the same donors and has provided some contemplative relief in its undergraduate center over the years. I know from personal experience that Amherst College, Williams College, Wesleyan University, Hampshire College, Mount Holyoke College, and Smith College have chapel spaces that can be expanded, pluralized, and "contemplativized," depending on the availability of motivated faculty who are willing to provide leadership. Certainly at Columbia University, both St. Paul's Chapel and Earl Hall are used by a number of different groups for various kinds of contemplative practices. I'm fairly certain that every liberal arts

college and university has available resources that can be used to support such practices.

2) Encouraging departments to introduce contemplative experience and expertise in whatever tradition as a recognized and rewarded accomplishment in the professor and the student. Just as knowledge of a particular text, ritual, doctrine, historical era, institution, and individual expressed in a thesis or other demonstration is evaluated and rewarded, so should knowledge of a particular meditation practice, gained by study of texts, exploration of institutions, and personal experience of the practice, expressed in a thesis or other demonstration, be evaluated and rewarded.

3) Encouraging individual scholars in the natural and social sciences to expand their research into physiological effects of various meditative disciplines. Professor Davidson at the University of Wisconsin has used magnetic resonant imagery to demonstrate certain well-developed mental capacities demonstrated by monks who are experienced in meditation.

4) Encouraging scholars in religious studies to research, translate, and publish more of the contemplative literature, technical as well as evocative, born of the contemplative disciplines. As I often point out, in the domain of contemplative development, we should not make the mistake of investing heavily in hardware possibilities and thus neglect the extraordinary software developed over millennia by contemplative cultures and traditions.

5) Encouraging media productions that inform about and instruct in the practice of contemplation, thereby reaching a wide audience, demystifying contemplation, and creating greater public acceptance of contemplation in the educational arena.

The opportunities are manifold for creative work in integrating contemplative practices into higher education, and we are grateful to the Center for Contemplative Mind in Society for the support it has given to faculty members at colleges and universities across the country to engage in this challenging work. We anticipate that their work will be multiplied in the years ahead as our society becomes more aware of the critical need for such practices.

3

CONTEMPLATIVE STUDIES

Can It Flourish in the Religious Studies Classroom?

HAROLD D. ROTH

The emerging field of contemplative studies reenvisions certain basic aspects of the existing models of teaching and research in higher education in order to foster a deeper knowledge of the nature of our existence as human beings in a world that is intricately interrelated on many levels. One way to accomplish this is to develop the study of contemplative traditions within established Western departments of religious studies. Another way to accomplish this is to develop a completely new field of academic endeavor that takes account of the emerging scientific work on the neurological foundation of the concentrated and relaxed states of mind attained by meditation and by a variety of other human endeavors, and applies them directly to our lives.

Contemplative experiences, while deliberately cultivated in many of the world's major religious traditions, occur extensively outside them as well and these are also worthy subjects for this emerging field. To limit this study to those experiences deliberately cultivated within religious traditions thus limits the consideration of their full breadth and range. Furthermore, to study them from within the methodologies of religious studies as an academic discipline is hampered by the extent to which Christian theological biases and historicist reactions against them still dominate the field of religious studies and prevent this field from an open-minded consideration of contemplative experiences. In this chapter I will attempt to demonstrate that such an open-minded consideration will only flourish if it is established as a totally independent field.

EUROCENTRIC ATTITUDES IN RELIGIOUS STUDIES

Writing in 1951, Joachim Wach baldly stated

> There can be no "godless" religion, and only a misunderstanding can make Buddhism and Confucianism into such. Buddhism and Jainism may have started as criticisms of the traditional or of any positive characterization of Ultimate Reality, but they soon developed into *genuine religions*.[1]

Wach was a pioneer in the history of religions who strove mightily to free the academic study of religion from Christian theological influences. Yet in this quotation and throughout his book, *The Comparative Study of Religions*, he makes an essentially theological assumption: that "genuine religions" must see God as the Ultimate Reality.

While this kind of unreflective ethnocentrism is understandable for someone thinking and writing almost seven decades ago, there are very concrete ways in which this still persists in subtle forms among scholars of religion in North America.

Popular and influential social scientific studies of religion in many ways exemplify this very limited understanding of religion. For example, the influential anthropologist of religion Pascal Boyer assumes that "supernatural notions" are one of the essential defining characteristics of religion and that these are caused directly by specific cognitive templates.[2] They include anthropomorphic ideas about God or gods, including intentional agency and they are never based on actual experience:

> It is also striking that the details of such representations [of supernatural agents' actions in the world] are generally derived not from what one has experienced but rather of what others have said . . . , from socially transmitted information, not direct experience.[3]

Drawing from Christian beliefs about the nature of God, considered *the supernatural agent par excellence*, Boyer generalizes his ideas to all religions without considering that there are religious traditions that put little or no stock in anything supernatural.[4] In his unreflective ethnocentrism, he demonstrates no awareness that in some of the major contemplative traditions of the non-Western world, such as foundational Daoism in China and Theravada Buddhism in South Asia, "supernatural" powers or forces are either absent or play a relatively insignificant role.[5] Henry Rosemont Jr. has unequivocally stated that these traditions simply do not presume the existence of a transcendent, supernatural realm:

No such metaphysical claims invest Buddhist, Confucian, or Daoist texts as I read them, and while these latter religions, and all others, have supernatural entities described in their oral or written canons, these entities remain altogether linked to the world.[6]

Clearly, Boyer and social scientists and scholars of religion who have proposed reductive and evolutionary attempts to "explain religion" are working with models of religion heavily influenced by their own personal cultural experiences, and demonstrate no awareness of the exceptions to their presumed universal assumptions about religion that are posed by the Asian contemplative traditions.

There is a second related issue that is just as deeply unreflective. It is the assumption that our European religious, philosophical, and now scientific conceptions of human experience contain its only possibly veridical models. Thus any tradition that posits veridical cognition that does not fall within these models is *ipso facto* mistaken. There are a number of key beliefs associated with this assumption, one of them being that human experience is totally conditioned by preexisting cognitive categories. This position is forcefully stated by Steven Katz in his influential essay "Language, Epistemology, and Mysticism": "*There are NO pure* [i.e., unmediated] *experiences.* Neither mystical experience nor more ordinary forms of experience give any indication, or any grounds for believing, that they are unmediated."[7]

Yet mystical traditions the world over argue that it is only when these mediating cognitive categories are stripped away that genuine intuitive knowledge and clear cognition can develop, yielding experience that is truly noetic, as William James put it.[8] Katz assumes that he, as a modern European child of the Enlightenment, understands what the world's great mystics have experienced, a form of ethnocentric hubris that parallels assumptions of European imperialists who dominated the world in the name of their cultural superiority.

The ultimate implications of this for the study of religion and cognition are far-reaching: namely, that mystical experience, and any subjective experience for that matter, cannot possibly be veridical. They can tell us nothing new or true about the world because we can only possibly cognize through the categories imprinted within us by our historical and cultural context. Subjective experience is thus relative and individualistic and has no claims to truth that anyone else must take seriously. Religious experience tells us only what our religion already knows, so there is absolutely no point in trying to understand or assess it because it yields no genuine "objective" knowledge. In Religious Studies departments throughout North America, lack of interest in religious experience (because of its lack of veridicality) has led to a scholarly shift to historicism, the approach to critical study that asserts that a text can only be understood as a product of the social, historical, and political forces of its time.

HISTORICIST REDUCTIONISM AND THE
RETREAT FROM RELIGIOUS EXPERIENCE

Unreflective ethnocentrism leading to a denigration of the value of religious experience is a principal reason why the open and unbiased study of contemplative experience can best be pursued outside the field of religious studies. This field has gradually moved away from its origins in Christian theology, first separating its mission from that of chaplaincy and second introducing what one scholar has called the "historical-scientific-philosophical study of religions committed to an underlying ideal of detached objectivity and value-neutral inquiry."[9] To a considerable extent, historical and social scientific studies have gradually come to dominate research and teaching in North American Religious Studies departments, as even a cursory examination of journals from the field will indicate.

I am not here to argue that historical and social scientific studies of different religious traditions are not valuable. Indeed this is not at all the case; they are extremely valuable in contextualizing religious experience and helping us to clarify differences between our own modern perspectives and those of the authors of ancient religious texts. In my own scholarship I have often done very detailed historical and text-historical studies of foundational Daoist religious and philosophical works.[10] However, the dominance of such scholarship in the field belies a deeper question: Why this almost total retreat from serious consideration of religious experience? Why has the role of subjective experience in religion been abandoned?

We can explain this in part because of the historical development of the field of religious studies. Because the entire field emerged from liberal Protestant theology in the immediate pre-War and post-War periods, issues that dictate the field derived from Eurocentric roots. For example, the following conceptual categories still dominate: soteriology (that discusses how people are saved and so implies a Power that does the saving); metaphysics (that implies a nonphysical, world-transcending supernatural power); ontology (that implicitly posits ultimate Being in the world); cosmogony (that implies that the universe had a unique and discrete beginning). All of these concerns betray an Abrahamic—and, in particular, a Christian—worldview that was presumed by our forebears to be universal.

To a great extent the strong emphasis on historical and social scientific models that now dominates the field of religious studies represents a forceful attempt to move the field away from Christian concerns and values and to develop a more neutral perspective from which to study all religions. Despite this, popular critics of the field such as Russell McCutcheon have completely missed this point: they mistake historicism and reductionism for "critical method," entirely ignoring the unreflective ethnocentrism that undergirds these methodologies. McCutcheon focuses on dividing scholars in the field into two camps: "critics" (who have this presumed position of neutrality) and "caretakers" (essentially theologians in disguise who seek to prove the truths of religion in the guise of value neutrality).[11] The only way to be critical for McCutcheon is to treat religion and religious phenomena as objects to be analyzed according to "naturalistic" historical and social contexts and hence devoid of epistemic value. Thus McCutcheon does not escape the ethnocentric assumptions of Wach, Boyer, and Katz. His concept of religion is totally derived from Abrahamic traditions: it is all about faith, belief, God, and the supernatural. This ignorance of the contemplative traditions of the non-Western world demonstrates the kind of continued failure of scholars of religion—who put such a high value on contextualizing the religions they study—to contextualize themselves.

This failure at self-contextualization is particularly ironic for those who consider themselves critical scholars of religion, because much of their historical and social scientific research is dominated by historicist agendas that assert that all aspects of religion, particularly the epistemic insights that derive from their practices, are totally determined by their historical and social context. Following this way of thought, religious experience is never to be studied from the insider, first-person perspective. That perspective is denied to scholars because we can study religion only from the outside in; only its external qualities are available to us; only the outer aspects of religion are potentially *veridical*.

European thought since Descartes and Kant has validated only "external studies," that examine only "objectively observable" aspects of religion: its institutions and how they interact with society, their internal power relations, and so on. This, in effect, basically excludes religious experience and human subjectivity from serious critical examination because they are internal. Yet it is precisely these internal experiences that for William James are the very heart of religion and that should be the very heart of any serious approach to studying both religion and human cognition. Thus for James the subjective religious experience of human beings (what he calls "personal religion") is the very essence of religion; yet it is ignored in the modern academy.[12]

This has far-reaching implications for the issue of whether or not we can study contemplative experience in departments of religious studies. By discarding the subjectivity of religion as a serious topic of rational inquiry, contemporary Western scholars of religion have abandoned the field entirely to religious practitioners, who may indeed place dogmatic faith in the truths of their religion as the primary article of practice. By turning our backs on the systematic exploration of religious subjectivity from the "inside out," scholars of religion have also cut themselves off from a valuable approach to the many problems of human existence, a valuable source of empirical knowledge that has been well developed in the contemplative traditions of Asia, and a potentially valuable method for studying these traditions.

I would argue that the very reason we have become so devoted to historicist approaches to religion is that the field of religious studies is still dominated by an ethnocentric bias. The limited view of human cognition that it entails developed from the struggles of the European Enlightenment and the split that arose therein between science and religion. Alan Wallace argues that this perspective had led to what he calls a kind of "metaphysical realism" that results in an "objectivist" view of the world whose principles are as follows:

1. The real world consists of mind-independent objects;
2. There is exactly one true and complete description of the way the world is;
3. Truth involves some sort of correspondence between an existing world and our description of it;[13]
4. It is not only possible, but desirable, for scientists and scholars to describe the world from the "God's-eye" viewpoint of a completely detached, objective, and value-neutral observer.[14]

As Wallace has cogently argued, this is the foundation of the "scientific materialism" that so dominates our modern understandings of the world and ourselves. What is missing is the very human subjectivity that is the basis of all our experience. On the scientific level, human subjectivity is the source for all the conceptual models we develop to explain the underlying structures of the world in the physical sciences and the underlying structures of consciousness in the cognitive sciences. All scientific experimentation used to establish these underlying "truths" is also a product of human subjectivity. Thus, despite all the principles of experimental science that attempt to establish objective standards for research, in the last analysis all these are derived by human beings and are therefore grounded in human subjectivity. Because of our headlong quest for scientific certainty in an objectivist-materialist world, we have ignored this important foundation, and this is true not only for scientists but for scholars of religion as well.

Ruling out the systematic exploration of human subjectivity because it is not a veridical epistemological source has given both scientific researchers and religion scholars a considerable amount of control over their subject matter and a rationale for their approach, yet at the same time it severely restricts it. If human cognition can be effectively reduced to the product of preexisting historical, social, and political forces, then it can be valuable to study only as a product of these forces and it provides no new insights in its own right. Yet the very history of human inventiveness flies in the face of this notion, for if people experience only what their culture imprints on them, how can anything new arise? Clearly something else must be going on. We cannot understand this something else without fully appreciating that importance of subjectivity. Furthermore, failing to explore human subjectivity, scholars of religion and social scientists remain blind to the very personal, subjective, and ethnocentric biases of their own approaches.

It is for these reasons I have concluded that the field of religious studies in the West is an unsuitable location for the open and unbiased study of contemplative experience. However, not all is lost: there are developments in other less ethnocentrically encumbered academic disciplines that are encouraging.

PROMISING DEVELOPMENTS IN COGNITIVE SCIENCE

There is an emerging movement in cognitive science that has broken free of western epistemological biases, asserting that human experience is fundamentally both *embodied* and *intersubjective*. Pioneered by the late cognitive neuroscientist Francisco Varela and his colleagues Eleanor Rosch and Evan Thompson, it describes an "enactive" approach to cognition, asserting that human cognition is fundamentally grounded in the subjective experience of our minds within a physical body and is hence both simultaneously subjective and objective.[15]

Varela, Thompson, and Rosch do not describe human cognition as a subjective representation of an objective world; it is, rather, the constantly shifting enactment of a myriad of worlds of experience that are context-interactive (simultaneously subjective and objective). Based on this research in cognitive science, we cannot ignore human subjectivity by the intellectual trick of pretending that it does not exist or is not relevant, as we find in ethnocentric religious studies. If we do this, we are living in what Zen master Jōshu Sasaki has called a "two dimensional" world, one in which I appear to stand apart from a preexisting objective world affirming truths from my position of a fixed self, as if it was the only one possible.

For Varela, Thompson, and Rosch, relying on Madhyamika Buddhist philosophy's nonreliance on either objectivity or subjectivity,[16] and for Wallace, whose work is in the training of consciousness through *shamatha* (meditative quiescence),[17] the realization of the fundamental groundlessness of human experience is a kind of intersubjectivity. Each of these thinkers posits somewhat different sources for the intersubjective world: "groundlessness" for one, the "substrate consciousness" for the other. What is clear is that none of these are possible to conceive of, much less experience, if we remain trapped within the ethnocentrism of studying contemplative experience as a product of exclusively social and historical forces. What is also clear is that the systematic training of consciousness through contemplative disciplines is a prerequisite for truly understanding and experiencing the role of the subjective in this intersubjective world.

The result of this cognitive research is the valorization of "first-person" experience in learning so crucial for contemplative studies. What Evan Thompson says about cognitive science is equally true of the study of contemplative experience in the major wisdom traditions of the world:

> I believe that a mature science of mind would have to include disciplined first-person methods of investigating subjective experience in active partnership with the third-person biobehavioral science. "First-person methods" are practices that increase an individual's sensitivity to his or her own experience through the systematic training of attention and self-regulation of emotion. This ability to attend reflexively to experience itself —to attend not simply to what one experiences (the object) but to how one experiences it (the act) seems to be a uniquely human ability and mode of experience we do not share with other animals. First-person methods for cultivating this ability are found primarily in the contemplative wisdom traditions of human experience, especially Buddhism. Throughout history religion has provided the main home for contemplative experience and its theoretical articulation in philosophy and psychology. Thus . . . religion . . . is . . . a repository of first-person methods that can play an active and creative role in scientific investigation itself.[18]

Ironically, despite the well-accepted role of religion as a repository of first-person methods and contemplative experiences, the current state of the field of religious studies makes it impossible for these experiences to be studied therein. One reason is that, for Varela, Thompson, Rosch, and Wallace, to truly study contemplative experience involves a systematic training of the mind to investigate itself, something that has been developed in the pan-Buddhist practices of *shamatha* and *vipashyana*—stopping and seeing, mental concentration and focused insight. Each of these scholars implies that these practices can be taken out of an exclusively monastic setting and used to develop what the latter calls a genuine "Contemplative Science." I see the natural home for this in the newly developing and independent discipline of contemplative studies. Why is this?

A truly non-ethnocentric study of the contemplative experiences would entail a number of things. The first is that we remain open-minded to them and do not *a priori* commit ourselves to the historicist reductionism that assumes that these experiences are epistemologically invalid. The second entails an admission of the fact that despite pretending to be "objective" and value-neutral, scholars of religion have their own subjective biases that are deeply enmeshed in their cultural presuppositions about the nature of religion and in their own personal experience of it. This has everything to do with how they pursue their study of religion, the kinds of issues they select, and arguments they attempt to prove. The third is that we pursue the study of contemplative experience from both third-person and first-person approaches, the latter involving direct experiential training in the introspective observation of experience.

What I am calling for is nothing other than what former University of California, Berkeley professor Frits Staal called for more than three decades ago in his pioneering work, *Exploring Mysticism*, a work largely ignored because of the deeply held ethnocentric biases of the field.

> If mysticism is to be studied seriously, it should not merely be studied indirectly and from without, but also directly and from within. Mysticism can at least in part be regarded as something affecting the human mind, and it is therefore quite unreasonable to expect that it could be fruitfully studied by confining oneself to literature about or contributed by mystics, or to the behavior and physiological characteristics of mystics and their bodies. No one would willingly impose upon himself such artificial constraints when exploring other phenomena affecting or pertaining to the mind; he would not study perception only by analyzing reports of those who describe what they perceive, or by looking at what happens to people and their bodies when they are engaged in perceiving. What one would do when studying perception, in addition, if not first of all, is to observe and analyze one's own perceptions.[19]

It is my contention that contemplative experiences, which include the mystical experiences of which Staal speaks and others of a more mundane nature, can most productively and accurately be studied by this dual approach combining third-person and first-person perspectives.

For the reasons given here, I do not think that departments of religious studies in the West can sufficiently free themselves from the pervasive influences of unreflective ethnocentrism to allow this kind of dual approach to be established. Where are we to develop this kind of dual approach that trains people in the historical contexts and the scientific explanations as well as the internal self-disciplines essential to the unbiased study of contemplative experience? It is my contention that we can best accomplish this within an independent discipline of contemplative studies.

THE FIELD OF CONTEMPLATIVE STUDIES

There is a developing new field of academic endeavor in North America devoted to the critical study of contemplative states of experience. Focusing on the many ways human beings have found, across cultures and across time, to concentrate, broaden, and deepen conscious awareness, contemplative studies is a rubric under which this research and teaching can best be organized. As we have developed the field of contemplative studies at Brown University, we conceive of it as the attempt to:

1) Identify the varieties of contemplative experiences of which human beings are capable;
2) Find meaningful scientific explanations for them;
3) Cultivate first-person knowledge of them;
4) Critically assess their nature and significance.

We study the underlying philosophy, psychology, and phenomenology of human contemplative experience through a combination of traditional third-person approaches combined with more innovative, critical first-person approaches. In other words, we study contemplative experiences from the following perspectives:

- Science: particularly psychology, neuroscience, cognitive science, and clinical medicine;
- Humanities: contemplative dimensions of literature, philosophy, and religion;
- The creative arts: the role of contemplation in both the creation and the appreciation of the visual and fine arts, creative writing, and in the various performing arts of dance, drama, and music.

Central to this approach is the understanding that contemplative experiences are not exclusively confined to religion. While methods to attain contemplative states of consciousness can most certainly be found in religious practices, such states can also be found in a wide variety of nonreligious practices such as making or listening to music, dancing, acting, writing poetry or prose, painting, sculpting, and even the intent observation of the natural world. Following the pioneering research on the state of optimal experience called "flow" by Mihalyi Csíkszentmihályi and his cohorts,[20] contemplative studies seeks to discover the complete range of experiences of attention, focus, tranquility, and insight and to demonstrate that even the most profound of them, those deliberately cultivated in the world's great contemplative traditions, are not of a fundamentally different kind than the most shallow; all occur on a continuous spectrum of experience that can be rationally identified, scientifically researched, and subjectively experienced.

The first of these major categories of contemplative studies includes more than four decades of scientific research into the nature of meditation and its cognitive impact. We can break down this research into four areas:

1. Clinical applications. Meditation has been applied clinically most often by using Mindfulness Based Stress Reduction (MBSR), and has been studied by

Jon Kabat-Zinn, by Zindel Segal, and by Ruth Baer, among others. Also studied are the medical applications of Transcendental Meditation and a variant of it studied by Herbert Benson, as well as the application of yoga, *qigong*, and *taiji*.[21]

2. Cognitive activity. This research, for example by Amishi Jha and by Stephen Kosslyn, explores how meditation influences cognitive functioning in both advanced and beginning meditators.[22]

3. Neurological measurements. EEG and fMRI research on both advanced and beginning meditators has been carried out by such researchers as Richard Davidson, Jonathan Cohen, and Cliff Saron.[23]

4. Positive Psychology, the scientific study of the strengths and virtues that enable individuals and communities to thrive, has developed in the past decade under the guidance of such researchers as Martin Seligman, Mihalyi Csíkszent-mihályi, and Jonathan Haidt.[24]

All these areas, taken together, might be considered "Contemplative Science."[25] Studying the scientific underpinnings of contemplative experience from perspectives that combine third-person and first-person approaches is beginning to yield fascinating results about what is going on in the human being who has contemplative experiences. Armed with this knowledge we may be better able to study, teach, and learn how to have contemplative experiences.

The second major category of contemplative studies is the humanities, and largely consists of studying the role of contemplation in philosophy (particularly phenomenology and philosophy of mind), literature, and the comparative study of religion. Critical first-person methods are just beginning to be developed in the study of religion but they are quite controversial. For example for nine years now, despite the best efforts of my colleagues, I have regularly taught a course entitled The Theory and Practice of Buddhist Meditation. This course includes both the regular weekly seminar of three hours *and* three one-hour "lab" sessions each week in which students try out meditation techniques that are directly related to the text we are reading in the seminars.[26] Because of the inherent biases in the field of religious studies, courses such as this one are often outliers, subject to intense scrutiny and criticism. Contemplative studies as an academic discipline is much better equipped to embrace and support such courses.

The third major category of contemplative studies is the creative arts. In it we explore the production of contemplative states of consciousness via the actual creation of art. For example, at Brown we have several classes in which students write their own poetry in class using cues and key words from their professor. We also teach a course on how the actual hearing of music affects the mind.

From the perspective of an educator, what is the point of all this?

1) In general, the purpose is to begin to give students a solid under-standing—both third-person and first-person—of the range of con-templative experiences they may encounter in their lives, both what

they are, how to understand them when they spontaneously occur, and how to deliberately cultivate them.

2) In particular, the purpose is to give students practical training in a range of techniques to attain calmness, tranquility, and attentional stability.

3) The attainment of states of calmness, tranquility, and attentional stability and focus are important tools to use in:

a) self-exploration and self-understanding; if the purpose of a university education is "to know thyself," there is no better means to do so than through contemplative training;

b) developing a sound grasp of the nature of consciousness as a basis for further philosophical and scientific studies;

c) first-person approaches to the study of contemplative experience cultivated in religious traditions.

William James well understood the importance of this type of training:

> the faculty of voluntarily bringing back a wandering attention, over and over again, is the very root of judgment, character, and will. . . . An education which should improve this faculty would be *the* education *par excellence.*[27]

We are finally reaching the point where James's pessimism about the existence of methods for training the attention can now give way to a new optimism about incorporating these methods as essential tools of higher education. I firmly believe that to do so will significantly broaden our perspectives on the nature and structure of human experience, breaking us out of the objectivism and "scientific materialism" that has dominated religious studies and the academy for far too long, and finally projecting us past a world of knowledge dominated by unreflective ethnocentrism into a fuller appreciation of a world in which subjective and objective fields of experience, in all their varieties, are on an equal footing. It is my conclusion that this can most fruitfully be accomplished by establishing a completely independent academic discipline of contemplative studies and that is what we have been attempting to do at Brown University.

NOTES

1. Joachim Wach, *The Comparative Study of Religions* (New York and London: Columbia University Press, 1961), 37. Italics added.

2. Pascal Boyer, "Gods and the Mental Instincts That Create Them," in *Science, Religion, and the Human Experience*, ed. James Proctor (Oxford and

New York: Oxford University Press, 2005), 244. Boyer's use of this term can only be described as deriving from common parlance. Neither in this article nor in his larger study, *Religion Explained*, does he attempt to provide a clear definition of this term. For the history of how such concepts led to the rise of "scientific materialism" in Europe, see B. Alan Wallace, *The Taboo of Subjectivity* (Oxford and New York: Oxford University Press, 2000), 41–56. For a study of these concepts in Christian theology see Paul Draper, "God, Science, and Naturalism," in William Wainwright, ed., *The Oxford Handbook of Philosophy of Religion* (Oxford and New York: Oxford University Press, 2005), 272–303.

3. Boyer, "Gods and the Mental Instincts That Create Them," 244.

4. Ibid., 247.

5. There are, of course, important contemplative traditions in Christianity that Boyer ignores; whether or not they hold "supernatural" beliefs is a contentious issue beyond the scope of this chapter.

6. Henry Rosemont Jr., *Rationality and Religious Experience: The Continuing Relevance of the World's Spiritual Traditions* (LaSalle: Open Court Press, 2001), 43.

7. Steven Katz, *Mysticism and Philosophical Analysis* (New York and Oxford: Oxford University Press, 1979), 26.

8. William James, *Varieties of Religious Experience: A Study in Human Nature* (New York: New American Library, 1958), 293. This is perhaps best seen in the early Daoist tradition, where the progressive emptying out of the contents of consciousness results first in a state alternately described as being completely empty, attaining the One, or merging with the Dao. This is then followed by the arising of an attachment-free cognition that spontaneously perceives, knows, and acts in complete harmony with the greater forces of the cosmos. For details on these processes see two articles of mine: "Evidence for Stages of Meditation in Early Taoism," *Bulletin of the School of Oriental and African Studies* 60, no. 2 (June, 1997): 295–314; "Bimodal Mystical Experience in the Qiwulun of *Chuang Tzu*," *Journal of Chinese Religions* 28 (2000): 1–20.

9. Sumner B. Twiss, "Shaping the Curriculum: The Emergence of Religious Studies," in *Counterpoints: Issues in Teaching Religious Studies*, ed. Mark Hadley and Mark Unno (Providence: Department of Religious Studies, Brown University, 1995), 33. Although written as a study of a particular department, it is a case study that is characteristic of the entire field.

10. See, for example, Harold D. Roth, *The Textual History of the Huai-nan Tzu* (Ann Arbor: Association for Asian Studies Monograph No. 46, 1992).

11. Russell McCutcheon, *Critics Not Caretakers: Redescribing the Public Study of Religion* (Albany: State University of New York Press, 2001) is probably the most direct statement of this thesis; *Manufacturing Religion* (New York and

Oxford: Oxford University Press, 2003) argues this critique in terms of the presumed clash between "insider" and "outsider" perspectives in the study of religion. His critique of the study of religion as a special *sui generis* phenomenon in the latter volume is not without merit, but he does not go far enough to break away from the European cultural presuppositions that support objectivist historicism and social scientific reductionism.

12. James, *Varieties of Religious Experience*, 42.

13. B. Alan Wallace, "The Intersubjective Worlds of Science and Religion," in *Science, Religion, and the Human Experience*, ed. James Proctor (New York and Oxford: Oxford University Press, 2005), 309.

14. B. Alan Wallace, *The Taboo of Subjectivity: Toward a New Science of Consciousness* (Oxford: Oxford University Press, 2004), 41–56.

15. Francisco Varela, Eleanor Rosch, and Evan Thompson, *The Embodied Mind* (Cambridge: MIT Press, 1991), 9.

16. Ibid., 217–54.

17. B. Alan Wallace, *Contemplative Science: Where Buddhism and Neuroscience Converge* (New York: Columbia University Press, 2006), 15–16.

18. Evan Thompson, "Empathy and Human Experience," in *Science, Religion, and Human Experience*, ed. James Proctor (New York and Oxford: Oxford University Press, 2005), 261–62.

19. Frits Staal, *Exploring Mysticism* (Berkeley and Los Angeles: University of California Press, 1975), 123–24.

20. Mihalyi Csíkszentmihályi, *Flow: The Psychology of Optimal Experience* (New York: Harper and Row, 1990).

21. The pioneering works in these areas are Jon Kabat-Zinn, *Full Catastrophe Living* (New York: Bantam Dell, 1990); Herbert Benson, *The Relaxation Response* (New York: Harper, 2000). See also Ruth A. Baer, "Mindfulness Training as a Clinical Intervention: A Conceptual Review," *Clinical Psychology: Science and Practice* 10, no. 2 (Summer 2003): 125–43; and Scott Bishop, Mark Lau, Shauna Shapiro, Linda Carlson, Nicole Anderson, James Carmody, Zindel Segal, Susan Abbey, Michael Speca, Drew Velting, and Gerald Devins, "Mindfulness: A Proposed Operational Definition," *Clinical Psychology: Science and Practice* 11, no. 3 (Fall 2004): 230–41.

22. Jha's lab at the University of Pennsylvania is doing cutting-edge research on the cognitive impact of contemplative practices. See, for example, her article, A. P. Jha, J. Krompinger, M. J. Baime, "Mindfulness Training Modifies Subsystems of Attention," *Cognitive Affective & Behavioral Neuroscience* 7, no. 2 (2007): 109–19.

23. The basic scientific research in these areas is voluminous. I refer the reader to the recent summary of research that focuses on Tibetan Buddhist meditation, Antoine Lutz, John D. Dunne, and Richard J. Davidson, "Meditation and Neuroscience: An Introduction," in *The Cambridge Handbook of Con-*

sciousness, ed. Philip Zelazo, Morris Moscovitch, and Evan Thompson (New York: Cambridge University Press, 2007), 499–555; see also two works by James Austin that present the neuroscience of Japanese Zen Buddhist contemplative experience: *Zen and the Brain* (Cambridge: MIT Press, 1998) and *Zen-Brain Reflections* (Cambridge: MIT Press, 2006).

24. Two leading works in this very new area are Martin Seligman, *Authentic Happiness* (New York: The Free Press, 2004); Jonathan Haidt, *The Happiness Hypothesis: Finding Modern Truth in Ancient Wisdom* (New York: Basic Books, 2006).

25. Wallace, *Contemplative Science*.

26. For a discussion of the pedagogical theory surrounding this, see my article, "Contemplative Studies: Prospects for a New Field," *Columbia Teacher's College Record Special Issue on Contemplative Education* 108, no. 9 (September 2006): 1787–1816.

27. William James, *The Principles of Psychology* (New York: Henry Holt, 1890), 1.424.

4

CONTEMPLATIVE STUDIES AND THE ART OF PERSUASION

The Institutional Challenge

LAURIE L. PATTON

M y interest in this emerging new field of contemplative studies comes from two sources. First, I have written about early Indian mythological and ritual texts, and the use of mantra in narrative and ritual, in ways that might be relevant for contemplative practices.[1] Second, in the last two years I have led a team that has had to justify this new initiative at Emory in contemplative studies to the higher administration. Fortunately, our team was successful in advancing that initiative. Let me focus on this second issue in this chapter.

PERSUADING THE DPP: MAKING THE SCIENCE-HUMANITIES CONNECTION WORK TO OUR ADVANTAGE

It seems to me that if Hal Roth's initiative at Brown, Anne Klein's initiative in pedagogy at Rice, and our initiative in both medical research and humanistic seminars at Emory are going to thrive, then a new way of talking about the value of the emerging field is necessary. To put it another way, in order for us to continue to be funded in some way that will let us do the kind of interdisciplinary work we are already doing, then contemplative studies as a field needs to be translated to the administration in a persuasive way. When I say "administration," I mean Deans and Provosts and Presidents, hereafter known as the DPP.

It is *easier* (not necessarily easy) to do this persuasion to the DPP in terms of science. The work of contemplative studies is especially intriguing in today's academy for two reasons. The first is that it dovetails with scientific inquiry and studies of neurology, psychology, and biological approaches to the nervous system. The second is that contemplative studies integrates with science in such a way that the onus of justification bears more on the scientists than on the humanists. In my own experience, scientists have to justify to their supervisors why they are interested in contemplative practices (rather than rheumatoid arthritis) far more than humanists have to justify partnering with scientists to study the roles of contemplative practices in our everyday bodily experience. Humanities' deans tend to like humanists partnering with scientists more than sciences' deans tend to like scientists partnering with humanists. This basic state of affairs is in the religionists' favor.

That basic observation being made, I think I would add that our describing the contemplative studies initiative to the DPP was successful not because it featured contemplative work *per se*, but because it provided a successful nexus of authentically interdisciplinary questions: we know that brains change, we know that psyches change, and we know that bodies change when we engage in contemplative practices. Description and measurement of these effects is just in its infancy and we need to do more. When presented in this way to the university funders, the rationale for contemplative studies was persuasive. It is important to note here that we specifically avoided saying anything about whether contemplative practices "work." The rationale had to be framed in terms of what we already know and the topics about which it would be good to know more.

CONTEMPLATIVE STUDIES AND NEW POSSIBILITIES FOR GOOD DESCRIPTION

We also know, from the humanist side, that these practices are poorly described by scientists who want to study them. When we first began to speak with one another at Emory, humanists were shocked at what the scientists all threw into a single grab bag of prayer, meditation, faith, attendance at church, and so on.[2] They seemed singularly unscientific in their descriptive practices. When we collaborated with them, intriguingly, scientists agreed with this statement. What they were describing was religion as a vague social force or set of practices that was not parsed in any detailed way that religious studies takes as normative in our field. In the context of contemplative studies, I encountered the first and perhaps the only time that scientists actually agreed that they could learn something from humanists. Thus the *Encyclopedia of Contemplative Practices* project, headed by John Dunne, was born.[3]

In addition to the exciting product of the *Encyclopedia*, the intriguing thing to me was that there was little argument, as there usually is, between scientists and humanists on this point. We all needed to learn how to describe, and describe more precisely—this was a shared intellectual goal about which there was very little controversy. I took this argument about description as well to the deans and provosts and presidents, and they all agreed. They agreed strongly enough that they thought the project eminently fundable.

It seems we have a new and intriguing development on our hands. Academic religious studies has typologies of contemplative experience in place and can engage with scientists in new and exciting ways—ways that are, moreover, fundable. The larger intellectual point here is very significant: good description is good description, whether it emerges from the scientific or the humanistic worlds.

CONTEMPLATIVE STUDIES AND ATTENTION SPANS IN CONTEMPORARY ACADEMIC LIFE

There is more to say about how to persuade administrators about the role of contemplative studies in the academy. This final perspective on contemplative studies comes not from the relative prestige of our topics of inquiry, but from a long-term interest in the ways in which we focus attention. When I was in graduate school I carried around a copy of Simone Weil's little piece "Reflections on the Right Use of School Studies with a View to the Love of God"[4] as a kind of inspiration. This is the essay in which she argues that learning languages is a kind of preparation for prayer. Rote memorization and the focus that it requires help us to confront our own stupidity as well as to sow the basic seeds for contemplation of God.

I loved this idea; I was learning Old Irish, German, and Sanskrit and felt very stupid indeed. More importantly, Weil's essay planted a seed in my mind that study is itself a form of contemplation, and needs to be marked that way—ritually marked. At a slightly earlier time I took a year to study in Edinburgh, where my study carrel at New College Divinity School was right next to that of a Dominican who crossed himself and said a prayer every time he sat down to study. In my twenty-year-old mind, it was a curiosity, but it kept recurring to me as I continued graduate work in religion. I became fascinated with the introductions and endings to the Sanskrit texts I read, many of them "framing" a text with a devotional prayer at the beginning and a statement of the *phalashruti*—the cumulative fruits of learning and reciting the sacred text—at the end. And many of the ancient Indian rituals that I have studied begin with a *samkalpa*, or declaration of intent. Now I am familiar with the Jewish prayer for scholars regularly recited by many Orthodox Jews before they sit down to study; it begins with a declaration that scholars create peace in the world.

All of these practices frame the basic act of study in a contemplative way, whether it is through recitation, declaration of intent, or devotion. They focus the act of study itself. In contemporary academic culture, we have lost such beginning and ending rituals for everyday acts of study. Convocation and the graduation rituals are hanging on by a thread in our academic practice. While convocations might have a contemplative tone to them, contemporary graduations surely do not. Neither ritual really has as its aim the focusing of attention. Yet, is it not the very thing that we complain about most in terms of the learning styles of our students? Some indeed argue that the intellectual "dark side" of our students' astonishing ability to multitask is their infinite distractability? Perhaps this is also their related inability to sustain an argument over the course of several paragraphs, whether it is in oral or written form?

Citing the recent studies of changes in learning styles here is not my point; we all probably have read them or know about them. Rather, my point is that contemplative studies has a larger, important role to play in the classroom because contemplative approaches move away from the kind of distracted and hasty instrumentality in which our students engage (what Paul Griffiths has called "reading for use"[5]) and back toward a sense that study and sustained attention are worthy acts for members of an academic community. Many of us in the contemplative practices seminar have agreed that contemplative studies as a field comprises far more than this, and many practices falling under the rubric of contemplative studies are about other things, such as the dissolution of attention. (To take a well-known example, *laya-yoga*, meaning the yoga of "absorption or dissolution," is named for that very idea.) Still, insofar as some contemplative pedagogy has to do with the training of the mind to stay in one place, then contemplative rituals designed to remind us that this is what we are doing when we study can be very useful indeed.

I am not advocating that we happily engage in the Dominican's prayer or the Jewish recitation, or even a watered-down pluralistic version of the same, where academics do their own rituals before they sit down to study (although they would be perfectly welcome to do so if they chose). Rather, I am thinking that this aspect of contemplative studies could challenge how we frame our classrooms at both their entrance points and their exit points. We might come up with a very important set of ritual frames that asks students to consider what they are doing in a noninstrumentalist way. To put it more precisely, we might help them to understand what kind of instrumentalism works well as a form of learning and what kind does not. We might connect the act of sustained attention with the disposition of rigorous analysis. We might begin and end our daily acts of learning with declarations of contemplative intention, either verbal or nonverbal.

While I would not rule out the more traditionally grounded rituals from specific religious traditions as a way of acting upon this idea, I also think that most of these rituals would need to be everyday rituals, and they would also need to be secular and to have a graceful way of entering into the secular study of religions within the academy. They would be small rituals of mindfulness, such as silence before the class begins discussion, or silence between one kind of discussion and another kind. They could be writing exercises in which students record intentions for that specific class. They could be exercises in which students are asked to contemplate the labor (*whose* labor?) that made the learning space of the classroom possible.

I mention this idea at some length because I think these small everyday approaches to contemplative studies in the secular learning environment could have a transformative effect on the negative effects of the increasingly distracted learning styles of our students (assuming of course that there are also positive effects). In the new classroom, students have a tendency toward multitasking, and "one-pointed" concentration is fast becoming a thing of the past in academic culture overall. Professors, too, are not immune to such a style of working; how many of us can recall a phone conversation with a colleague where we also hear them typing in the background?

Perhaps such transformative effects could be a way to persuade those Deans, Provosts, and Presidents who might be listening. We could even call those effects better "learning outcomes" because these are the kinds of results that the DPP themselves seek. In addition to the strong cases made here from highly experienced teachers of contemplative studies, those interested in the effects of contemplative studies on learning styles in general might productively study learning outcomes of students more practiced in contemplative concentration. These studies would make the most persuasive case possible to the DPP.

I am sure Simone Weil would never have thought her essay, written as it was in the throes of European upheaval and the personal ambiguity of existing between two religions, could help the "learning outcomes" of twenty-first-century classrooms. She probably would be suspicious of creating academic rituals, but she never feared the unexpected. Nor should we, as we move between our own ambiguous worlds within the academy.

NOTES

1. See my *Myth as Argument: The* Brhaddevata *as Canonical Commentary* (Berlin: DeGruyter, 1996); *Bringing the Gods to Mind: Mantra, Poetry and Ritual in Early Indian Sacrifice* (Berkeley: University of California Press, 2005).
2. As mentioned in Paul N. Duckro and Philip R. Magaletta, "The Effect of Prayer on Physical Health: Experimental Evidence," *Journal of Religion and Health* 33, no. 3 (Fall 1994): 211–19, the very definition of prayer in order to operationalize it for a scientific study is notoriously difficult, and over which there has been considerable disagreement (213). The scientists in our

group seemed frequently to refer to studies of Christian prayer, Buddhist meditation, Muslim prayer, Hindu yoga and Jewish chanting as if they were the same thing. Even in the more recent literature, there is considerable overlap of categories. (For example, in "Preferred Prayer Styles and Anxiety Control," *Journal of Religion and Health* 44, no. 4 [Winter 2005]: 403–12), J. Irene Harris, Sean W. Schoneman, and Stephanie R. Carrera do distinguish between prayer styles and provide an excellent review of the literature dealing with the difficulties of defining prayer in a social scientific way. However, the article still lacks a rigorous description of the cognitive process that self-reported "prayer" of those in the study actually involved. As religionists, we found this imprecision of categories rather daunting, and we were fortunate that our scientific colleagues agreed readily.

3. See http://www.emory.edu/religions&humanspirit/Religion%20pages/Contemplative%20Studies.htm.

4. Simone Weil, "Reflections on the Right Use of School Studies with a View to the Love of God," in *Waiting for God* (New York: Harper Collins, 2001 [reprint of 1951 edition]), 57–67.

5. Paul J. Griffiths, *Religious Reading* (New York: Oxford University Press, 1996).

II

THE CONTEMPLATIVE
PROFESSOR

5

FROM CONTENT TO CONTEXT TO CONTEMPLATION

One Professor's Journey

FRAN GRACE

THE POWER OF LIVED TRUTH

Truth resides in every human heart, and one has to search for it there.
—Gandhi[1]

This chapter offers a first-person account of my inner-outer evolution as a professor. The purpose is not to be exemplary but to animate the reader's own self-clarification and joy of teaching. Rather than encourage readers to adopt contemplative pedagogy, this chapter gives an account of why this professor decided to do so. The account is of interest to the current book because I began my career as the proverbial "last person you would ever expect" to teach meditation, and now I teach all of my classes in our university's Meditation Room, which is one of the first "contemplative classroom" spaces in the country. What happened?

I have discovered that all of my academic work emerges from an inner pursuit of truth. People become uneasy with interior reflection in academic settings, as if the life of the mind had nothing to do with the heart, body, and spirit. Experiential knowledge is sometimes seen as suspect in academia and in certain Christian theologies. This suspicion certainly held true in the church of my upbringing: "We have the scripture, *not* experience!" A similar principle seems to hold true in current academia, where third-person theoretical "outsider" knowledge is often viewed as more trustworthy than first-person experiential "insider" knowledge.

However, we find that experiential knowledge tends to be authoritative in daily life. When we want to know the taste of chocolate, we are more satisfied by eating it than itemizing its chemical constituents. Parents sending a child off to college want to know what the school is like by going for a campus visit, since the college guidebooks give only part of the story. As a hiker, I prefer to hear about the conditions of a trail from the person coming down off the summit, not the person reading a guidebook at the trailhead. Only the hiker who has "been there" that day can tell me whether the seasonal stream is flowing or not.

Theoretical (third-person) knowledge is valuable, but actualized (first-person) knowledge transmits certitude. In other words, lived truth transmits a clarifying coherence on the nonverbal level. Indeed, experimental scientific research of the last twenty years suggests that the nonverbal transmission of truth carries well beyond the single listener: perfected coherence within a person has a direct effect on the collective good and planetary health. The "personal" inner life may not be, in the end, personal at all. Individuals and groups who have attained high levels of lived truth coherence benefit the world, via a nonlinear "field" effect.[2] Newtonian physics and its billiard-ball-mode of linear causality bounded to the material plane, where a particular object moves another particular object by direct strike, seems to be giving way to a new paradigm wherein the tiniest movement (of a material *or* interior nature) *any*where has nonlinear reverberations *every*where.[3] The nonlinear impact of truth is referred to in Pali Buddhist literature, where truth statements of an existential nature are seen to change a course of events, often alleviating crisis. In the *Milindapanha*, we find this comment on the power of truth declarations: "Making an assertion of the truth they can cause rain to fall, fire to go out, they can ward off poison and do various other things they want to do."[4]

The "Map of Consciousness" developed by clinical scientist and modern mystic David R. Hawkins, synthesizes East-West spiritual literature, quantum physics, and nonlinear dynamics. One of Hawkins's key findings, matching those of quantum theorists David Bohm and Henry Stapp, is that inner development benefits the world: "We change the world not by what we say or do, but as a consequence of what we have *become*."[5] We are part of the whole, so our lived truth benefits the whole.

WALKING THE LABYRINTH

Since lived truth has a poetic rather than linear logic to it, this account unfolds via the circular inward-outward journey of the Labyrinth. I have been walking the Labyrinth as a contemplative practice since I was a college student traveling in Europe on a semester abroad program. In France, I visited the magnificent Chartres Cathedral and felt drawn to its eleven-circuit Labyrinth (twelfth century CE). Stepping into it, I knew I was entering into the collective field of devotion spirited by centuries of pilgrims who had walked its unicursal path to the Center. Prior to this Christian eleven-circuit Labyrinth, the seven-circuit Labyrinth existed in Cretan, Celtic, and Hopi cultures, as well as Jewish mystical texts.[6] Unlike a maze, the Labyrinth contains no tricks or dead ends. Its purpose is not to confuse but to clarify. Similar to other meditative methods, walking the Labyrinth facilitates a quieting of the left-brain thinking patterns characteristic of ordinary beta-wave activity, and it correspondingly enhances right-brain noetic insights characteristic of alpha and theta brain activity. The Labyrinth is "nonlinear"; the path takes you through its four quadrants in a nonsequential way. Suddenly, as with life, you may find yourself in the opposite quadrant from what you expected.

There is no single right way to walk the Labyrinth—fast, slow, skipping, kneeling, scooting, it does not matter. The unicursal path dissolves the common illusions of "the grass is greener elsewhere"; "my life should be different from what it is"; or "that other person's path is more right (or wrong) than mine." Inevitably, if you stay the course, the circular path leads you into your own deepest wisdom and back out to the world again.

The circular journey inward-then-outward is an archetypal imprint found in many religious traditions (e.g., spiral, medicine wheel, mandala, circle of life, circumambulation of the Kaaba at Mecca). Carl Jung called the circular pattern "an archetype of wholeness." Clinically, he noticed that many patients resolved their psychic turmoil after drawing or painting spontaneous (nondiscursive) "mandalas."[7] Subsequent research has confirmed the healing effect of rituals, meditations, and art therapies based on the circle form, known as the "torus" in mathematics. Jung suggested that the human psyche has an inexorable drive to uncover its wholeness by "circumambulating" its center.[8] Walking the Labyrinth is a body form of that inward motion; it facilitates the shedding of self-deception and the revelation of one's true nature. In contemplative Christianity, walking the Labyrinth is said to be patterned according to three inner "powers" or "stages" of Christian mystical tradition: purgation, illumination, and union.[9] I will take these three movements as the turning points of my journey.

As the reader will see, these inner movements correspond to three major pedagogical shifts in my development as a professor. I began my teaching career defaulting to a *content-based (third-person)* approach that emphasized information. Next, I explored *context-based (second-person)* teaching that involved interactive dialogue and community engagement. Most recently, I developed *contemplative (first-person)* learning methods that cultivate interior awareness, creative epiphanies, and compassionate understanding. My religious studies courses now consciously integrate the three pedagogical movements (content, context, contemplation) and three inner "powers" (purgation, illumination, union).

PURGATION

Life smoothes us, rounds us,
perfects us, as does the river the stone.
And there is no place
that our Beloved is not flowing . . .
though the current's force
you may not always like.
                              —St. Teresa of Avila[10]

When I first started the professor's life, I thought I knew a lot. Seven years of graduate training, three master's degrees, and a doctorate "with honors" gave me the impression that I knew more than I actually did. I assumed that my principal task in teaching was to impart the scholarly knowledge that I had been privileged to acquire. In other words, education was about *content*. Since I had not been trained in pedagogy during graduate school, I imagined that the correct style of teaching was what I had experienced from professors: lectures that organized information according to the professor's interpretative preferences. When I showed up for my first tenure-track teaching position, I noticed that most of my eight department colleagues lectured in this style. They thoughtfully prepared PowerPoint slides full of informational content, and they evaluated students based on their retention and analysis of this content. I studied their pedagogy, went to their classes, took notes from them, and sought to customize my own courses according to their style.

My first teaching job was at a church-related liberal arts university, well known for its conservative views. For my entire adult life, I had been a faithful member of this Protestant denomination. I served as a church missionary for two years after college, and, at the time of my hire as a faculty member, was married to a minister in the church. My first steps on the path of the professor were that of the confident Christian believer, loyal to her church and its traditions, including the prohibition of women's leadership in worship: "Women, be silent in the church" (I Corinthians 14:34). When the university's student newspaper interviewed me as a new hire, they queried, "What is it like to be the first and only full-time female religion professor here? Are you a feminist?" "Of course not!" was my impatient response. But the question had a lingering effect on me. In the classroom, I felt an extra determination to prove that I was just as authoritative in my content expertise as my male colleagues. I made sure my classes were "rigorous" (I relished student complaints about how "hard" my classes were), and I would not tolerate any of "that warm, fuzzy, navel-gazing fluff."

Asserting my authority in the classroom, however, was not the only reason I disparaged interior learning. There were also unconscious fears about stillness.

"Meditation is a doorway for the devil" was the warning from our preacher when I was in high school, and it still lurked in my unconscious two decades later. "Do not be idle. Keep your hands and mind busy. The devil, your enemy, lies in wait." Stillness was linked with "sloth," so I never allowed more than a few seconds of silence in the classroom. I filled the time with content, data, outlines, concepts, theories, and talking, talking, talking. "Besides," I told myself, "I want them to get their money's worth." Talking was productive; silence was a waste of time.

The initial inward movement on the Labyrinth is one of purgation, or un-learning. The walker sheds ignorance and limiting self-views. One of the first beliefs about teaching that I shed was "You have to teach the way that others teach." As long as I clung to that belief, I would never discover a pedagogy that fulfilled my potential as a professor. In my third year of teaching, I realized that I was not an effective teacher following the style of my colleagues; though success-ful for them, it was not natural for me. Exertions to "prove oneself," I discovered, are not nearly as worthwhile as healing the insecurities that underlie such com-pensatory strains.

I also saw the limitations of a strictly "outsider" view of religious traditions. Would we not have a fuller understanding of religious practitioners if we left the walls of the classroom and met them in person? So, I began to experiment with interactive and experiential learning assignments. In contrast to the third-person stance of my content-based lectures, these new methods aimed at second-person, contextual learning: peer discussions, in-class visits from community practition-ers, service learning, and field trips. We went to Skid Row in Los Angeles to work with a shelter program. We visited a diversity of religious sites in Southern California. In class, we had guest experts from local religious organizations who spoke of their faith and practice from an insider perspective and responded to student questions. Students reported in class on their visits to various religious congregations, including the university's official congregation held on campus.

The shift to include dialogue with "insiders" changed everything. It was as if the electricity of learning had switched to "on." When class time ended, the con-versations spilled out into the courtyard! The students bubbled over with enthu-siasm about the hands-on experiences and learning from religious insiders, and they became astute in applying the theoretical literature to the phenomena they observed. Religion had come alive for them as a topic of study.

Within weeks, I was called into the chair's office. My teaching seemed to be "stirring up trouble." He advised me to stay away from classroom discussions about the students' experiences at the on-campus church because they were sometimes critical of church tradition. This conversation was a turning point. I could see that even as my teaching came alive, my university was not a good fit for the professor/person I was becoming. In addition to the pedagogical changes,

I began to explore an inner vista beyond the sectarian wall I had lived behind for most of my life.

Especially desirous of cultivating a calmer presence for the benefit of my students, I entered a three-year certificate program in spiritual direction and contemplative practice, taught by religious sisters in the Archdiocese of Los Angeles. I faced my lifelong fear of silence and stillness as "the devil's gateway" and touched the peace of what Catholics call contemplative prayer. The apophatic nature of this method, which involved the dropping of all names and concepts about God, harmonized with an emerging agnostic part of me that had no interest in naming nonphysical phenomena. The medieval contemplative manual *The Cloud of Unknowing* recommended letting go of all concepts and dogma about God—even the holiest ones. The method entailed the gathering of one's "naked intent" onto a single word such as "love" in order to subdue mental distractions and bypass intellectual curiosity: "Why do you suppose that this little prayer of one syllable is powerful enough to pierce the heavens? Well, it is because it is the prayer of a whole being."[11]

I was delighted to experiment with quiet "beingness" if I did not have to theologize it. Still, the silence was not easy. I realized that the earlier religious indoctrination about the "devil" had covered over a deeper dread of silence that was best expressed by seventeenth-century philosopher Rene Descartes. After a series of mental experiments, he decided that the certainty of his existence depended upon his thoughts: "For it might possibly be the case that if I ceased entirely to think, that I should likewise cease altogether to exist."[12] So, there it was. The real fear was not the child's fear of a devil but the adult's terror of nonexistence. If I am not the intellect, what am I? It would be several years before I met a teacher who could show me the way through that terror to the peace that lay underneath it all along. There was indeed existence without thoughts, as the sages throughout history have declared. But this is getting ahead of the story.

By the fourth year of teaching, it felt riskier to stay where I was than to leave. The resignation was painful because I was leaving the only spiritual community and academic world I had known. Also, I feared failing the many women, young and old, who had placed their hopes on me to be an agent of change toward greater gender inclusivity within the institution. I hoped, however, that honoring my own joy would be the better gift than staying out of loyalty. I do not presume to know which choice would be best for others, as each person has her own purpose with reference to the collective good.

Gratefully, a new educational community welcomed me and my work. It was a private, nonreligious university whose pedagogical hallmark was engaged, experiential, community-based, and interactive learning. Serendipitously, the campus has one of the finest outdoor Labyrinths in the country, with this inscription:

Walking the Labyrinth

Your life is a sacred journey,
and it is about change, growth,
discovery, movement,
transformation,
Continuously expanding your vision of
what is possible,
Stretching your soul, learning to
see clearly and deeply,
Listening to your Intuition,
Taking courageous challenges at
every step along the way.
You're on a path, exactly where you are
meant to be right now.
And from here, you can go forward,
shaping your life story into a magnificent tale of
Triumph, of Healing, of Courage, of
Beauty, of Wisdom, of Power, of Dignity,
and of Love.

Whereas the first place had emphasized the singular authority of the professor and *content* in teaching, the new place emphasized the facilitating role of the professor and the interactive *context* of learning. While excited about this new circuitry, I felt ill-equipped for it. But pedagogical praxis was the air my new colleagues breathed, and they generously brought me up to speed with books, lunch conversations, and class visits. They were committed to nurturing my highest excellence as a teacher, even though my methods turned out to be very different from their own.

With such an encouraging context, I put myself fully into experimenting with the range of "engaged" pedagogies.[13] I asked students to see each other as "living texts" of expertise from their multiple "contexts" of life experience: gender, race, ethnicity, socioeconomic class, sexual expression, and personality type. I designed second-person interactive formats that engaged students directly with the readings, their own life histories, the local community, and each other: fishbowls,[14] debates, group presentations, guest speakers, practitioner panels, dance, spoken word, and community service work. This expansion to include "eco-social context"[15] was transformative for students, as the life narratives they heard from peers and community practitioners expanded their heart-minds beyond presumed viewpoints.

Inspired by bell hooks, I sought to educate the "entire person—mind, body, spirit—always lovingly."[16] However, looking back, I see that my pedagogical goal to educate the "whole person" faltered because I myself was not "whole," especially when it came to the third aspect of hooks's "body-mind-spirit" triad. Still stung by religious rejection, I tended to highlight the downside of religion: moralism and dogmatism. Influenced by Paulo Freire's *Pedagogy of the Oppressed*,[17] I assumed that education should liberate students from systems of oppression, and I included religion in that mix. "Religious faith is something that you outgrow" was my (mostly unconscious) assumption.

My work as a teacher, as I saw it back then, was to crack open the insulated worldviews of my students, unsettle them, revolutionize them, and liberate them from the societal bonds of suffering. Truthfully, however, the courses seemed to surface suffering rather than reveal a path out of it. Students lined up at my office hours like the wounded from a battlefield. The courses had not empowered them as ethical agents; they often *reacted* rather than *responded*. Students reacted unconsciously to each other and our texts, without awareness of their own part. Sometimes our second-person interactions shut down dialogue instead of opening it, because the inner source of a prejudice had not been observed and was projected onto the other person. The courses taught students the importance of their humanity, but not how to cultivate their wholeness. They learned about sociopolitical power, but not the power *within*. Therefore, they often spoke from a place of pain rather than agency. In sum: I was doing triage, not teaching.

As my four years at the second institution came to a close, culminating in tenure, I shed another layer: the illusion that I could teach others about social liberation without having pursued my own inner liberation. My exhaustion told me that I was not teaching from a place of lived-truth coherence: How could I give to others what I had not realized within myself? I began to understand why Gandhi had asserted the primacy of self-mastery in the process of collective liberation: "One drowning man will never save another. [If] slaves ourselves, it would be a mere pretention to think of freeing others."[18] How was I going to teach students the way out of suffering when my own life imploded with it?

ILLUMINATION

> Know that studying is also a great veil.
> Man goes into it, as if he has gone into a well or a moat.
> Then at the end he regrets it, because he comes to know that
>   he was kept busy with licking the pot so that he would be
>   held back from the subsistent, endless food.
> After all, words and sounds are the pot.
>
> —Shams-iTabrizi[19]

As I began my first sabbatical, I had little idea of the shift about to happen. I had been granted tenure at a university I truly enjoyed, yet I felt restless, exhausted, and disheartened. Weary of living from the neck up, my plan was to complete a degree in holistic healing. Just before I sent the tuition check, a dear nonacademic friend advised me: "You really think you can *study* your way to a healed life? The problem is not that you don't know enough. The problem is that you don't know who you are. Get over your fear and face yourself. The problems and the solution are both there, inside of you." I gave up seeking another degree; instead, I went within.

What I saw was not all pretty: underneath the surface of success boiled unresolved resentments and painful insecurities. I felt despair about my life and could see no way out. Spanish mystic St. John of the Cross used the apt metaphor "dark night of the soul" to describe the interior "denuding" prior to "union."[20] What was gestating in this "darkness"? I had no idea.

"What is dark night for the world is day light for the soul."[21] This principle turned out to be true, in spite of my skepticism. Through a synchronicity of events, I came upon a book that unveiled the "day light" for me. The book ended with a brief account of the author's spontaneous Enlightenment. As a scholar, I had studied mystics and sages for years, yet I had never come across a firsthand account of mystic realization so crystal clear and subjectively compelling as this account. His consciousness seemed to be of such veritable lived truth coherence that it induced impeccable clarity within me. I felt compelled to make a trip to see him, and that encounter redirected the course of my life.

I do not presume that others would find him to be helpful. As we know from academic teaching, different students are drawn to different teachers, and it is impossible to decipher the exact reasons for this. Nor do I presume that a "teacher" in physical form is the answer for others. I have seen people emerge from despair similar to mine with the help of other fields of coherence—music, nature, pilgrimage, support groups, therapy, love relationship or loss of one, healing from cancer, near-death experience—the list of catalytic possibilities is endless. For reasons I still do not understand, it was an eighty-year-old male sage that mirrored to me the truth of my life.

The discovery of this teacher for my inner life was profound, perhaps in the way that it would be for an initiate in any field of human learning to come upon a "coach" or "mentor" or "master" who had attained the highest degree of excellence in that field: the music composer who meets a Mozart, the physicist who meets an Einstein, the writer who meets a Jane Austen, the painter who meets a Rembrandt. In the vast literature on the inner sciences, a principal requirement specified for advancement is the guidance of a "realized master." This would be true for any field of endeavor. When I was a competitive tennis player, I sought out the best tennis coach I could find. In the realm of interior work, I needed instruction and transmission from a realized teacher. Contemporary Sufi philosopher Seyyed Hossein Nasr calls this realized state "the ultimate goal of human life, the crown of human existence."[22] Before encountering this sage, my academic interpretation was that Enlightenment did not exist except as fantasy in the minds of well-meaning religious people. But this third-person theoretical interpretation fell away in the presence of a real sage.

I remembered Rumi (Sufi master of the thirteenth century) and the famed encounter with his teacher, Shams. Rumi was an erudite theology professor and Shams a traveling dervish. Suddenly, out of nowhere, Shams appeared in the marketplace and asked Rumi a question that yanked him out of his scholarly sobriety and into a whirling intoxication of heart-stirring poetry and salvific joy. Shams was a living fire, and Rumi's heart ignited from the contact. Shams told him: "Intellect takes you to the threshold, but it doesn't take you into the house." He explained: "Whoever is more learned is further from the goal. The more abstruse is his thinking, the further he is. This is the work of the heart, not the forehead."[23] Christian mystics and Zen masters affirm a similar path to illumination: the ripening from intellectual erudition to experiential heart-knowledge. Dogen, thirteenth-century Zen master, realized that his sitting meditation would benefit others more than his book knowledge: "I stopped reading recorded sayings and other texts. I sat wholeheartedly and clarified the matter."[24]

With my teacher's enlightened consciousness as a guide, I put the books aside and "sat wholeheartedly." To initiate this inward focus, I spent several weeks in a rustic cabin, off the grid, down a rough, dirt road in the middle of an Oregon forest. There was no cell phone, computer, email, electricity, or indoor plumbing. I hiked downhill through snow to get to the compost toilet, and I heated the cabin with a woodstove. In this isolated and simple space, I faced several years' worth of jagged inner pieces.

In the years previous, I had grown exhausted from a way of teaching and "doingness" that aimed at changing external behaviors and institutional structures of justice. I saw in myself, students, and colleagues that behaviors could *appear* more just while inner prejudice remained. How could I eliminate the prejudice from the inner core of consciousness itself? The teacher taught me that when the source (heart-mind) is radiant with compassion, then the outflow (actions) cannot help but be compassionate—much like an uncontaminated water source effortlessly pours out pure water. He taught me to see myself as consciousness itself, rather than the contents of consciousness; in other words, to see myself as the screen upon which the movie is projected, or as the light of the projector itself, rather than a character in the movie. I started to pay more attention to the silence underneath all sounds than to the sounds themselves. This radical shift in perspective made possible the dropping away of mental patterns that had carried a lifetime of suffering. Through contemplative practice, cultivation of positive inner states became possible: attention, compassion, contentment, forgiveness, and stillness.

When I returned to work after my sabbatical, colleagues and friends remarked that I appeared happier, healthier, and calmer. As the years have passed, I recognize this period as one of inner transformation from a state of incoherence to one of lived-truth coherence. There is obviously much further to go, for as I let go of one barrier to compassion, another reveals itself. The gaps in my inner evolution are ever before me.

The primary point is that those first-person experiments out in the woods changed me radically as a teacher and scholar. I learned that meditation had the capacity to reduce suffering—without drugs, without cost, and in a way that activated a person's own ethical agency and refined the mind itself. Meditative practice seemed to offer a means to fulfill the purpose of what I understood liberal education to be: to foster "excellence, private and public," "train the mind," and "hold the habitual vision of greatness."[25] I left my solitary retreat knowing that my teaching and writing would be different than it had been. I came to see religious studies as a field rich in resources and methodologies for inner liberation and thereby foundational to the classical liberal arts aim to "know thyself." Eager to return to the classroom, I intuited that the interior (contemplative) dimension would complete the informational (content) and interactive (context) dimensions characteristic of my previous teaching.

UNION

> . . . Let me
> keep my mind on what matters,
> which is my work,
> which is mostly standing still and learning to be
> astonished.
> The phoebe, the delphinium.
> The sheep in the pasture, and the pasture.
> Which is mostly rejoicing, since all the ingredients are here,
> which is gratitude, to be given a mind and a heart. . . .
> —Mary Oliver, "Messenger"[26]

The final movement of the Labyrinth is the outward movement of "Union." In my current understanding, "union" means to be gratefully united in my heartmind with the potential for greatness that lies within all of us and with the forces of healing, beauty, wisdom, and love that exist in the world and all realms. It means to be of service to my students and to the community at large.

The work I do with students now integrates all three modes:

- Third-person (discursive analysis)—content
- Second-person (communal interaction)—context
- First-person (interior awareness)—contemplative

For example, the Seminar on Compassion course I developed several years ago carries this description: "Explores what it means to live a life of compassion through these lenses: 1) biographical models such as Gandhi, Nelson Mandela, the Dalai Lama, Mother Teresa, Viktor Frankl, and Mary Oliver; 2) the compassion teachings of the world's religions; 3) first-person investigation of compassion practices." Students read seven books, complete twenty hours of community service, carry out six contemplative "applied inquiry" assignments, and write an exam that requires competency in all three areas: content analysis, dialogic-communal skills, and interior cultivation.[27] We investigate what Paul J. Griffiths refers to as "maximal greatness": "If there are any trans-cultural universals in the sphere of religious thinking, it is probably that among them is the attempt to characterize, delineate, and, if possible, exhaustively define maximal greatness."[28] We study those rare individuals who love "beyond boundaries" and who are breathed by a universal compassion that goes beyond self, family, and nation to encompass all sentient beings.[29] When asked, these exemplars emphasize that unconditional compassion emerges from the rigor of inner examination, not social activism or rational analysis. Nelson Mandela told an interviewer who had asked him how it was possible to endure twenty-seven years in prison and walk out with his hand extended in forgiveness: "I had twenty-seven years to accomplish the most difficult task in life, which is to change *oneself*."[30] By changing himself, he changed the world. Much like the rising of the sea level lifts all ships, so the radiance of compassion within a human heart lifts all humanity.

Although ethically challenging, first-person contemplative methods bring a sense of completion to my pedagogy. They empower students to anchor themselves within their own body-mind-heart wholeness. It is so easy for students to default to the authority of another, especially that of the professor. Third-person critical thinking takes students a long way toward being independent thinkers, but in my experience, it is the first-person contemplative investigations into the nature of mind that liberate the students from their intellectual and emotional dependencies on others, including the professor. Like most people, they do not want to take responsibility for the thoughts in their own heads. Over time, the interior task that initially felt so daunting becomes empowering. At first, students are horrified at the contents of their thoughts: "I want to win the argument at all costs"; "I didn't realize how much self-hatred was there"; "I seem to be judgmental about everyone"; "My mind is rarely focused; it flits from thing to thing." Within a few weeks of meditation, they are usually able to experience the capacity to *observe* their mental phenomena. With that observer capacity activated, they are no longer the victims of their mind's knee-jerk reactions to the ideas of others or their own life conditions. Struggles such as test anxiety, attention problems, panic attacks, past resentments, or eating disorders begin to lessen their hold, and students express a new confidence as learners and sense of moral freedom as humans.

Nearly all students comment that meditation and contemplative assignments have made them more aware of others, more open-minded to those who are different from them, and more capacious to mitigate their selfish or self-sabotaging drives. Self-knowledge is, paradoxically, the fulcrum to self-transcendence and genuine service to others. Given the power of contemplative methods to catalyze what Robert Thurman calls an "inner revolution,"[31] it flabbergasts me to hear the drubbing of contemplative education as "selfish," "oppressive," or "socially, politically escapist."[32] On the contrary, contemplative process is the spade that can uproot selfishness and indifference. From what I see, we will not have a better world until we have changed the only world that is ever truly in our command: our own inner world.

Moving outward from the center of the Labyrinth has a quiet but steadfast discipline to it. Contemplative teaching requires a razor-edge dedication to the students' highest good, not only in verbal or written communication, but also at the energetic level. Therefore, I daily aspire to several specific personal goals in my teaching. First, I refuse to take credit for the students' inner discoveries, and instead mirror back to them the internal locus of their delight, even when they want to project it onto me or the class. Second, I am aware that each student may need something unique from me in the teaching, and so I strive to discern what specific "medicine" serves each student, whether leniency or strictness, philosophy or practice. Third, I seek to avoid all situations where I would be "taking" from them—intellectually, emotionally, financially, psychically, energetically, professionally. Fourth, I have learned that each seed sprouts in its own time far beyond what I can know of its circumstances, so there is a letting go of being attached to the outcomes. Peace prevails when I love the work for its own sake, with no thought given to the results or to receiving thanks.

> When one has let go of
> the fruits of action,
> one joined to yoga
> gains full peace.[33]

The outward movement of "union" means to be of service to the greater community as well. In 2007, our university opened one of the first "contemplative classrooms" in the country.[34] The classroom is a spacious, serene, and inviting learning space with meditation cushions, yoga mats, and kneeling benches. The space facilitates inner inquiry, quiet reflection, and the realization of knowledge from within and experientially. Several faculty members teach our curricular courses in the Meditation Room, and we also offer weekly free, nonacademic community meditation classes for staff, students, faculty, and locals. This contemplative space is a physical reminder for us that "sustainability" begins as an inner reality. Planetary health depends upon interior wealth. In a recent document written by our department members, "Our Vision for a Sustainable Department," we concluded:

> The "rat race" is not what we want for ourselves, and it is not the model of personhood and citizenship we want to give our students. We hope to offer our students not only historical and textual information about sustainability, life meaning, wholeness, universal responsibility, and nonviolence, but also our own lives as living testimony—what Viktor Frankl called an "existential example": "A professor [does not] give meanings to students. What they may give, however, is an example, the existential example of personal commitment to the search for truth."[35]

In forging a sustainable department life, my colleagues and I expressed our hope that we might be an "existential example" for "the search for truth" to unfold clearly and compassionately in the *union* of personal joy and community health, in service to the flourishing of all. The inward-outward movement of the Labyrinth illuminates a "mystic truth" that verges on becoming scientific truth: the breakthrough of the one benefits the many.[36] The journey inward may be one of solitude but is not, at its best, for oneself alone.

NOTES

Thanks to the following people for edits and comments on early drafts: Judith Simmer-Brown, Martha Stortz, Toby Frank, Patty Topel, Elizabeth Cheatham, and Meena Sharify-Funk.

1. M. K. Gandhi excerpt in Eknath Easwaran, *Gandhi the Man* (Tomales, CA: Nilgiri Press, 1997), 47.
2. Scientists are finding ways to measure the physics of energy fields. A basic discovery is that coherence exists first within the "field" before it exists in form. The highest degrees of coherence are found in enlightened beings, whose inner "energy field" of compassion emanates a beneficent and healing effect. See Russell Targ and Jane Katra, "Close to Grace: The Physics of Silent Mind," *Spirituality and Health* (July/August 2003), http://www.spirituality health.com/NMagazine/articles.php?id=3 (accessed 3 June 2008); David R. Hawkins, *Power vs. Force: Anatomy of Consciousness* (Sedona: Veritas Publishing, 1995); and Valerie Hunt, *Infinite Mind: Science of the*

Human Vibrations of Consciousness (Malibu: Malibu Publications, 1996 [1989]). In Hunt's lab at UCLA in the 1980s, she pioneered a way to measure the auric frequencies of healers using radio wave signals. The highly coherent energy fields of the healers catalyzed a phenomenon of "coherence" in the frequencies of the clients, which facilitated physical healing. Jill Bolte Taylor, *My Stroke of Insight: A Brain Scientist's Personal Journey* (New York: Viking Press, 2008); this Harvard neuro-anatomist suffered a near-fatal brain stroke requiring an eight-year recovery during which she observed that human beings are energetic fields that radiate either coherence or incoherence. The Institute of HeartMath Research Center found that the cultivation of heart coherence through contemplative methods has physical and academic benefits, and that individuals' inner field coherence is related to the earth's magnetic field, a correspondence also suggested by Roger Nelson's "random number generator" research at his lab in Princeton. See "Global Coherence Initiative" at http://heartmath.org (retrieved 30 July 2009).

3. David Bohm, *Wholeness and the Implicate Order* (New York: Routledge, 1980); Bohm's quantum physics posits the unfolding of physical material existence (explicate order) from an invisible field of consciousness (implicate order). Henry Stapp, *Mindful Universe: Quantum Mechanics and the Participating Observer* (Berlin: Springer, 2007). William Tiller, Walter Dibble, Michael Kohane, *Conscious Acts of Creation: Emergence of a New Physics* (Walnut Creek, CA: Pavior Publishing, 2001); this double-blind experimental research at Stanford found that the specific intentions held in mind by highly coherent individuals (longtime meditators) altered actual material substance (e.g., pH balances). Biologist Rupert Sheldrake terms the nonlinear connection of mind a "morphogenic field"; so, one person's breakthrough redraws the collective "m-field" such that Roger Bannister's record-breaking time for the race makes the same attainment more possible for others. *The Sense of Being Stared At and Other Unexplained Powers of the Human Mind* (New York: Three Rivers Press, 2004).

4. *Milinda's Questions*, translated from Pali by I. B. Horner (London: Luzac, 1963), 166–72. Thanks to colleague Karen Derris for this reference to truth statements in Buddhist literature. In ancient Indian literature, "acts of truth" bring cosmic response, and this is carried on in the Pali traditions of Theravada Buddhism.

5. David R. Hawkins, *Eye of the I* (Sedona: Veritas, 2001), 69. See his *Power vs. Force: Anatomy of Consciousness* (Sedona: Veritas, 1995) for background to the "Map of Consciousness."

6. Lauren Artress, *Walking a Sacred Path: Rediscovering the Labyrinth as a Spiritual Practice,* revised and updated (New York: Riverhead Books, 2006 [1995]), 45–57. For guidance on the contemporary usages of the Labyrinth

as a contemplative method, consult the organization established by Artress: http:www.veritiditas.org.

7. See C. G. Jung, "A Study in the Process of Individuation" and "Concerning Mandala Symbolism," in his *The Archetypes and the Collective Unconscious*, Bollingen Series XX (Princeton: Princeton University Press, 1969), 290–354, where he reports on his clinical work with patients using the mandala form. A more recent applied study is that of Judith Cornell, *Mandala: Luminous Symbols for Healing* (Wheaton, IL: Quest Books, 1994), which includes an essay on Jung's pioneering work with mandala forms. Meditative use of the mandala is illuminated beautifully in *Mandala: The Architecture of Enlightenment* by Robert A. F. Thurman and Denise Patry Leidy (London: Thames & Hudson Ltd., 1997). This research influenced me recently to develop a contemplative-based, semester-long Mandala Project for my Psychology and Religion course; the assignment includes meditation, walking the Labyrinth, weekly spontaneous creations of "mandalas," self-inquiry, and research into symbols.

8. Harold Coward, "Mandala and Circumambulation," in *Jung and Eastern Thought* (Albany: State University of New York Press, 1985), 49–52.

9. Dionysius the Aeropagite (the sixth-century CE "Pseudo-Dionysius") delineates a foundational mystical theology of "the three powers" (purgation, illumination, union/perfection) in his texts "Celestial Hierarchy" and "Ecclesiastical Hierarchy," both in *Pseudo-Dionysius: The Complete Works*, trans. Colm Luibheid and Paul Rorem (New York: Paulist Press, 1987).

10. Found in Daniel Ladinsky, *Love Poems from God: Twelve Sacred Voices from the East and West* (New York: Penguin Compass, 2002), 292.

11. *Cloud of Unknowing*, ed. William Johnston (New York: Doubleday, 1973), 96.

12. Rene Descartes, *Meditations on the First Philosophy in Which the Existence of God and the Distinction between Mind and Body are Demonstrated*, Great Books of the Western World, Vol. 31 (Chicago: University of Chicago Press, 1952), 79.

13. Key resources were: Maurianne Adams, Lee Anne Bell, Pat Griffin, eds., *Teaching for Diversity and Social Justice: A Sourcebook* (New York: Routledge, 1997); Jane Tompkins, "Pedagogy of the Distressed," *College English* 52 (1990): 653–60; Ira Shor, "Education Is Politics: Paulo Freire's Critical Pedagogy," in *Paulo Freire: A Critical Encounter*, ed. Peter McLaren and Peter Leonard (New York: Routledge, 1993), 25–35; bell hooks, *Teaching to Transgress: Education as a Practice of Freedom* (New York: Routledge, 1994); bell hooks, "Engaged Pedagogy," *Women/Writing/Teaching* (Albany: State University of New York Press, 1998).

14. "Fishbowl" is a discussion technique in which a small group sits in the center to discuss while the larger group sits around the outside, listening and eventually trading places with members of the center circle.

15. Thanks to Beth Blissman for lessons on eco-social contexts, and to Grace Burford and Sid Brown for regular encouragement and discussion on life and pedagogy through the years.
16. bell hooks, *Women/Writing/Teaching* (Albany: State University of New York Press, 1998), 237.
17. Paulo Freire, *Pedagogy of the Oppressed*, thirtieth anniversary edition (New York: Continuum, 2000 [1968]).
18. M. K. Gandhi, *The Essential Gandhi: An Anthology of His Writings on His Life, Work, and Ideas*, ed. Louis Fischer (New York: Vintage Books, 2002), 108.
19. *Me and Rumi: The Autobiography of Shams-iTabrizi*, trans. William C. Chittick (Louisville, KY: Fons Vitae, 2004), 45.
20. John of the Cross, *Selected Writings*, ed. Kieran Kavanaugh (New York: Paulist Press, 1987).
21. Swami Vivekananda, "Commentary on the Bhagavadgita," San Francisco, May 28–29, 1900, read by Christopher Isherwood at the Hollywood Vedanta Society, August 17, 1975. Vedanta Video Archives.
22. Seyyed Hossein Nasr, "In the Beginning Was Consciousness," *The Essential Seyyed Hossein Nasr*, ed. William C. Chittick (Bloomington, IN: World Wisdom, 2007), 229.
23. *Me and Rumi: The Autobiography of Shams-iTabrizi*, 39, 46. For a modern poetic remembrance of this encounter between the "scholar" Rumi and the "angel" Shams, see Mary Oliver's poem "The Return" in *What Do We Know* (Cambridge: Da Capo Press, 2002), 9.
24. Zen Master Dogen, *Beyond Thinking*, ed. Kazuaki Tanahashi (Boston: Shambhala, 2004), 9.
25. "The Great Conversation: The Substance of a Liberal Education," Vol. I, Great Books of the Western World (Chicago: Encyclopedia Britannica, 1952), 2–3, 26. Thanks to Gabe Valencia.
26. Mary Oliver, *Thirst* (Boston: Beacon Press, 2006), 1.
27. The course is described further in Grace, "Breathing In Suffering, Breathing Out Compassion," *Spirituality in Higher Education Newsletter* 5, no. 2 (May 2009): 1–10; and Grace, "Pedagogy of Reverence," *Religion and Education* 36, no. 2 (Summer 2009): 102–23.
28. Paul Griffiths, *On Being Buddha: The Classical Doctrine of Buddhahood* (Albany: State University of New York Press, 1994), 59.
29. John Makransky, *Awakening Through Love* (Boston: Wisdom Publications, 2007).
30. Nelson Mandela, televised interview with Oprah Winfrey, archived in *Twentieth Anniversary Collection: The Oprah Winfrey Show* (Hollywood: Paramount Pictures, 2005).
31. Robert Thurman, *Inner Revolution: Life, Liberty, and the Pursuit of Real Happiness* (New York: Riverhead, 1999).

32. Most recently, I heard this attack on contemplative education from an otherwise outstanding teacher who holds an official position of leadership in the area of pedagogy, within the American Academy of Religion organization.

33. *The Bhagavad Gita*, 5:12, trans. Laurie L. Patton (London: Penguin Books, 2008), 64.

34. For more on the Meditation Room, see the documentary film, *A Semester Within: Exploring Meditation* (2008), Fran Grace (writer, director, executive producer) and Richard Spencer (director, co-producer, editor). The film includes classroom footage and student interviews.

35. Viktor Frankl, *Man's Search for Ultimate Meaning* (New York: Basic Books, 2000), 119.

36. The "mystic truth" of the Labyrinth and its scientific correlates in mathematics and sacred geometry are discussed by Dr. David R. Hawkins, public lecture on "Peace" in Prescott, AZ, August 9, 2009, DVD (Sedona, AZ: Veritas Publishing, 2009). Other scientists have discussed the power of inner attainments for the collective: David Bohm refers to the "implicate order" and Rupert Sheldrake to the "morphic field" as sources of nondual consciousness out of which visible transformations unfold or emerge. See: "The Enfolding-Unfolding Universe: A Conversation with David Bohm," interviewed by Renee Weber, *The Holographic Paradigm and Other Paradoxes: Exploring the Leading Edge of Science*, ed. Ken Wilber (Boston: Shambhala, 1985), 44–104; "Extended Mind, Power, and Prayer: Morphic Resonance and the Collective Unconscious, Part III," *Psychological Perspectives* 19, no. 1 (Spring 1988): 64–78.

6

THE COLLECTIVE DYNAMICS OF CONTEMPLATIVE PRACTICE

CHRISTOPHER M. BACHE

As contemplative studies becomes an established part of our university curriculum, it will do more than influence the content of what we teach and the manner in which we teach it. It will also tend to expose the workings of the collective psyche in our classrooms. Our contemplative traditions have extensive history with these dynamics, but the academy does not. While our spiritual traditions have placed great value on the insights of interdependence and the transparency of self to a deeper collective matrix, our academic institutions for the most part have committed themselves to an "atomistic psychology" that emphasizes separation and self-autonomy—one mind per brain. As a result, introducing practices that have the capacity to initiate persons into this deeper matrix will hold some surprises not only for our students but for our colleagues as well.

I have been a professor of religious studies at a public university in northeastern Ohio for over thirty years. While I have incorporated meditation into a few of my courses, I have done so only in a limited fashion. In this respect, I probably represent a transitional pedagogy, something between the conventions of the past and the more robust contemplative pedagogies represented by others in this volume. In the conservative setting in which I have taught, I felt it was important for me to maintain a clear distinction between my private life and my professional work on campus. In my private life, I cultivated an active spiritual practice, drawing primarily from Buddhist and shamanic traditions. In my professional life, I worked as a more or less traditional academic, teaching courses in world religions, Eastern religions, psychology of religion, Buddhism, and transpersonal studies. As a matter of professional ethics, I kept these two domains separate from each other. I did not discuss my personal practice with my students and few knew about this side of my life. And yet what I discovered was that nature did not honor the boundary I had so carefully drawn.

As my spiritual practice deepened over the years, a variety of "paranormal" phenomena began to surface in my classroom, if one wishes to use that term. My mind and my students' minds began to become more porous to each other in striking ways. Spiritual breakthroughs at home sometimes triggered shockwaves among my students on campus. Over the years, as I entered progressively deeper states of consciousness, the number of students being affected increased and the impact intensified. Eventually these energetic and cognitive resonances became such a prominent part of my teaching that I had no choice but to explore what was driving them in greater detail. I carefully observed what was taking place in my classes, read the consciousness literature extensively, and experimented with how to work with the powerful forces involved. Over time, this inquiry profoundly changed how I teach and eventually resulted in the publication of *The Living Classroom: Teaching and Collective Consciousness*.[1]

If a professor's "private" spiritual practice can trigger effects like those I am going to describe here among students who were neither aware of their professor's practice nor (in most cases) doing practice themselves, it seems reasonable to suggest that these effects could be even more pronounced where professors and students are doing contemplative practice together on a regular basis.[2] In my experience, these practices not only illumine the great *depth* of consciousness, they also *activate* the great *breadth* of consciousness. Therefore, if we are going to initiate our students into these practices, we should be prepared to manage this activation when it occurs and to help our students understand it. These dynamics challenge the conventional psychological and pedagogical paradigm and invite us to take our teaching to a more conscious, more intentional level.

RESONANCE IN THE CLASSROOM

About five years after I began teaching, a student came up to me after class one day and said, "You know, it's strange that you used the example you did in class today, because that's exactly what happened to me this week." In my experience, I had simply reached for a random example to illustrate a point I had been making, but what had been random for me turned out to be poignantly significant for him. When he heard his recent life experience coming back to him in my lecture, it snapped him to attention. It was as if he had been given a personal invitation to get more deeply involved in the course.

The first time this happened, I brushed it off as mere coincidence, but it continued to happen often enough that eventually I could no longer dismiss it. In the years that followed, it became a not uncommon occurrence in my classes. My students were finding bits and pieces of their recent life experience, or the experience of a close family member, in my lectures. Without my intending it, without my even being aware when it was happening, my consciousness seemed to be tapping into some kind of informational field that held their life experience. (I should mention that I have never considered myself particularly psychically sensitive. In fact, before these events, I had always thought of myself as something of a psychic brick.)

One evening, for example, I was teaching a night course in Eastern religions with about thirty students. In the middle of my lecture, I found myself taking a little detour in which I described an account of a Zen master who had had an accurate precognitive intuition of his impending death, similar to accounts Sushila Blackman later published in *Graceful Exits*.[3] I had never talked about this account in this lecture before. It was just a little aside, something dropped in to add a little anecdotal interest to the discussion we were having about the capacities of the mind.

After class, a silver-haired elderly lady came up to talk with me. She was not part of our usual group but had been brought to class that night by a friend who was worried about her. Her husband had died three months before, and her friend thought she was languishing at home and needed to get out of the house. In the conversation that followed, she told me this story. Her husband had been a used car salesman in good health. Several weeks before his unexpected death, he had cleared out most of the cars from his lot and gotten all his financial paperwork in order. A few days later, he and his wife were watching TV in the evening when he put down his newspaper and, in a way that was quite out of character for him, turned to his wife and said, "Darling, I just want you to know that if I died tomorrow, you've made my entire life worthwhile." A week later, he died in his sleep.

What she wanted to know was whether I thought her husband might have been unconsciously aware that he was going to die, like the person I had described in my lecture. I said that it sounded like a possibility, and this thought was comforting to her. This led to a longer conversation in which she described the challenges his passing had created for her. In the midst of her grief, she then got in touch with how overprotective he had been and how she was now being given the opportunity to develop herself in ways that his well-intentioned care had always prevented. That very night, she decided to return to college, where she thrived for several years, allowing many new doors to open in her life.

When these things first started happening in my classroom, I was in the early stages of both my career and my spiritual practice, and here the plot thickens. To make a very long story short, as my spiritual practice gradually deepened through the years, these synchronicities became more frequent. It was as though by entering more deeply into conscious communion with the underlying fabric of life, the threads of that fabric were being activated around me. The experience of depth seemed to be triggering the emergence of greater breadth, as though depth and breadth were two different dimensions of a seamless fabric.

Not only were these cognitive resonances becoming more frequent, they were also targeting increasingly sensitive areas in my students' lives. It was as though a radar had been activated that was operating below the threshold of my egoic awareness, a radar that zeroed in on some part of their life that was hurting or constricted. Sometimes it touched a question they had been holding for years, or triggered an insight they had been searching for, something they needed to find before they could take the next step in their development. Sometimes it lanced a private pain that had been festering inside them. In this mysterious communion that opened between us, it was as if my students' souls were slipping messages to me, giving me hints on how I might reach them—telling me where they were hiding, where they were hurting, and most importantly, what ideas they needed to move forward.

As the years passed and the process deepened, my students also began to have unusually deep experiences related to some of the concepts I was presenting in class. It was as though they were being activated by more than just the ideas, as though they were somehow being touched by the actual *experience* of these realities that now lived in me to some degree because of my practice.

I have taught more sections of Introduction to World Religions than I care to remember; it is a staple in our department. When students hear the perennial truths of the world's spiritual traditions simply spoken, when they are reminded of things long ago forgotten but always present at the edge of their awareness, there is sometimes a spark of recognition that can explode into a flame. This flame is contagious and sometimes stimulates sympathetic resonances with other students in the room. Students may collectively feel their energy shift to different centers of awareness, though they may not understand what is happening at the time. Symptoms of "chakra-opening" and "kundalini arousal" may begin to manifest. Energy runs, hearts open, and insights arise.[4]

These can be very powerful experiences for students. One sophomore described such an experience in an essay she wrote at the end of the semester. It happened to her on a day when I was describing the Buddhist understanding of the relationship of individual mind to nondual consciousness. To convey this point, I sometimes use the analogy of a tree, contrasting leaf-consciousness (the personal mind) with tree-consciousness (nondual consciousness). In this exercise, I invite the students to imagine that the leaves of a tree are individually self-aware but not yet conscious of the life of the tree they are part of, until the moment of breakthrough. It is a powerful metaphor that I save until I think the class is ready to absorb its full import. On this particular day, this young woman experienced the following:

> The thing that hit me the hardest of all that we talked about in class was tree-consciousness and leaf-consciousness. It was what brought everything together for me. What made me understand everyone's

interdependence and stopped me from living in fear. I was so moved that it took everything that I had not to cry in class, not from sadness but from being hit by a life-altering realization. It made an emotion rise in me that I had never felt before and I wasn't really sure how to react to it.

Another student, a woman in her mid-thirties, summarized a similar experience in a different course in the following way:

Sitting in class, I felt like I was inside one of those glass ball snow scenes that folks use as paperweights. Shake the ball and mass confusion begins with flakes of fake snow swirling all around. . . . I couldn't *hear* the lecture. My mind struggled to focus and stay with your words, but I was missing it. . . .

Later . . . at home . . . alone. It would all return to me, the lecture. . . . Mostly feelings. Tears. Recognition. Understanding after I let it simmer for a while. Realization that if I didn't grab at it, it would be there waiting, this knowledge. These tiny bright spots of revelatory insight. I'd journal. I'd cry. Sometimes light and gentle, warm feel-good crying. Sometimes sobs, wracking and exhausting. I THOUGHT I WAS LOSING MY MIND A FEW TIMES. . . .

The result? I'm becoming who I was *long* ago. The field by-passed my intellect and went directly to my heart to pry it open. . . . I now know what I had deeply buried in me for years, and the gift of the pick and shovel for the ongoing process comes from being in the energy of the folks in our classroom. It didn't come from me alone.

I should mention that it was not my intention to trigger such deep existential reactions among my students. In fact, fearing that they were out of place in a university setting, I often tried to damp them down, but I found that this was impossible without damaging the teaching process itself. Whenever my students and I would gather and simply cover the day's assignment, these things would spontaneously occur without my consciously intending them. It was as though fire was lighting fire. When we would simply focus on the task of sharing understanding, these *resonances of living experience* would spring up—not always, but often—drawing students into heightened states of awareness.

THE CHALLENGES OF SELF-TRANSFORMATION

Most of the students who were touched by these dynamics experienced them as uplifting, even exhilarating "Aha!" moments. For some students, however, the

process presented them with difficult personal challenges. As the spiritual literature makes clear, purification is often the companion of liberation. Before we
can realize the greater being that we are, we must confront and release what is
holding us back from realizing this potential—some habit of thought, some
emotional constriction. When some of my students were activated by what I
believe is a life-enhancing process, their systems began a process of spontaneous
detoxification—a shedding of old patterns, old ways of thinking and feeling. I
do not believe this would have happened to them if they had not been ready for
it at a deeper level, even inviting it. They entered this transformational process
because they were ripe for it.

These cathartic activations became particularly pronounced during a period
of several years when I was undergoing a series of powerful transformative experiences in my practice that were breaking me down at very deep levels. The
details of these experiences are not important here and are described in my book
Dark Night, Early Dawn.[5] Many spiritual traditions describe a phase of inner
work that involves dissolving the sense of boundary between self and other. They
describe an experiential membrane that marks the border between one's individual mind-field and surrounding fields of awareness. On the near side of this
membrane, the world appears to be composed of separate beings, each with their
seemingly private existence. On the far side of the membrane, the world appears
as an integrated whole, a continuum of energy that is unfathomably complex
and extravagantly beautiful. When a practitioner is transitioning through this
territory, standing at the interface of these two paradoxically compatible realities,
powerful synchronicities with surrounding persons sometimes manifest.

As my inner work came to focus on this boundary, triggering the purifica-
tions that typically accompany this transition, some of my students simultaneously began to undergo very difficult challenges in their lives. Most of my
students did not enter these waters, of course, and passed through my courses
untouched by these dynamics, but some did enter them. Those who did so
sometimes felt themselves coming to a breaking point in their lives or a moment
of supreme risk-taking. It was as though they and I were being drawn through a
collective death-rebirth vortex together, a vortex that was breaking all of us down
in different ways, uprooting deeply buried pains, and challenging restrictive bar-
riers in our lives.

Some students chose to end bad marriages or to heal wounded ones. Others
left careers they had outgrown but were still holding onto. (Thirty percent of the
students at my university are older, nontraditional students.) Some began to
confront their addictions and others to reapproach persons from whom they had
been estranged for a long time. One woman in her mid-forties hints at the profound disruption of her inner and outer worlds that occurred during this period
when she began to spontaneously recover painful memories of child abuse, in a
course on Buddhism, of all places:

> During and after having been in your classes, my internal world became increasingly chaotic as demons from painful psychological gestalts began to emerge, and eventually coloring my external world too, challenging everything I thought I was and dissolving familiar reference points. . . . As I struggled to break through powerful gestalts of pain, you spoke to and nourished my soul, making it possible for me to move more deeply into my spiritual journey.

Obviously the phenomena I am describing raise important pedagogical and ethical issues. As my students came to me with these reports and I saw how deeply they were being affected by this mysterious alchemy that had opened between us, I was more than a little shaken myself. Neither of us had solicited this connection, yet here it was. Did I need to protect them from what was happening? Obviously this was not what they had consciously signed up for when they enrolled in my course. How does one ensure informed consent when the dynamics are so involuntary and beyond the pale of current academic discussion?

While the activation some of my students experienced during this period was quite powerful, there were no casualties and many positive breakthroughs. On the rare occasion when a student's self-transformation became particularly turbulent, I referred him or her to a gifted therapist in the area with whom they could process what was emerging in a safe setting.

While these kinds of responses might be expected in certain types of courses, such as a counseling course, this was not the case for the kind of courses I was teaching. Rather, these events seemed to be the *indirect effect* of our simply coming together to learn. It was not the content of the course that seemed to be driving these effects, but something deeper. I believe it had something to do with the interaction of our subtle life energy at a fundamental level. What was triggering these effects was not what I was *doing* but rather what I had *become*. They were being evoked less by what I was saying than by what I was, or more accurately, by what we were together.

THE ECOLOGY OF CONSCIOUSNESS

Whatever description scientists eventually give the fundamental level of reality that underlies space-time and its relation to consciousness,[6] the experiences of my students appear to demonstrate a simple principle: *clarified states of consciousness are contagious.* My efforts to realize deeper states of awareness seem to have caused my person to begin acting as a kind of lightning rod triggering sparks of a similar awakening among those students who were receptive to this influence. Like ripples spreading across water, this is an utterly natural effect. When one person begins to throw off layers of egoic conditioning and awaken to clearer, more inclusive states of awareness, surrounding persons will be affected. Our spiritual ecology simply does not permit private awakening. *The ecology of consciousness is an inherently collective ecology.*

Though this suggestion is still regarded as heretical in most academic circles, it raises fewer eyebrows in spiritual communities, which have long known that persons undergoing deep transformation affect those around them in subtle ways. The devotee and author Satprem, for example, discusses this phenomenon in his biography of Sri Aurobindo, where he writes:

> Sri Aurobindo and the Mother would realize that transformation is not just an individual problem but one involving the earth and that no individual transformation is possible (or at least complete) without some degree of collective transformation. . . . It should be noted that each time Sri Aurobindo and the Mother had some experience indicating a new progress in the transformation, the disciples, without their even knowing anything about it, experienced in their consciousness a period of increased difficulties or even revolts and illnesses, as if everything were grating. Now we begin to understand how things work.[7]

Similarly, scholar-practitioner Mike Sayama mentions this phenomenon in his book, *Samadhi*. In his discussion of the dynamics of *ch'i*, Sayama quotes the Japanese healer Kaneko Shoseki, who observes:

> Apart from the normal communication between men through language and action there is another quite different sort of mutual influence. It is that of the rhythm of the Original Strength which permeates all human beings and Nature. Through it every individual thing . . . is connected with every other. If then one who is further removed from the working of the Primordial Force is close to one who lives more in accord with it, the rhythm of the Primordial Force will certainly be transmitted from the one to the other. The latter without knowing it exerts a good influence on the other.[8]

CONCLUSION

If my students could share one message with teachers of contemplative studies, I think it would be this. If you are an educator who is doing a form of spiritual practice that has the capacity to activate deep levels of the unconscious, especially at the level of the collective psyche, you can expect to stimulate sympathetic resonances with at least some of your students. These resonances will likely be more pronounced if you are meditating with your students on a regular basis. This is a natural and unstoppable effect of practice, a manifestation of the inherent wholeness of consciousness at deep levels.

Furthermore, in addition to the energetic resonances between teacher and student, when a class meditates together, there is a compounding effect generated by the *group field* of the class as a whole. Though I do not have the space to discuss this second part of the equation here, readers will find an extensive discussion of it in *The Living Classroom*. There I draw upon Rupert Sheldrake's concept of morphic resonance to explore the compounding effect learning has on groups and the emergence of a true collective intelligence in the classroom.[9]

To teach conscientiously in a world where minds are separate at one level and yet "entangled" in a unified field at another calls for a more intentional pedagogy than the separatist, atomistic psychology of the Newtonian-Cartesian paradigm. The new paradigm emerging in science today emphasizes the inherent connectivity of life and the powerful tendency of nature to synchronize its many parts into larger wholes.[10] Accordingly, the pedagogy emerging within this new paradigm will recognize the innate connectivity of consciousness and the distributive effect of specific states of consciousness. Contemplative studies has an important role to play in this transition.

NOTES

1. Christopher M. Bache, *The Living Classroom: Teaching and the Collective Consciousness* (Albany: State University of New York Press, 2008).
2. "Spiritual practice" is being used here as a broader category than "contemplative practice" and includes all practices designed to initiate one into and deepen one's experience of spiritual reality, such as shamanic work, yoga, meditation, vision quest, prayer, fasting, deep body work, among others. "Contemplative practice" refers more narrowly to various forms of meditation practice.
3. Sushila Blackman, *Graceful Exits* (New York: Weatherhill, 1997).
4. In Indian yoga and medicine, the *chakras* (or "wheels") are centers of consciousness and bioenergy believed to exist in the subtle body. Traditionally there are seven chakras, each associated with a major nerve ganglion in the body and reflecting a specific kind of conscious awareness. Together the chakras are said compose the entire range of human experience from the primitive fight-or-flight response to highly spiritual nondual awareness. *Kundalini* (literally, "coiled") is described as the bio-spiritual energy that animates the chakra system. This energy rests at the base of the spine, and as it rises it "opens" the various chakras, activating their potential for certain kinds of experience and insight. Gopi Krishna, *Kundalini* (Boston:

Shambhala, 1997); Lee Sannella, *The Kundalini Experience* (Lower Lake: Integral Publishing, 1987).

5. Christopher M. Bache, *Dark Night, Early Dawn* (Albany: State University of New York Press, 2000).

6. Amit Goswami, *The Self-Aware Universe* (New York: Tarcher/Putnam, 1995); Ervin Laszlo, *The Interconnected Universe* (Singapore: World Scientific Publishing, 1999), *The Connectivity Hypothesis* (Albany: State University of New York Press, 2003), *Science and the Akashic Field* (Rochester: Inner Traditions, 2004).

7. Satprem, *Sri Aurobindo, or The Adventure of Consciousness* (Pondicherry: Sri Aurobindo Ashram, 1993), 291.

8. Michael Sayama, *Samadhi* (Albany: State University of New York Press, 1986), 80–81.

9. Rupert Sheldrake, *A New Science of Life* (Los Angeles: J. P. Tarcher, 1981), *The Presence of the Past* (New York: Vintage, 1988), *The Rebirth of Nature* (New York: Bantam, 1991).

10. Howard Bloom, *Global Brain* (New York: John Wiley and Sons, 2000); Stewart Kaufman, *At Home in the Universe* (New York: Oxford University Press, 1995); Dean Radin, *Entangled Minds* (New York: Pocket Books, 2006); Steve Strogatz, *Sync* (New York: Hyperion Books, 2003).

7

THE MINDFUL TEACHER AS THE FOUNDATION OF CONTEMPLATIVE PEDAGOGY

RICHARD C. BROWN

Contemplative pedagogy flourishes when it involves the interplay of the mindful presence of the teacher with effective instructional methods. Much has been written about "best practices" in contemplative education, but the personal presence of the teacher is an important foundation demonstrating that curricular implementation and subject mastery alone are not enough. Contemplative pedagogy demands that the teacher engage fearlessly in a dynamic relationship with the learning process on both personal and professional levels. Presence is not accidental; it is cultivated through meditative practices that open and clarify the heart and mind of the teacher, facilitate communication, sharpen the intellect, and foster creativity.

Yet, effective contemplative pedagogy requires more than the teacher's meditative practice. Many teachers who meditate or practice other contemplative disciplines struggle to marry their mindfulness meditation to their teaching. Quiet sessions on a meditation cushion can contrast sharply with the complex dynamics of the classroom. Experienced contemplative practitioners develop clarity and stability of mind, but how can such qualities be transferred skillfully into the classroom?

This exploration will focus on how the development of inner meditative discipline gradually progresses into outer contemplative pedagogy. Using mindfulness meditation as an illustration, we will explore how that practice develops skills that can gradually infuse teaching presence and instruction, and become the basis of effective contemplative teaching.

MEDITATION AS A FOUNDATION
FOR CONTEMPLATIVE PEDAGOGY

There are, of course, many different meditative practices, but in this essay, sitting meditation with its mindful focus on breathing will be considered the foundation. This form of meditation develops certain qualities relevant to academic pursuits, including being present in the moment, clarity of thought, and emotional equanimity. Many forms of breath meditation exist, but for this purpose we will explore the form used by many, but not all, of the faculty at Naropa University. Drawing from the Buddhist tradition of *shamatha-vipashyana* (mindfulness and awareness), meditation at Naropa is taught not as religious practice but as a "first-person" method for self-discovery and learning.[1] In our training of contemplative teachers, we begin with a foundation of mindfulness developing into heightened awareness as a foundation for a variety of contemplative pedagogies for the classroom.

The form of meditation has three dimensions—posture, breath, and working with distractions. The sitting posture in meditation is upright, still, open, and solidly grounded. The posture is firm and contained, and yet the body is receptive to inner experiences and to the environment. The eyes, ears, and all the senses are alert, but passive. This balance between a contained form and openness to experience is a principle throughout meditation that makes the practice relevant for dealing with everyday life and teaching. For instance, form and openness create a powerful balance in the contemplative teacher. Strong, confident teacher presence that is also open and receptive to students makes for dynamic and trustworthy learning relationships.

The second dimension of meditation is mindfulness of breathing. Attention is focused on ordinary breathing; no special breath techniques are involved. Attention on the breath seems to have a naturally calming effect. Taking a deep breath or two has become a common centering practice in sports and as a response to stress in everyday life. For the teacher in the classroom, a few focused breaths can have the same effect, especially when combined with a well-aligned, upright posture. Focusing on the breath as it is makes an easier transition to using breath awareness as a tool while teaching.

The third dimension, closely related to breath awareness, is working with distractions. When attention to breathing wanders in meditation, the instruction is to briefly notice where the attention has strayed and come back to mindful breathing. For instance, we might notice that our attention has strayed to thinking about some intriguing question, planning a conversation with a colleague, or perhaps simply daydreaming. Interestingly, we are taught that in meditation we do not instantly return our attention to breathing. Instead we take a quick moment to notice what has captured our attention. In this way we become aware of the habits of our mind. The meditation session, however, is not the time to analyze these patterns. We simply notice, let go, and, without judgment, return our attention to the breathing. Contemplation, reflection, or analysis of our habitual patterns is a separate practice. Thus, we develop "familiarity" (one definition of "meditation"[2]) with our habits of attention. As our meditation practice deepens, we find ourselves returning to the present moment more naturally and frequently.

Noticing wandering mind and bringing it back to awareness of breathing is at the heart of the practice, but is easier said than done. Our natural emotional and conceptual vitality tend to complicate this very simple focus. For instance, during meditation when our attention to breathing has been absent for a while, we may have a tendency to castigate ourselves for being undisciplined, to criticize the practice itself as being impossibly difficult, or to conclude that this was not the most conducive circumstance for meditation. When we notice ourselves being critical, judgmental, or analytical, we gently let that go and return to breath awareness. We cultivate the skills of being precise, open, and unattached no matter what our state of mind.

The meditative ability to notice when our attention has strayed and to gracefully and readily come back to the matters of the present moment is very useful while teaching. With practice contemplative teachers develop facility and ease with the natural vacillations in our attention. As our compassion toward our own patterns deepens, our attention remains more constantly present. These calming and synchronizing practices seem to foster equanimity and reduce the danger of burnout.

APPLICATIONS OF MEDITATION IN TEACHING

How can mindfulness-awareness practice be useful in developing contemplative pedagogy? Moving from mindfulness on the meditation cushion to mindfulness in the classroom takes a lot of practice. One way to begin this transition is to bring tangible reminders of mindfulness practice into the classroom. A particular object placed on our desks or somewhere in the classroom can serve as a reminder of mindfulness while we are teaching. A small piece of driftwood or a stone collected on a retreat could serve as a reminder to notice, let go, and wake up to the present moment. If our classroom culture is open to the notion that we are exploring mindfulness, then the purpose of the object might be shared with the class. If not, it can remain a silent personal reminder.

The meditation posture itself suggests that being mindful of our body, uncommon in academic teaching, can also aid in the transition. There is little appreciation of mindfulness of body as an enhancement to our teaching. While teaching we might even forget we have bodies. But just as in meditation, when our physical bodies are upright, receptive, and present, we are more able to directly contact our inner resources and be more responsive to our students. Thinking and communicating are often more creative and fluid.

We can strengthen our physical presence while teaching by noticing our sense of touch. Taking a moment to feel the weight of our bodies in our chairs or the texture of the book we are holding can bring us back into the present moment. The practices of mindful standing or walking are also useful. Similar to sitting meditation, in walking or standing meditation our focus is on our feet touching the floor. When our attention strays, we gently return our attention to the direct sensory experience of touch. In teaching these practices can center and stabilize us. Mindfully walking en route to our classrooms is a wonderful way to ground ourselves before teaching; likewise with some thought we can find moments for standing meditation throughout the teaching day. For example, while students are taking a few minutes to discuss a question with the person next to them, the teacher can do standing meditation, unbeknownst to anyone.

For the contemplative teacher, the breath can also have meaning as a reminder of a meditative state of mind. Breathing is the perfect metaphor for a basic premise of contemplative pedagogy: interconnectedness, or "interbeing," as Vietnamese Zen master Thich Nhat Hanh calls it.[3] Our inner experience is directly related to all that exists "outside" of us. When we are aware of the interconnectedness between our personal presence and the learning experiences of the students, our teaching becomes more deeply synchronized. Noticing our breathing during teaching can remind us of interbeing and becomes a way to soften any sense of separation we may feel from our students. We begin to meet them more directly with greater openness and compassion. Spending a moment or two noticing our breathing can center and connect us with the shared learning environment. A contemplative student-teacher wrote:

> I have noticed that [meditation] has a profound impact on my disposition and focus. I am calmer and more encouraging in one-on-one encounters. I find that I am a better listener because I don't have so many random thoughts bouncing around inside my skull. My students seem to respond positively to this by not holding their bodies as tensely and making more eye contact with me. They also seem to allow themselves to take more academic risks, venturing educated guesses. . . . [4]

RELATING WITH THOUGHTS AND EMOTIONS

Another basic application of meditation practice is developing clarity about how our minds function during teaching. The meditative mind is less apt to mindlessly run through old thought patterns. Just as in meditation, when we notice we have lost our awareness of our thoughts while teaching, we could nonjudgmentally take a breath or two and resume more mindfully. Mindfulness of our thoughts promotes a more creative inner dialog. What we are teaching becomes more dynamic in our own minds and, thus, fresher for our students. Even when we are teaching the same old material, we can be more present with it, rather than mindlessly rummaging through the same old thoughts.

As instructors lecturing passionately about our subjects, we can even forget that we are actually communicating with students. When we are mindful of our thoughts and speech during teaching, and at the same time are aware of interconnectedness with our students, then we can more easily notice how they are responding to classroom dynamics. Thus, we can tailor our pedagogies to meet the students' needs in the moment.

As we loosen our grasp on our conceptual activity, common concerns that arise among new meditators are the fears that we may lose our train of thought, that we may become so disconnected that we cut off communication with our students, that too much openness will not leave time to cover the material, or that we will look like doddering fools. With practice we develop more grace and confidence in mixing focused mind with spacious mind. This inner/outer awareness furthers the development of a more creative, supple mind.

It is not just our thinking processes that can separate us from a deeper learning relationship with our students. Emotional reactivity is also at play. Highly educated instructors are often loath to admit that their emotional responses can negatively affect their students' learning experiences. Indeed, many would maintain that emotions should play no role in teaching, with the possible exception of the enthusiasm and joy for the subject. However, emotions are always active in human experience, from extremely subtle feelings to stormy outbursts.[5] Emotions are most clearly apparent in communications with individual students in or outside of class, but they also appear in every dimension of education. For example, when we read a student paper, we can feel delight, confusion, or irritation.

In meditative practice we do not reject our emotions, even when they are troublesome—they are an indispensable and valuable resource. As we mindfully meditate we become familiar with our emotions—notice and touch the feeling, gently let go, and return to breathing. Gradually we become accustomed to the arising of feelings and notice how we respond emotionally. For example, one morning's meditation might be preoccupied by a situation involving a student, and we notice emotionally charged thoughts as they rehearse possible scenarios. We return to breathing, but the charge of the situation may remain very strong. The thoughts and accompanying emotions keep returning. As we patiently keep coming back to the breathing, we begin to see how our thoughts and feelings are intertwined. Gradually we become aware of the distinctions between the two and the tangle begins to loosen. We begin to notice more precisely how irritation toward the situation is affecting our thinking and communication. It is often found that when encountering a similar situation while teaching, teacher responses are more balanced. Learning to experience emotions directly and to express them moderately and compassionately is a key element in contemplative education. A contemplative student-teacher wrote:

> I find myself reacting less to aggression and disruption from students, as well as having more space for their difficult reactions and emotions. . . . It is not so much that the specifics of meditation create a specific way of being. It is more that the entire process, sitting each day, simply all of it, has contributed in allowing a tiny bit more space in my awareness so I can stop and notice my reactions. I can then consciously make a choice, or at least be aware of the possibility of making a choice, as to how I want to act.[6]

Challenging situations could be viewed not as distractions, but as opportunities for insight and deepening our teaching.[7] For example, in a class discussion, a student might question our deeply held ideas. When we are unaware of our emotional responses, we tend to unconsciously limit discussion and the exploration of ideas. From a mindful perspective, we could notice our attachment to the idea and whatever emotions are associated with it. Thus, we are not so easily blindsided by the unconscious entwinement of thoughts and emotions. They become a less potent complication or disruption. Whether we react defensively or are pleased by the courage of the student, our inner awareness allows us to be more fully present and open in the discussion. Mindfulness does not necessarily mean that we would change our ideas or approach; only that we are better able to tolerate ambiguity and paradox, and utilize tension creatively. Communication with others seems easier and more straightforward, and empathy is stronger. We could become both clearer about our inner life and also kinder to ourselves. Within a new sense of ease, fresh perspectives can often arise.

WAIT TIME

How do these inner meditative skills more fully manifest in observable pedagogical practice? When we examine one established pedagogical method, Wait Time, we can see how mindfulness enhances a time-honored pedagogy. Wait Time was developed in the 1970s,[8] and since then it has been studied and expanded upon.[9] In the Wait Time method, the teacher pauses three seconds after asking a question to the class before selecting a student to respond. Studies found that when Wait Time is used, more students are poised to respond to the question and that higher-order thinking skills improve.[10] This assures that more than just the quick-thinking students are being engaged in class discussion; the practice also helps the students who leap quickly to respond by giving them more time to reflect. The second part of the Wait Time method involves the teacher allowing three seconds after a chosen student has finished responding. These studies showed that often after the pause, the same student would frequently offer an additional, deeper, and more thoughtful response. Thus, the outcomes of Wait Time indicate that it could be a contemplative pedagogical method. However, any "contemplative" method can be perverted. Without contemplative experience we teachers might just be biding our time during the three-second pause. Our physical presence might be projecting blankness or discomfort, or we might be mindlessly solidifying our own notions of the "correct" response. The presence of the teacher during the three seconds communicates a great deal to the students about how that time is used.

Wait Time can become a *contemplative* method when the teacher uses the three seconds for a brief awareness practice. A variety of such practices can be done quickly. Standing meditation allows us to notice our body, feel the floor beneath, and relax. It could be a time when we become aware of what we expect the students to say, and we let go of that expectation. It could be three seconds in which we notice our emotional state, and use the time to synchronize with our emotional tone. If our feelings seem too strong and might impede the discussion, we could modulate them. The pause could be a time to simply make a silent connection with our students. In general, Wait Time can be a pause during which we open freshly to ourselves and the class, and prepare to meet the responses with unbiased eyes and ears.

> I have really been observing how I use time. . . . Wait Time, silence, pauses. . . . just watching myself and my students. I find that as I experiment with infusing spaces of time around questions and directions, before and after answers and within transitions, the whole rhythm of the room changes. It feels more fluid, less solid.[11]

To get the best results from the Wait Time approach, contemplative or otherwise, the teacher needs to prepare the students. When they understand how to use the three-second pause as a time for reflection or contemplation of the question, they are less likely to become impatient. I have found that most students quickly become comfortable with the brief silence and use it beneficially.

Of course, there are times when it is best not to wait—times we must jump in or interrupt the discussion. But being able to pause is an important skill for teachers. Pausing during teaching is not easy to learn, but practicing silence and stillness in our daily meditation practice can give us the experience and the courage to pause before responding in a classroom setting. From those moments of stillness, we can choose the skillful means necessary for that situation. Something new and unexpected may arise in the gap, or our habitual or learned responses may become fresher, more appropriate. Embodied pauses can enliven learning both for teachers and students and, indeed, for the sake of the subject itself.

THE MINDFULNESS BELL AND PAUSES

There are other teaching methods that more directly involve the students in contemplative pauses. The mindfulness bell, used by Thich Nhat Hanh in his teaching, has been adapted for contemplative classroom practice.[12] At predetermined intervals throughout the class period, typically ten to twenty minutes, a small bell is sounded. Class lectures or discussions pause and everyone listens to the sound of the bell. When the bell can no longer be heard (two to three seconds), learning activities resume with the person who was last speaking. The standard instruction for what to do during the pause is similar to meditation: simply listen to the sound of the bell. When thoughts or emotions arise while listening, return to the sound itself. I use the mindfulness bell regularly in my classes and find that students adjust easily to the rhythm when it is used consistently. I notice that the tempo of the class settles and students appreciate the gaps.

We can also use pauses in the middle of a class at our discretion to create openness in the atmosphere. This can be particularly helpful when the discussion becomes heated or greatly intensified. Parker Palmer describes using periods of silence in his teaching "when the words start to tumble out upon each other and the problem we are trying to unravel is getting more tangled."[13] It is important to mention that using pauses in this way is not intended to silence students or to shut down the emotional intensity. We use such pauses to notice our breathing as a way of modulating our strong feelings, not suppressing them. Where appropriate, students could be asked to do the same, or just feel their physical presence on their chairs or follow a few breaths.

> These gaps can come in any form and at any time; they need not be anything extraordinary. A gap between my own words, between and within an exchange with another, a gap between direct instruction and practice, between classes. . . . I notice that if I am mindful, the gaps continually present themselves.[14]

As mindfulness and awareness deepen we can gradually extend our inner skills to create more overt contemplative learning environments. Pauses in discussions may improve the pacing, rhythms, and transitions of class periods and semesters. The same principles begin to enhance content presentation, curriculum, and learning environment design. We contemplative teachers find that mindfulness-based strategies sharpen the students' mastery of content while deepening and personalizing their learning experience. At its best the journey toward contemplative pedagogy begins and always returns to the discipline of the mindful teacher.

NOTES

1. Shinzen Stephen Young, "Buddhist Meditation," in *The Buddhist Religion*, ed. Richard H. Robinson, Willard L. Johnson, and Thanissaro Bhikkhu (Belmont: Wadsworth, 1982), 226–35.

2. Ibid., 229. *Bhavana*, literally, "familiarity," is the term in Sanskrit Buddhist texts.

3. Thich Nhat Hanh, *Being Peace* (Berkeley: Parallax Press, 1987), 83–102.

4. All quotations are taken from student journals from the MA in Contemplative Education program, Naropa University. Student initials and dates indicate contributors. DG 2008.

5. John Wellwood, *Awakening the Heart* (Boston: Shambhala, 1983), 81.

6. MKH 2009.

7. Richard C. Brown, "Taming Our Emotions: Tibetan Buddhism and Teacher Education," in *Nurturing Our Wholeness: Perspectives in Spirituality in Education*, ed. John P. Miller and Yoshiharu Nakagawa (Brandon: Foundation for Educational Renewal, 2002).

8. Mary Budd Rowe, "Wait-Time and Rewards as Instructional Variables, Their Influence in Language, Logic and Fate Control." Paper presented at the National Association for Research in Science Teaching, Chicago, IL, 1972.

9. Robert J. Stahl, *Using "Think-Time" Behaviors to Promote Information Processing, Learning, and On-Task Participation: An Instructional Module* (Tempe: Arizona State University, 1990); G. Claxton, "Thinking at the Edge: Developing Soft Creativity," *Cambridge Journal of Education* 36, no. 3 (2006): 351–62.

10. Kenneth Tobin, "The Role of Wait Time in Higher Cognitive Level Learning," *Review of Educational Research* 57 (Spring 1987): 69–95.

11. JG 2008.

12. Thich Nhat Hanh, *Being Peace* (Berkeley: Parallax Press, 2005), 109–11.

13. Parker Palmer, *To Know as We Are Known: Education as a Spiritual Journey* (San Francisco: Harper Collins, 1993), 80.

14. DG 2008.

8

COMPASSION BEYOND FATIGUE

Contemplative Training for Educators and Other Helping Professionals

JOHN MAKRANSKY

ORIGINS OF THE COMPASSION BEYOND FATIGUE WORKSHOP

Compassion Beyond Fatigue is the name of a contemplative training workshop that I developed for people in helping professions, including teachers and professors. In the workshop, guided meditations ease participants into a state of simple presence and compassionate connection with others. I have adapted these meditations from the "natural ease" tradition of Tibet (*dzogchen*) so as to make them accessible to people of all backgrounds and faiths. The purpose is to provide participants with contemplative techniques that can help them to alleviate burnout and compassion fatigue, to replenish energy and motivation, and to become more fully present to others. This essay describes the development of the program, its aims, some of the meditations taught, and how they inform the work of teachers and other helping professionals.

I began offering the Compassion Beyond Fatigue workshop in 2007 in the continuing education program at Boston College's Graduate School of Social Work. Since then I have offered it in diverse professional settings that have included educators, therapists and clinical psychologists, social workers, social justice activists, health care providers, pastoral counselors, and ministers.[1] The process that led to this workshop started seven years earlier when I began exploring new ways to adapt Tibetan Buddhist meditations of compassion, reverence, and wisdom so as to make them more fully accessible to Western participants in meditation retreats sponsored by Buddhist centers.[2] Many of those who attended were teachers, professors, and people in other service professions. A number attended multiple retreats and made a daily practice of the meditations. Many of these told me that they experienced more satisfaction and greater effectiveness in their work as they became more fully present to their students or clients. Several asked me to make the meditations available to a wider public of helping professionals in the secular world. As a result, I began to offer a Compassion Beyond Fatigue workshop in diverse professional settings in 2007. In September 2008, together with Leah Weiss Ekstrom and Julie Forsythe, I cofounded a new organization, the Foundation for Active Compassion, which provides contemplative training for people in all types of social service and social justice professions.[3]

AIMS OF THE COMPASSION BEYOND FATIGUE WORKSHOP

The meditations taught in the workshop aim to address three kinds of professional need which are elaborated in the following sections:

1) Alleviating Burnout and Compassion Fatigue—Teachers and others in helping professions can benefit from tools to alleviate burnout and compassion fatigue. The meditations in this workshop help participants access a level of awareness beyond the dynamics of stress and burnout, where they can find deep rest, a sense of inner safety, and replenishment of energy and motivation.

2) Becoming More Fully Present to Others—Teachers and other helping professionals are taught the importance of listening with full attention, of connecting to students or clients in their deep worth, and of discerning their hidden strengths. But *how* are these professionals to enhance in *themselves* the capacities of presence, connection, equanimity, patience, and motivation that are needed to fulfill those tasks? The meditations in this workshop are designed to help participants evoke and increasingly actualize those capacities.

3) Enhancing One's Ability to Effect Change—Teachers, social activists, and others in helping professions must often challenge dysfunctional patterns of behavior in students, clients, and communities. Meditation tools can help them find more of the equanimity and inner strength needed to do so skillfully, while strengthening their compassion for everyone involved. [4]

Alleviating Burnout and Compassion Fatigue

At the beginning of each workshop I ask participants to tell what brought them there. Many report that they suffer from stress and burnout—feeling overwhelmed by frustrations with their students, clients, colleagues or dysfunctional institutional structures. There are feelings of resentment at being underappreciated or misjudged. There are sometimes harsh self-judgments—blaming oneself for disappointing interactions and outcomes.

Workshop participants often use the term "compassion fatigue" in a broad way to signify their loss of compassionate connection to those they serve. Statements like these are common: "I used to be so eagerly concerned for my students' welfare, but after years of teaching I feel so worn down that I've lost interest in them. It frightens me how little connection I now feel to my students." "I used to have so much compassion for my patients. Now it feels like I'm on autopilot." "I feel as though I have been giving and giving and giving and don't *have* any more to give. *I* need to be replenished, but don't know how."

Difficult external circumstances are the triggers for these problems, but people who come to this workshop want to continue in their professions. At work, they feel that they are caught in a self-perpetuating cycle of habitual reaction that they don't know how to free themselves from. They want to see if a contemplative practice can help them address this inner need at a deep level.

To help alleviate burnout and compassion fatigue, people need to find a place of inner refuge, a quality of awareness that is prior to the turmoil of ego reaction—a place of deep rest from their own reactivity and of profound replenishment for their energy and motivation.

There is a powerful contemplative method that can help the mind relax to that degree, a method that I adapted from Tibetan traditions for people of any faith or background to explore. The meditator vividly brings to mind loving, inspiring figures from her past and *communes* with them—*receiving* the energy of their loving compassion so deeply into her body and mind that her habitual, self-focused patterns of thinking and reaction can unwind and relax their grip. The meditation is done slowly, step-by-step, until the posture of self-concerned worry and reaction begins to fall apart of itself, accompanied by a sense of relief. When thoroughly familiarized with the practice, the mind can learn to relax so fully that it settles into its most natural, preconceptual state of simplicity, openness, and unobstructed awareness—a most profound letting be. That is where the deepest rest and replenishment are found.

Meditation One—Deep Replenishment: Communion, Union and Release into the Natural State

Bring a few people to mind with whom you have felt happy, completely safe, well, and loved (referred to here as "benefactors"). They can include people from any stage of your life, such as a favorite relative, teacher, camp counselor, mentor, or friend. Your benefactors can also include deeply spiritual figures past or present whose presence in the world, or whose words, have inspired you— your spiritual ancestors.

Envision your benefactors' smiling faces before you. Imagine that they are sending you the wish of loving compassion—the wish for your deepest well-being, happiness, and peace. Notice the joy of holding their smiling faces in mind. When you feel that joy, the meditation has already begun. It is the joy of sensing others *commune* with the goodness of your very being—your deep worth beyond all limiting value judgments.

Feel the loving energy of this communing. Imagine it as a soft radiant energy, like a gentle, shimmering mist that comes from your benefactors and showers down upon your whole body and mind. Receive that soft, loving energy into every part of your body. First receive it deeply into your upper body, into every part of the face, head, neck, shoulders—letting all areas of tension soften and relax under its gentle touch. Then receive this soft radiant energy gradually into the middle part of your body: chest, back, abdomen, arms, and hands all the way down to your fingertips—allowing the gentle radiance to permeate every cell; letting bodily tensions relax under its touch. Finally receive the energy into each part of your lower body: torso, thighs, legs, all the way down to your toes— letting every part of you be loved.

After a little while, receive that loving, radiant energy into every part of your mind: into each layer of tension and worry; every feeling of difficulty, frustration, longing, sadness, grief, anger. Allow every feeling and thought in the mind, even as it arises, to be thoroughly permeated by this healing energy—sensing every part of you as loved. Do this for some time.

Then receive the loving energy into the subtlest feelings of holding onto your self, of holding onto anything at all. In this way, let yourself be tenderly swept away to merge into oneness with your benefactors and surroundings in that radiant energy. At this point, release the visualization and let your body and mind fall completely open. Allow all thoughts, feelings, and perceptions to just arise and dissolve of themselves like wispy clouds in sky-like openness. Let the mind rest in a state of utter simplicity and total expansiveness, allowing all to be just as it is.

This completes the first meditation.

To bathe so thoroughly in such loving energy, letting it permeate every thought and feeling, can be profoundly healing for the dynamics of burnout described earlier. When there is sufficient familiarity with this meditation, at the final stage of release, the mind can arrive at a simple, preconceptual level of awareness that is prior to ego reaction and discursive thinking, a place of most profound rest, peace, and renewal—as if dropping below the choppy waves of a raging sea into its calm depth. In Buddhist terms, this is the place from which our inmost capacity of tranquility and wisdom is heard. It is from this place of deep inner peace and safety that we can best embody a sense of peace and safety for others.

Becoming More Fully Present to Others

The second meditation follows from the one just completed. By letting our benefactors commune with our fundamental goodness and by deeply receiving loving energy (in the first meditation), we learn to relax into the ground of our being prior to all reactive thought—to find rest and replenishment in the openness and simplicity of preconceptual awareness. From that very place, in the second meditation, we can sense the same essential goodness, dignity, and potential of all other persons around us, beyond anyone's limiting value judgments. We can commune with others in their deep worth and potential, just as our benefactors have done with us. To commune in this way is to tap our capacity for fuller presence to others, more positive energy, equanimity, discernment, patience, and compassion. Meditation Two thus moves *us* into the position of benefactor in relation to others—including our students or clients—bringing out our preverbal capacity for communing, connecting, and affirming the best in them.

In the second meditation we repeat the first meditation, then continue with the further instructions as follows.

Meditation Two—Deep Connection: Taking the Position of Benefactor for Others
Begin by repeating Meditation One until you reach the final stage: letting the mind rest in its most natural state of simplicity and total openness. Sense the quiet power of that simple, undivided awareness.

After a little while, again recall your benefactors' smiling faces, this time imagining them *behind* you and just above. Feel the joy of holding their smiling faces in mind, sensing them commune with your essential goodness beyond anyone's limiting judgments. Feel the loving energy of this communing, imagining it as a gentle radiance that permeates your whole body and mind. Mentally repeat the wish of loving compassion *for yourself* so as to receive that energy even more deeply into your whole body and mind: "May this one have deepest well-being, happiness, and peace."

After a little while, bring to mind a person such as a family member, neighbor, student or colleague, and imagine him in front of you. While continuing to receive the loving energy from your benefactors behind, as if you were a windowpane, let that radiant energy come *through you* now to the person envisioned before you. Imagine this loving energy pervades his whole body and mind. As you do so, mentally repeat the same wish of loving compassion *for him*: "May this one have deepest well-being, happiness, and peace." While repeating that wish in your mind, commune with the goodness of his very being beyond limiting judgments, affirming him in his deep worth and dignity.

When you are familiar with the practice thus far, you can let the energy and wish of loving compassion gradually extend to further persons around you in

widening circles, communing with each in their essential goodness and worth
beyond limiting judgments, repeating the same wish for them all: "May they
have deepest well-being, happiness, and peace." Do this step-by-step in widening
circles at your own pace, including more and more of the persons and beings all
around you.

After doing this for some time, imagine that the benefactors behind you dissolve into their loving energy and that energy dissolves into your heart. Then
imagine that your heart, one with your benefactors, radiant like the sun, extends
the same loving energy and wish to all persons in all directions at once, communing with them all in the goodness of their very being: "May all beings have
deepest well-being, happiness, and peace."

Finally, let yourself be swept away by the loving energy, so that you merge
into oneness in its radiance with all those beings and surroundings. Release the
visualization, letting your body and mind fall completely open, letting all
thoughts, feelings, and perceptions arise and dissolve of themselves like wispy
clouds in sky-like openness. Let the mind rest in a state of utter simplicity and
total expansiveness, allowing all to be just as it is.

This completes the second meditation.

In Meditation One, we received the loving energy of benefactors and merged
with them, permitting the mind to relax into its most natural state of simplicity
and openness. In Meditation Two, we drew upon the quiet power of that preconceptual awareness to bring out its capacities of connection and loving energy
for others. By permitting our benefactors to commune with *our* deep worth and
potential, we learn to commune with others in *their* deep worth and potential—
including our students or clients. In this way, we learn to be more fully present
to others in a simple, direct, and deeply affirming way, beyond everyone's narrow
judgments, reactions, and prejudices.

Progressing in Practice and Applying It in Life and Work

Not everyone who attends these workshops is motivated to take up the meditations in a regular way. But many do. For them, I offer these tips for progress in
practice.

Do daily practice of the first meditation—communing with and deeply
receiving loving energy from benefactors, merging into oneness with them, then
letting your mind come to rest in its most natural state of simplicity and openness.
Do that daily for weeks or months before proceeding to the second meditation.

When you take up the second meditation in daily practice—widen the circle of other persons with whom you commune day by day, while extending loving energy. When you feel the power of loving communion to be strong and stable at one stage of the meditation, you are ready to progress to the next stage, extending the energy and wish of loving compassion in wider and wider circles.

When you start to practice the second meditation regularly, try to do so in the morning. When you imaginatively extend loving energy to others in the morning meditation session, consciously include all the people that you will see and work with that day. When you are familiar with this practice, to meet those very people at your workplace triggers the gestalt of your morning meditation: bringing you back to simplicity, openness, and compassionate connection with them. When this begins to happen, the quality of your presence to students and clients changes. Less distracted by habitual reactions, you can be present to others in a simpler way, connect preverbally to them in their deep worth and potential, listen more fully, sense their hidden strengths, and respond more creatively as the natural outflow of the compassionate communing that is already happening.[5]

If you are a teacher, during morning meditation, envision yourself receiving the radiance of loving compassion and letting it radiate through you to all your students. Later, when you step into your classroom, you begin communing with your students, radiating the energy of compassionate connection below the radar of narrow, self-concerned judgments—theirs or yours. Let your wish for your students' well-being help evoke their capacities for discernment, compassion, and joy in learning. Teachers and professors familiar with this practice tell me that they are amazed at how much more enjoyable and effective their classroom has become for themselves and for their students.

Enhancing the Ability to Effect Change

Notice how the second meditation extends the power of compassionate communing impartially to all other persons. All of us are socially conditioned toward limiting value judgments that are largely subconscious to us—judging some people as intrinsically more worthy of our concern, others as much less worthy. These meditations undercut that social conditioning, helping us to connect impartially to the immeasurable value of each person that transcends all limiting value judgments, including our own.

Although people in helping professions are routinely taught the importance of relating equally to the dignity and potential of all our students or clients, this can become merely an empty ideology if no specific way is provided to actualize the ideal in the quality of our presence to others. These meditations provide specific methods for gradual progress in that direction. The impartial, nonjudgmental quality of loving compassion in these practices concerns *value* judgments. It does not, of course, imply that we should avoid making the judgments needed to help people learn or address their problems.

Social justice teachers and activists find the impartial quality of compassion in this practice especially meaningful. Many activists are motivated by anger at injustice and hatred for those who maintain the unjust social structures. Indeed, some consider this a primary motivation for their work, the other motivation being care for the victims of injustice. The activist may see himself as a champion for some and a scourge against others. But this can become self-defeating. Anger and hatred are painful to be around. They drive away potential supporters, trigger rage in one's opponents, polarize communities, and often burn out the social activist who gets consumed by his own rage.

The meditation practices herein provide a different paradigm for social activism. Activism does *not* require two different motivations—compassion for some and hatred for others. *One* motivation—wise, enduring compassion—provides what is needed to challenge *different* people *in different ways*. People who suffer from injustice may need to be challenged to recognize their dignity and power to effect change. People who support unjust conditions may need to be challenged to recognize their connection to the poor and marginalized and their own greater human potential. Rather than being *for* some and *against* others, these practices structure a way to be *for everyone*, and *from* that very concern, to challenge different people differently. This approach is what can energize the social activist and inspire those around her for the long haul, like Gandhi, Martin Luther King, and Thich Nhat Hanh have done.

Many teachers are social activists in their own spheres of influence, challenging not only their students but also parents and communities in support of children and their education. Here is one example. When a teacher or school counselor senses abuse in the home, she may sympathize with the student while harboring rage at the parent. Yet such parents were themselves often abused as children. To be present in a way that holds everyone involved in deep care, even as you *challenge* dysfunctional behavior, is more effective than suppressed rage. A contemplative practice that holds all in wise compassion can become deeply healing, first for the teacher herself, then for all those with whom she works.

CAN NON-BUDDHISTS TAKE UP THESE PRACTICES?

Someone might ask, since these meditations draw upon Buddhist understandings of reality, is it possible for non-Buddhists to take them up? The meditations presented here adapt practices of compassion, reverence, and wisdom from Tibetan Buddhism for a diverse, modern audience.[6] They draw upon a Tibetan Buddhist (*dzogchen/mahamudra*) understanding that the underlying nature of our minds—prior to habits of thinking—is an unobstructed awareness of utter simplicity and openness that possesses a tremendous capacity of impartial love and compassion. Taking up these meditations requires exploring that understanding of the mind's nature in contemplative practice.

Certainly there are people whose beliefs would not permit them to explore in this way. However, in the past nine years of contemplative retreats and workshops, I have taught these meditations to thousands of Christians and Jews (including theologians, priests, ministers, and rabbis) and to many others of no formal religion, who have had no difficulty finding a place in their worldviews to explore these meditations in a serious way. Many of these people have taken up the practice regularly and reported the benefits mentioned previously. Self-selection seems already to be answering the question. Indeed, what I most often hear from religious Christians and Jews is deep appreciation for the light these meditations have shed upon their own traditions and spiritualities. On the one hand, as the meditations described here expose how much mental energy we usually spend in narrowly self-centered distractedness, fear, and aversion, they help illumine Jewish and Christian understandings of sin as a real human problem. At the same time, for many Christian and Jewish practitioners, as these meditations evoke the power of presence and impartial compassion from beyond the narrow patterns of their egos, their faith in a transcendent power of love is reaffirmed.[7] Nonreligious participants, on the other hand, often express gratitude at discovering more of their own human capacity for inner peace and impartial compassion.

NOTES

1. Compassion Beyond Fatigue workshops are listed at: www.johnmakransky.org, "workshops and retreats," and at: http://foundationforactivecompassion.org/.
2. See my recent book, *Awakening through Love: Unveiling Your Deepest Goodness* (Boston: Wisdom Publications, 2007) for fuller explanation of the meditations and how they were adapted from Tibetan praxis. I developed these techniques over the past nine years while teaching mainly in meditation retreats sponsored by Dzogchen Center (www.dzogchen.org), and also in retreats at the Barre Center for Buddhist Studies (www.dharma.org/bcbs) and Rangjung Yeshe Gomde, Austria (www.gomde.de/eng/).
3. For information on the Foundation for Active Compassion and its social justice and social service programs, see: http://foundationforactivecompassion.org/.
4. My thanks to Leah Weiss Ekstrom for many informative discussions on the concerns and needs of social service professionals that informed my articulation of the three aims listed here. Thanks also to Julie Forsythe for many

instructive discussions on social justice activism and service, and to Cathy
Cornell for sharing her developing reflections on compassion fatigue, secondary trauma, and contemplative practice.

5. For detailed explanation of progress and integration of practice in life and
   work, consult *Awakening through Love*, chapters 5–7.
6. On principles of adaptation, see *Awakening through Love*, introduction and
   chapters 1 and 2.
7. For one such example, see *Awakening through Love*, 240.

9

FIELD NOTES FROM A
DAOIST PROFESSOR

LOUIS KOMJATHY

FROM THE HUT TO THE ACADEMY

I walk over the needle-strewn path beneath a canopy of Douglas-fir, hemlock, and cedar. I find my way along the narrow, rain-soaked trail, eventually reaching the door to my thatched meditation hut. It is sparsely furnished, free of unnecessary objects—a small cot, writing table, books, and meditation mat. I take my seat on mat and cushion and begin practicing Daoist quiet sitting (*jingzuo*). Internal stillness merges with external silence. The silence takes in everything. Wind and the rustling of leaves. A kingfisher calling in the distance. After completing the meditation session, I stand up, stretch, and open the rough-hewn door. As I cross the threshold, I encounter thirty pairs of eyes looking at me. Some seem curious, others hungry, and still others frightened. These thirty students are in my Daoism class, having found their way through the forest along many different life paths. When I stand in front of them as their teacher, does it make a difference that I am a Daoist and a contemplative? What is the relationship between the meditation hut and the academy?

Much of academic life may be compared to solitary meditation, though an appreciation of and opportunities for contemplation itself seem increasingly rare within university life. There is no doubt that a "capitalist model of education" has become dominant in the academy: production, consumption, and service (in the sense of the "service industry") too frequently define academic success. Where is the time for contemplation? Indeed, few people seem capable of engaging in deep reflection and conversation, or of recognizing the contributions of philosophical insights derived from contemplative practice. Some of us may opt out of academic life, seeing it as incompatible with our inner commitments. In Daoist literature, for example, we encounter Lü Dongbin, a Tang dynasty literati-official who abandoned an official career in order to practice internal alchemy. In other words, the "hut" may be compelling in its own right. To pursue contemplative life may mean that one finds oneself as a recluse in early retirement, rather than a court official who has attained promotion in the imperial bureaucracy. But, even though academic life may be analogous to Lü Dongbin's Yellow Millet Dream,[1] for those of us who are dreaming the dream, we should dream big. Can we envision a fully integrated life as contemplative scholar-professors who seamlessly cross the threshold of hut to academy and back again?[2]

By "contemplative" and "contemplation," I do not simply mean meditative praxis; contemplation cannot be reduced to mere technique. Contemplation involves heightening awareness and attentiveness. This awareness may then inform one's daily life. Daoists frequently speak of this interplay in terms of developing clarity and stillness (*qingjing*), and emphasis on these psychosomatic conditions is one connective strand throughout the Daoist tradition. For example, chapter 45 of the fourth-century BCE *Daode jing* (Scripture on the Dao and Inner Power) explains, "Clarity and stillness are the rectification of the world." These technical meditation terms receive one of their clearest expressions in the eighth-century CE *Qingjing jing* (Scripture on Clarity and Stillness; DZ 620):

> Perfect stillness resonates with things.
> Perfect constancy realizes innate nature.
> Constantly resonating, constantly still,
> There is constant clarity, constant stillness. (1b)[3]

Other contemporaneous, Tang dynasty Daoist texts describe this as a five-stage process: 1) great agitation; 2) decreasing agitation; 3) equal agitation and stillness; 4) increasing stillness; 5) great stillness. Through quiet sitting, stillness deepens. Daoist contemplatives locate themselves in the internal silence at the ground of being, which from a Daoist perspective is the Dao. As stillness deepens, clarity increases. This is the capacity for discernment and spiritual insight. Consciousness becomes purified of defilements and distortion, returning us to our basic humanity and goodness. It then becomes possible to see things from a more all-encompassing perspective, and to develop ways of relating based on mutual respect and mutual flourishing. Thus, for Daoists, meditative practice is both solitary and communal; on a more integrated level, it informs and is expressed in the Daoist's daily life.

My personal practice is Daoist quiet sitting, a form of apophatic meditation that centers on internal silence and nonconceptual, contentless awareness. It finds clear historical precedents in the earliest Daoist scriptures and remains one of the primary forms of contemporary Daoist meditation. Briefly stated, Daoist quiet sitting involves stilling and emptying intellectual and emotional activity. This is not a forced or contrived activity; rather, one simply allows thoughts and emotions to dissipate naturally. The practitioner enters stillness. In terms of its basic commitments and guidelines, it resembles other practices such as Quaker silent worship and Soto Zen meditation. For this form of meditation to be "Daoist," there is of course an informing worldview and communal context. In my case, the study of Daoism is not restricted to reading and translating classical Chinese texts or examining fragmented artifacts in an attempt to reconstruct lost worlds. My understanding of Daoism is deeply informed by participant-observation in Daoist communities, both in mainland China and the United States. This includes formal commitment to and affiliation with the Daoist religious tradition.

Many challenges result from being a "scholar-practitioner." I do not always find it easy to cross that threshold from the hut to the academy, so to say. The most difficult challenge is how to address the negative view of religious practice that seems to prevail in the academy. I have come across this negative view at every turn, from a variety of sources: Protestant Christians, secularized Protestants, spiritualists, and adherents of secular materialism or social scientific reductionism. These various segments of the academy assert what I see as a highly questionable view that religious adherence necessarily leads to prejudice, manipulation, and distortion. But my experience reveals that the opposite may, in fact, be true: critical religious adherence may not only lead to a greater degree of reflectivity and self-awareness, but it may also provide important insights into *lived religiosity*. Such insights, I have found, enrich rather than compromise my research and teaching as a scholar in religious studies.

BEING A DAOIST PROFESSOR

How has Daoism enriched and guided me as a professor? What does the tradition I study and practice teach me about pedagogy? Reflection on and application of the study of Daoism has transformed my pedagogical practice in specific "Daoist ways." By taking Daoism seriously on its own terms, I have discovered principles and practices that may be applied to classroom teaching and learning. One dimension of my contemplative pedagogy involves actually engaging in critical inquiry on teaching (reading relevant books and speaking with colleagues, for example) and developing an applied and experimental approach to student learning. According to chapter 41 of the *Daode jing*,

> When the highest adepts hear about the Dao,
> They are diligent in their practice of it.
> When the middle adepts hear about the Dao,
> They wonder whether or not it exists.
> When the lowest adepts hear about the Dao,

> They laugh loudly and mock it.
> If they did not laugh, it would not be the Dao.

This passage is, of course, referring to the Dao as the sacred or ultimate concern of Daoists, but there are many *daos* ("ways") in human existence. One is the "way of teaching." Reframing the passage under this light,

> When the most committed teachers consider teaching,
> They are diligent in their reflection and practice.
> When less committed teachers consider teaching,
> They wonder whether or not it is important.
> When the least committed teachers consider teaching,
> They dismiss and ignore its relevance.

As we deepen our level of pedagogical reflexivity and practice, we become more committed to facilitating student learning.[4] We become more aware of the motivations behind our teaching, the means by which we teach, as well as the importance and relevance of our subjects. We also realize that our being and presence in the classroom, our physical embodiment and nonverbal communications, are as influential as conventional podium postures.

Being a Daoist professor means that I attend closely to listening. By this, I do not simply mean listening to the students' insights, questions, and concerns; I also mean listening to aspects of interpersonal relating with which they may not even be aware. The aforementioned insights about committed teachers may, in turn, be combined with the following passage on classical Daoist meditative praxis:

> Make your aspirations one. Don't listen with your ears; listen with your heart-mind. No, don't listen with your heart-mind, listen with your *qi*. Listening stops with the ears, the heart-mind stops with recognition, but *qi* is empty and waits on all things. The Dao gathers in emptiness alone. Emptiness is the fasting of the heart-mind. (*Zhuangzi*, chap. 4)

This passage urges me to become attentive to what I am listening to. Some teachers are listening to institutional limitations. Others are listening to student dissatisfaction or apathy. Still others are listening to their own insecurities and reactions. From a contemplative perspective, it is possible to overcome this conditioning, habituation, and reactivity; we can train ourselves to listen to something else, to discern what lies beneath appearances. For example, many students who denigrate the relevance of a course are actually limited by their own preconceived ideas or habitual tendencies of perception. A sensitive teacher finds ways to reveal and transform such cognitive and behavior patterns. Internal silence and stillness are essential for this task. Every classroom, every teacher, every student, and every group of students has its own energetic quality. Such influences and patterns of interaction may be a source of joy or a source of distress. By abiding in a state of open receptivity, we become more aware of our own strengths and weaknesses as teachers and of the possible opportunities and challenges of specific learning contexts.

This is where "nonaction" (*wuwei*) *as a Daoist practice* may be applied (see *Daode jing*, chaps. 2, 3, 38, 43, 48, 57, 63, and 64). *Wuwei* is a Daoist technical term related to effortless activity, or doing nothing extra. Parallel principles include "embracing simplicity" and "decreasing desires" (*Daode jing*, chaps. 19 and 37), and "loosening the tangles" and "untying the knots" (*Daode jing*, chaps. 4 and 56). We can find ways to teach, to facilitate student learning, in which our own egos are submerged in a larger communal vision. Our own educational values, concerns, and objectives (to be discovered by each teacher) become more prominent in our courses. Such commitments may be expressed in a more subject-centered and person-centered classroom.

Also relevant in this respect is the classical Daoist emphasis on "nonknowing" (*wuzhi*). In chapter 2 of the *Zhuangzi* we find the following:

> Suppose you and I have had an argument. If you have beaten me instead of my beating you, then are you necessarily right and am I necessarily wrong? If I have beaten you instead of your beating me, then am I necessarily right and are you necessarily wrong? Is one of us right and the other wrong? Are both of us right or are both of us wrong? If you and I don't know the answer, then other people are bound to be even more in the dark. Whom shall we get to decide what is right? Shall we get someone who agrees with you to decide? But if he already agrees with you, how can he decide fairly? Shall we get someone who agrees with me? But if he already agrees with me, how can he decide? Shall we get someone who disagrees with both of us? But if he already disagrees with both of us, how can he decide? Shall we get someone who agrees with both of us? But if he already agrees with both of us, how can he decide? Obviously, then, neither you nor I nor anyone else can decide for each other. Shall we wait for still another person?
>
> But waiting for one shifting voice [to pass judgment on] another is the same as waiting for none of them. Harmonize them all with the Heavenly Equality, leave them to their endless changes, and so live out your years. What do I mean by harmonizing them with the Heavenly Equality? Right is not right; so is not so. If right were really right, it would differ so clearly from not right that there would be no need for argument. If so were really so, it would differ so clearly from not so that there would be no need for argument. Forget the years; forget distinctions. Leap into the boundless and make it your home![5]

And according to chapter 71 of the *Daode jing,* "To know that you do not know is best; / To not know that you are knowing is sickness. / Only by being sick of sickness are you not sick."

These passages teach me that strong attachment to my own opinions inhibits conversation, and every perspective has inherent limitations. The classical Daoist recognition of the limitations of rationality and knowledge tempers the academic tendency toward hyper-intellectualism and authoritarian discourse. It helps to reframe teaching and learning in terms of inquiry, a communal discourse informed by every engaged and committed participant. We recognize the partial nature of any perspective, and this creates openness toward the perspectives of others. Why? Because we ourselves may not fully understand what we teach and why we teach. This aspect of a Daoist worldview also inspires us to investigate alternative views of consciousness and human flourishing. Dominant approaches to education as well as our very social and institutional locatedness may be as much of an impediment as an aid to student learning. For example, is there a type of learning that can only be attained with physical movement? Should walking have a place in teaching and learning?

I would thus suggest that the religious traditions that we study and teach may inform our own teaching and learning. In addition to clarifying pedagogical practice, our subject matter may become our conversation partner and create contexts for inquiry with our students. In contemplating Daoism, I find alternative views of human flourishing: from self as landscape and alchemical crucible; to place-specific community as a manifestation of the Dao; through clarity and stillness as the source of social transformation. These views challenge dominant American value systems, especially the emphasis on desire-based existential modes and material acquisition. They challenge the prevalence of uninformed opinions, conspicuous consumption, the cult of celebrity and fame, and "entertainment" based on humiliation and denigration. We may thus turn the subject matter of our classrooms back on ourselves: how do specific religious views and practices challenge our own pedagogical approaches? How can they be used to challenge students to reflect critically on their own learning and motivations? For example, why is a memorial at the former site of the World Trade Center ("Ground Zero") so important from a Daoist perspective?

DAOIST INTERNAL ALCHEMY:
TRANSFORMATIVE MOMENTS IN THE CLASSROOM

The Daoist tradition invites me to see education as transformative process. Whether teachers acknowledge it or not, they influence the lives and perspectives of students. Education imprints students. On some level, it even acculturates and domesticates them. The most committed teachers understand this and teach with awareness, intentionality, and care. They also make space for creativity, spontaneity, and wildness.

Internal alchemy, a model of Daoist practice and attainment that became dominant from the late Tang dynasty (618–907) onward, provides a possible map for the process of transformation. One way of understanding Daoist internal alchemy involves the refinement of *yin* qualities into their *yang* counterparts.[6] Here yin and yang diverge from the standard associations of female/receptive/stillness/earth and of male/assertive/activity/heaven, respectively. In internal alchemy, yin often refers to negative or harmful qualities and existential modes, while yang refers to positive or beneficial qualities and existential modes. Like Daoist alchemical practice, teaching and learning involve transmutation, or alchemical transformation. That transformative process entails cognitive and behavioral shifts: from ignorance to understanding, from rigid conviction to open inquiry, from inherited limitations to unimagined possibilities.

I witness these shifts in the classroom, especially as a result of contemplative-based assignments that give students direct personal experience with the subject matter. This type of learning catalyzes "critical first-person" perspectives in class discussion. In my Contemplative Traditions course, for example, students are required to choose a particular contemplative method and to practice it regularly throughout the semester. They study the religious and historical context for that practice and also have the opportunity to hear directly from a practitioner of that religious tradition about the practice. Thus the first-person contemplative learning goes hand-in-hand with conventional third-person historical-critical methods.

This combination of learning methods catalyzes an alchemical process for some of the students. One student, who chose Dominican prayer as her personal contemplative practice, came to a profound respect for the religious tradition she studied. She realized that the power of a practice may come from its connection to a community of practitioners: "It's a Catholic practice. I'm Christian, but not Catholic. You have to be part of the Catholic tradition to really practice Dominican prayer. Maybe even be a Dominican." The class members subsequently had conversations on the tradition-based nature of certain forms of contemplative practice, on the ways in which contemplative practice is always informed by the specific worldviews, concerns, commitments, contributions, and limitations of community and tradition.

In addition to the transformative effect of individual, first-person investigation of subject matter, something beneficial seems to happen when the class sits together in silence. Recently, in the Contemplative Traditions course, I applied my Daoist meditation practice to the classroom. We sat silently for five minutes at the beginning of a given class. Why do this? There are various rationales for introducing such "learning exercises" into education, including creating an environment more conducive to learning, helping students deal with stress, providing an experiential basis for conversation about religious praxis and embodied being, meeting students in a place of open inquiry and existential search, and so forth. These and other benefits of making space for "meditation in the classroom" were noted by students in my Contemplative Traditions course. For example, one student remarked during a class discussion, "I never knew how confused and chaotic my mind was. I'm completely distracted. I have no attention span. How can anyone learn like this?" In a journal entry, another student wrote, "Meditation is helping me calm down and relax. . . . In class, I can concentrate more and be fully present."

OPENING THE THATCHED DOOR AND
REMEMBERING THE FOREST COMMUNITY

With respect to contemplative pedagogy, to "meditation in the classroom," I have benefited from the tradition that I study and in which I participate. Daoist quiet sitting as well as similar apophatic and quietistic meditation practices develop awareness, attentiveness, and interior silence. Such qualities have the potential to frame classroom learning. While some teacher-scholars may have reservations about introducing actual contemplative practice into university education, there can be little doubt that fully embodied presence and deep listening exert a beneficial influence on students' academic and personal development. We become more capable of meeting our students, including their aspirations, fears, and disappointments. We may abide in a state of unagitated encounter and open receptivity that makes space for their own process of becoming fully human. We may become a model for a contemplative mode of being, a way of life rooted in clarity and stillness. Such a commitment offers an alternative to conventional academic tendencies toward egoism, domination, pettiness, and rigidity. Daoism thus gives me specific insights into the contributions and limitations of knowing and learning, including those of university education and academic intellectualism. It reminds me that there are many dreams, from Zhuang Zhou's dream of a butterfly's life to Lü Dongbin's dream of millet. I am dreaming too. But in the process, I find Daoist existential and ontological models that inform my pedagogy, a pedagogy that remembers a meditation hermitage and the forest community.

NOTES

1. According to standard Daoist hagiographies, Lü Dongbin (b. 798?) was a Tang dynasty literati-official who abandoned an official career in order to practice internal alchemy. The Yellow Millet Dream is one story related to

this decision, wherein Lü realizes the absurdity of pursuing fame and reputation. For one account see Livia Kohn, *The Taoist Experience* (Albany: State University of New York Press, 1993), 126–32.

2. If one has affinities with the Daoist emphasis on "embracing simplicity" (*baopu*) and "decreasing desires" (*guayu*) (*Daode jing*, chaps. 19 and 37) and the principle of "non-contention" (*wuzheng*) (*Daode jing*, chaps. 66 and 81), one may know the "joy of fish" (*Zhuangzi*, chap. 17) and be able to "drag one's tail in the mud" (ibid.).

3. Unless otherwise indicated, all translations are my own.

4. More recently, I have found Parker Palmer's *The Courage to Teach* (San Francisco: Jossey-Bass, 2007) and David Finkel's *Teaching with Your Mouth Shut* (Portsmouth: Boynton/Cook Publishers, 2000) to be books on pedagogy worthy of critical reflection. I have also benefited from many conversations with colleagues about teaching.

5. Burton Watson, *Chuang-tzu: Basic Writings* (New York: Columbia University Press, 1964), 43–44.

6. Conventionally speaking, *yin* and *yang* relate to what may be referred to as "traditional Chinese cosmology." They are complementary and interrelated cosmological principles. This cosmology became utilized in Chinese medicine and particular Daoist worldviews.

III

CRITICAL ISSUES IN
CONTEMPLATIVE TEACHING

10

TRAINING THE HEART RESPONSIBLY

Ethical Considerations in Contemplative Teaching

JUDITH SIMMER-BROWN

Our universities have had excellent reasons for their powerful emphases on analytic skills, objectivity, and scientific and social-scientific methods in third-person investigation. Among other considerations, these methods have assured fairness, respect, personal privacy, and objectively determined standards of academic excellence as the benchmark in higher education. They have also carried with them a body of ethical criteria that has guaranteed professionalism in our fields.

As we identify the imbalance resulting from overemphasis on exterior learning, and endeavor to introduce more interiority in our higher educational environments, we must address the corresponding ethical concerns that naturally arise. It is important that we invite our students into greater personal reflection without violating their privacy, or without exerting undue influence on their spirituality or religious convictions in their process of exploration. It is also important that we retain our responsibilities as evaluators without standing in unwarranted judgment of their personal experience.

These are particularly important matters in the field of religious studies. As our discipline charted a course to establish legitimate academic departments at public universities in the 1960s and '70s, we departed from the often-confessional stance of sectarian religious universities and institutions. As the ethics of contemplative education emerges, it is important that the field of religious studies steps forward as a leader in navigating the challenging waters of these considerations. Our discipline has weathered storms of higher education's sectarian past, and has developed criteria for studying religious doctrine, symbol, and practice within the appropriate historical and cultural contexts in which they were developed, honing strong methods for third-person investigation. Now is the time for religious studies to step forward as a leader in the ethics of the first-person investigations of contemplative pedagogies, and their utilization in our classrooms.

THE QUESTIONS

A small group of senior faculty at Naropa University inaugurated the first in a series of faculty contemplative pedagogy seminars in the summer of 2007, attracting a select group of twenty-five visiting faculty from a variety of North American colleges and universities, and from a range of academic fields.[1] After five days of exploration together, our closing session solicited "remaining questions" that the group might wish to consider in future conversations.[2]

1) What are appropriate motivations for introducing meditation into one's classroom?

2) What kinds of qualifications are necessary for a faculty member to introduce a contemplative practice in the classroom? For example, should a contemplative practice be taught by a faculty member who is not deeply steeped in that practice, such as loving-kindness meditation?

3) How do we deal with the potential for coercion in the contemplative education classroom? That is, how can we appropriately use our power as teachers to educate without attempts to convert or proselytize?

4) What is the difference between the faculty member who uses contemplative pedagogy and a spiritual teacher? What is the difference between an academic instructor and the therapist?

5) What are the implications of using Buddhist or other traditions' religious practices divorced from their roots and contexts—such that "mindfulness" becomes popularized as mere relaxation (like yoga has become in the United States)?

6) How can we evaluate or grade meditation and the contemplative components of our courses without violating the ethics of "dual relations" in our classrooms?

7) As contemplative teachers, how do we create pluralistic, inclusive, and respectful atmospheres in our classrooms while fostering contemplative values in education?

These specific questions have been helpful to me, as a longtime contemplative educator, in thinking through the ethical considerations of my teaching. I have chosen to foreground these questions as the foundation for our conversation in this chapter.

Naropa University was founded in 1974 by Tibetan Buddhist meditation master Chögyam Trungpa Rinpoche as a learning community based on contemplative pedagogy, and it has served as a vanguard in the field since that time. A small and cohesive group of faculty has worked together to develop educational methods that differ from the religious practices one may find in retreat settings associated with Buddhism, Christianity, Judaism, or other religions, appropriate to our diverse student body, faculty, and staff. In my three decades on this faculty, I have benefited from countless conversations on these matters as we charted our course, dealing with many of the issues that have arisen in these seminar questions. We have not definitively answered these questions; in fact, there are many issues I will discuss about which some of my colleagues have drawn very different conclusions. I hope you will take the questions as a discussion piece to your own heart, to your contemplative colleagues, and to your departments, if they are inclined to discuss them.

WHY TEACH MEDITATION IN THE CLASSROOM?

There are numerous reasons why religious studies professors have brought meditation into their classrooms. For many, like myself, the first compelling reason is our own journeys of cultivating interiority in our personal lives and our desire to include this aspect in our academic lives. This is not motivated by a desire to proselytize, as some of our colleagues may quickly presume, but by a sense of how the inner life nurtures wholeness, confidence, intellectual creativity, and compassion in our experience, and promises to do so also for our students. This is how we understand good education.

Many of us pursued higher degrees in our fields because of the potent sense of the importance of the inner life. Of course, most of our graduate programs rightly sought to quell the inappropriate propagation of religious beliefs in our classrooms, and trained us in objectivity and scholarly methods in religion. Some of our mentors even encouraged us to develop contempt for religious doctrine and practice, no doubt because of the wounding of previous generations of scholars who had to undergo indoctrination in church-related colleges and universities.

Contemplative education is not indoctrination or the propagation of religious beliefs. Most of the contributors to this book have also been trained in meditation traditions that do not advocate belief systems as primary, no matter what our disapproving colleagues have said. Instead, these traditions have encouraged the cultivation of an interior life. Just as religious studies has properly moved its center of gravity away from the Judeo-Christian tradition, dominated by the Protestant establishment, to include broader perspectives about what is religious, we must change our reactivity to narrow notions of religious practice. In Asian religious traditions, *praxis* rather than doctrine is primary as any scholar of these traditions can attest.[3]

Still, it is important to articulate what we are doing when we introduce meditation into the college classroom. We are not introducing religious practices; we are developing new teaching pedagogies. We are not creating little Buddhists, Hassidim, Sufis, Daoists, or Trappists. We are returning to the roots of liberal education in the West. These roots are grounded in the development of depth and wholeness that synchronize with intellectual rigor. Education was meant to "draw out" (L. *educare*) the brilliance of the student through respect and training. Contemplative disciplines were inherent in medieval education, they continued in liberal education, and contemplative pedagogies have the potential to return the transformative qualities to our educational endeavors.

Another reason we bring contemplative pedagogy into the classroom is the yearning of our students. What we encounter in our classrooms reflects what we have learned about student expectations for spiritual content and inner development in their higher education experience. The Astin report for the Higher Education Research Institute at UCLA (HERI) surveyed 112,000 matriculating freshmen attending 236 diverse colleges and universities across the country, finds this:

> The study reveals that today's college students have very high levels of spiritual interest and involvement. Many are actively engaged in a spiritual quest and in exploring the meaning and purpose of life. They are also very engaged and involved in religion, reporting considerable commitment to their religious beliefs and practices. As they begin college, freshmen have high expectations for the role their institutions will play in their emotional and spiritual development. They place great value on their college enhancing their self-understanding, helping them develop personal values, and encouraging their expression of spirituality.[4]

The Astins report that three-fourths of college freshmen say that they are searching for meaning or purpose in their lives; nearly half of the students surveyed consider it "essential" or "very important" to seek opportunities to help them grow spiritually. Two-thirds reported that they derive strength, support, and guidance from their spiritual or religious beliefs.[5] They additionally expressed the expectation that college will help them develop emotionally and spiritually.

Religious studies, in particular, has a great deal to offer such students. Of course, we can include curriculum that ponders the Big Questions, and we should. But didactic learning alone has limits, and shifting the *way* we teach can have a significant impact on how students develop in our classrooms. We can educate our students about religious traditions while also teaching them related contemplative skills to access the interiority they seek.

QUALIFICATIONS FOR CONTEMPLATIVE EDUCATORS

What kind of preparation do we need to introduce meditation in the classroom, and what responsibilities are implicit in such an undertaking? This first matter has to do with the qualifications necessary for trustworthy presentation of a meditation practice or contemplation in the classroom. Certainly, the classes described in section 4 and the exercises and activities presented in section 5 require more than a pocketful of techniques learned in a weekend workshop. When we give students tools to open to their inner lives, they must be tools with which we are deeply familiar. Meditation entails a subtle journey that has many potential pitfalls that can be harmful to the student; it is important that we ourselves know how to avoid these pitfalls from our own experience, so that we can guide students gently, with integrity, through their own journey of self-discovery.

At Naropa, we have the delightful advantage that faculty who are already contemplative practitioners seek teaching positions where they can begin to integrate their academic training with contemplative perspective. Once here, most of them have no idea how to proceed—I certainly did not when I first arrived in 1978. I taught in very traditional third-person methods for the first three to four years of my Naropa teaching, completely stymied about how to maintain academic rigor while employing contemplative methods in the classroom. As I interacted with my colleagues, especially the performing artists and psychologists, in collaborative work, together we experimented on each other about how to bring a self-reflective method into our classrooms. Gradually over the years, I have developed different pedagogies for my different academic classes, endeavoring to customize methods appropriate to the subject matters of those courses.

The main point is that it takes time, reflection, and experimentation for even the most seasoned contemplative practitioner to find appropriate, responsible, and effective pedagogies for their classrooms. It is very helpful to seek colleagues who can serve as sounding-boards for our work, and to carefully and consistently gather feedback from our students. Most of all, however, it is critical to have an ongoing personal contemplative practice that provides the depth and context for whatever pedagogies we practice in our classrooms.

As several of our contributors have indicated,[6] long before we bring pedagogies into our classrooms, we bring our contemplative minds to ourselves, our students, and the subject areas that we teach. Those minds have an invisible but powerful effect on our students, and often provide resonance for the interior journey long before there is an explicit invitation for such a journey. This is perhaps the first step to becoming a qualified and responsible contemplative educator.

For those educators who wish to bring contemplative pedagogies directly into the classroom, what should the training standards be? Just as we examine the academic credentials of our candidates, we need to develop criteria, establish equivalencies, and evaluate preparation for our contemplative educators as well. Of course, one of the most effective ways we can bring this expertise into our classrooms is to carefully select meditation teachers, checking their qualifications in the spirit of these criteria, and then create appropriate contexts for their presentations to our students. In the curriculum committee and search committee settings at Naropa, we have asked for information regarding the lineages of training for our faculty who wish to introduce contemplative practices. Eclectic training may signal lack of depth or clarity in experience, and self-made meditation teachers are deemed untrustworthy. Has this person been authorized by her lineage teacher to teach the practice she wishes to introduce? What previous teaching experience does our candidate have? Generally speaking, we do not approve courses or hire faculty to teach contemplative courses that cannot pass this muster.

IS MEDITATION IN THE CLASSROOM A TROJAN HORSE?

Given the sectarian history of church-related colleges, another delicate issue has to do with the perceived attempts to convert or proselytize within the context of introducing contemplative pedagogies in the classroom. Critics of contemplative education suggest that contemplative education is a "Trojan horse" that allows "things that might otherwise be deemed inadmissably religious [to] be smuggled into the educational arena."[7] Such worries appear to come from three directions. Conservative Christian movements consider contemplative pedagogy to be threats to both public and Christian institutions. They perceive the widespread introduction of yoga, for example, as either Eastern or "New Age" missionary conspiracies designed to convert the secular West, or to dilute the Christian message.[8] From the opposite direction, Constitutional scholars and jurists worry that the "moment of silence" is a Trojan horse for conservative religious forces of American culture to return prayer to the schools.[9]

In a third area, within religious studies, the assumption of such criticisms is that the Protestant establishment is still working full force (and many think it is[10]) to bring an individualized, personalized understanding of spirituality back into the classroom, unencumbered by social and institutional understandings of religion. This is fundamentally the criticism leveled at the New Age understanding of spirituality, and it is assumed that this is what contemplative educators are doing. Parker Palmer, luminary of the "spirituality in education" movement, is singled out for special criticism in this vein.[11] Eugene Gallagher comes close to accusing Palmer of proselytizing in his call to reintegrate spirituality in the classroom:

I suggest that much of Palmer's work can be read as the record of his efforts to re-make his job *and the jobs of many others* (teaching) in the image of his vocation ("the quest for god"). In fact, at times Palmer comes very close simply to asserting that the two are virtually inseparable, or that no one can do that type of job without having the same type of vocation.[12]

This type of criticism comes from religious studies scholars for whom religion is defined, first and foremost, as doctrinally based and mission driven, following the Western Protestant model. After decades of struggle to assure that religious studies is a respectable academic discipline, free of the sectarian agendas of religious practice in schools, these colleagues are working overtime to oppose contemplative pedagogy, perceived to be returning the classroom to dreaded sectarian agendas. These Eurocentric biases create specters that are primarily Western that do not reflect the profile of religion in the non-Western world. Within the Buddhist, Daoist, and Hindu expressions of religion, missions of this kind are for the most part unknown, and religious identity comes not from belief so much as from community, symbol, and practice. It is time for religious studies to transcend its Eurocentric bias and develop some broader understanding of religion such that this Protestant specter can be laid to rest.

Still, within a paradigm like that of Asian religions, the contemplative professor must be savvy about students' expectations that she become a spiritual mentor. What is the difference between the college professor and the spiritual teacher or guru? Between the academic instructor and the therapist? Once meditation is in the mix, it is easy for the students to turn to the instructor for focused spiritual guidance, and we must be prepared for this. When students engage in an interior journey, we cannot keep our office hours' conversations limited to due dates for papers or performance on exams; part of our responsibility is to support the students' unfolding self-discovery, while refraining from taking on the inappropriate role of actual spiritual direction. We must explore these parameters in order to fulfill our responsibilities as educators while not exploiting our students at the time of their greatest spiritual vulnerability.

REFRAINING FROM APPROPRIATION

As contemplative educators, it is important to cultivate respect for context and tradition as we present interior pedagogies in our classrooms. This is an especially important consideration in our discipline of religious studies, which has developed skillful methods for contextualizing religious practice within the traditions in which they were developed. While we are not teaching religious practice *per se* in the classroom, many of our pedagogies are informed by these practices, and it is important that we respect the milieus in which they were developed. This requires that we bring forward our third-person perspectives as scholars and train our students accordingly.

For example, the practice of *hatha-yoga* (Sanskrit for "mastery of physical energy through union") has become immensely popular during this period of the early twenty-first century, becoming for many a physical discipline to develop flexibility, strength, and balance without any particular reference to the mind. Most contemporary practitioners of yoga are completely unfamiliar with the religious and cultural roots of the Indian tradition that place it within a sophisticated philosophic context and a variety of practices that do not involve the *asana* postures.[13] For the most part, the phenomenon of "modern yoga" is sheer cultural appropriation, and many teachers and professors in other disciplines are introducing it in their classes without context.

If we as religious studies professors were to introduce *hatha-yoga asanas* in our classes without naming them within the context of their history, philosophy, and culture, it would be irresponsible. This does not mean that we must teach *hatha-yoga* only in a Hinduism class, but it does mean that we must take responsibility for our own training and perspective, and include that in our presentation of this discipline in the classroom. It is also a "teachable moment" to demonstrate to students the importance of respecting cultural context for religious practice. One effective way to do this is inviting guest teachers with the appropriate credentials to teach a contemplative discipline while we provide the academic context for the study of a contemplative discipline.

The same can be said for mindfulness practices such as *shamatha-vipashyana* (Sanskrit for "calm-abiding and insight") from the Buddhist traditions, or any such pedagogy we teach. There are currently many adaptations of this widespread practice in a variety of Asian settings, but the principles of mindful attention have a certain consistency throughout. Given the popularity of mindfulness meditation in many settings in contemporary North America and Europe, many who practice mindfulness are unfamiliar (and often uninterested) in the variety of cultural and historical settings in which the practice was developed, and know nothing of the sacred texts that support the practice.

Certainly, mindfulness as a phenomenon is not "owned" by any specific tradition, as Alan Wallace's Shamatha Project has shown.[14] William James famously spoke about repeatedly bringing the wandering attention back to focus as the educational pedagogy *par excellence*.[15] Studies on attention in psychology and science have shown the power of training attention, and a wide range of non-Buddhist philosophers and researchers, from Simone Weil and James Hillman to Jon Kabat-Zinn and Aldous Huxley have praised the cultivation of focused attention as key to the development of contentment, learning of skills for adaptation, and management of psychological and physical pain.

Outside of the laboratory, the phenomenon of mindfulness practice has its longest and most explicit occurrence within religious traditions, especially Buddhism. When we introduce mindfulness practices into our classrooms, we owe our discipline the respect to present the historical and cultural settings in which the lineages of mindfulness practice were formed. To be balanced, it would also be helpful for us to include other traditional settings in which attention was similarly trained, as among the Christian Desert Fathers and Mothers,[16] in writings of the Muslim and Hindu traditions, and from Hassidim.

When we take responsibility for demonstrating the importance of third-person investigation within the context of contemplative pedagogy, we have plenty of ripe opportunities for exploring religious phenomena, contemporary culture, Orientalism and its accompanying Occidentalism, and such topics that are the bread and butter of our field. These conversations will be of benefit to our students in both a personal, interior way and in their ability to cultivate critical perspectives about the cultures in which we live.

CONTEMPLATIVE RIGOR—EVALUATION AND GRADING

How do we evaluate and grade student work when first-person investigation is the medium? This is an issue with which we have grappled for decades at Naropa University. The dilemma can be stated very simply: how can we create an environment that supports student self-discovery if we evaluate that discovery? Our students are at a variety of stages of development in personal awareness, and it is difficult to imagine how grading criteria would support their individual development. On the other hand, if evaluation has no role in contemplative pedagogy, are we conveying to our students that these aspects of our courses are "freebies," not important in the overall scheme of things? Should we not uphold "contemplative rigor" as well as academic rigor?

Over the decades, my Naropa University colleagues and I have discussed extensively how to evaluate the contemplative components of our courses, and we have created certain ground rules. It is important that faculty avoid "dual relationships" with students, and that we never evaluate or grade our students' meditation practice itself. In Naropa's dedicated meditation courses, students have non-grading meditation instructors with whom they have strictly confidential meetings. A portion of their grade is based on whether these meetings occur, according to semester confirmations from the meditation instructors.

In general, students must be given choices about what specific contemplative practice that they do to fulfill course or department requirements. Still, the choices cannot be too broad, or TV-watching could be called a practice. At Naropa, we are most interested in mindfulness-type practices that can be traced to spiritual lineages from the world's wisdom traditions, and these are fulfilled in our undergraduate curriculum by elective offerings in T'ai-chi Ch'uan, aikido, contemplative brush calligraphy, ikebana, Centering Prayer, yoga, Jewish meditation, or *shamatha-vipashyana*. For an individual course, however, it is difficult for one faculty member to present these practices, and so outside resources must support such a curriculum.

What can we evaluate? While we do not evaluate contemplative practice itself, we can determine that the student participated in the practice he has chosen in the class on a quantitative level, and this is reflected in the "participation" portion of the grade. In order to ensure that students who do not wish to engage in contemplative practice are not in our courses, it is important to advertise in our course descriptions and syllabi, during the drop and add period, that contemplative practice is a required part of our course. Once they are enrolled and have participated, we can teach our students how to communicate about first-person investigation, whether from meditation, contemplative exercises in class, or in life.

Of course, when students begin to communicate personally, at first they share superficially whether they "like" something, or not. That is unacceptable in my classes; I insist that students begin to draw on their own insights and experience in a way more sophisticated than a mere "reaction." They may begin with anecdotes, but I guide them to reflect, in the present moment, on their insights rather than turning to plotlines to explain their views. Eventually they draw richly from the depths of their reflections, improving their ability to engage in first-person investigation and to trust themselves as participants in their own education.

My paper-grading rubric for undergraduate writing places one-third emphasis on "comprehension," which is the third-person investigation, including confirmation they have read the assignment, followed the argument, identified the evidence, and "done their homework." An additional third is based on "integration," which means that they have reflected on what they have studied and can support, challenge, or add to what they have studied with an articulation of their own personal experience and insight. An additional third of the paper grade is based on the "mechanics" of their writing, the actual structure of the paper; the fluency of writing; the grammatical, spelling, and syntax elements that make a paper "work." An excellent paper is the successful assimilation of all three of these elements.

The main point is that we need to show respect for both the first- and third-person aspects of our courses, ensuring rigor that is both academic and contemplative. Just as it is demanding to develop the critical perspectives that weigh the strength of philosophic arguments or the veracity of research findings, we need also to weigh students' abilities to articulate their insights and their abilities to probe the depth of their experience, not being content with a first glance.

Real creativity and brilliance come from the joining of these two kinds of rigor, and they prepare students for inquisitive interaction with the world and with themselves.

CONTEMPLATIVE EDUCATION IN A PLURALISTIC SETTING

As contemplative teachers, how do we create a pluralistic, inclusive, and respectful atmosphere while fostering contemplative values in education? Even when we do not introduce contemplative pedagogies such as mindfulness exercises as religious practice, it is easy for students to feel that they must be Buddhist in order to be properly mindful, Christian to be properly prayerful, or that our pedagogies do not include their own religious traditions or spiritual leanings.

Rather than perpetuate the myth that none of us have religious leanings or spiritual yearnings in our private lives, professors in many disciplines are coming out of the closet to engage issues of religious identity, but they are unsure how to do so. Harvard's Mark U. Edwards Jr. argues,

> there's the larger world where religious conviction and practice is shaping political, economic, and social life in ways impossible to overlook or ignore even in our ivory tower. . . . Religious conviction burns through attempts to confine it to chapel services, dorm-room discussions, and topical courses. In these changing circumstances, the default mode [that true intellectuals and scholars are not religious] will no longer do.[17]

But how we emerge from this myth is terribly important, and as religious studies professors, we must do so responsibly, drawing on the best perspectives of our discipline.

Rather than being the dirty word that it has been in church-related colleges and universities, "pluralism" is an important, positive element in the educational environment in which contemplative pedagogy is introduced. While there are many definitions of pluralism, I have found that of Harvard's Diana Eck most helpful. She speaks of pluralism as the recognition that truth is not exclusively (or inclusively) the property of any one religious tradition, and that the myriad understandings of truth or the "ultimate" in religious traditions provide an opportunity for celebration and dialogue rather than providing obstacles to be overcome. She adds: "It does not mean giving up our commitments; rather, it means opening up those commitments to the give-and-take of mutual discovery, understanding, and, indeed, transformation."[18]

This does not mean that the religious studies professor needs to "lead" with religious or spiritual identity (or nonreligious worldview, for that matter), but it does suggest that hiding it may be more dangerous and insidious than allowing it within a carefully developed context of pluralistic sensibilities. When we allow ourselves transparency in this way, we also encourage it in our students, and acknowledge the potency of identity issues into our classroom interactions.

This cannot be done well without concomitant training in the basics of dialogue skills, so that an atmosphere of respect can grow and flourish. One of the popular courses in our department is my Interreligious Dialogue class, in which students study the rapidly changing demographics of religion in America, showing (in Eck's words) "How a Christian country has become the most religiously diverse nation on earth."[19] Because such an environment needs training in pluralism, dialogue, and the dynamics and complexities of religious and spiritual identity, the course includes actual dialogue training between classmates, with guests from the faculty and the surrounding community, and with religious communities along the Colorado Front Range. In all of this, I ensure that every student, no matter whether religious, spiritual, or not, feels respected and valued for whatever interiority he or she wishes to share. For example, when a student makes a derogatory comment about Christian prayer or Muslim communalism, I ensure that we "own" our own biases and invite my Christian or Muslim students to share their responses, and how it feels to be disparaged this way. By the end of the semester, my students have developed the ability to deeply listen to religious "others" and to surface the inner dialogue that sometimes contains inherited prejudice and stereotypes.

In conclusion, if contemplative approaches to religious studies are to flourish and enrich the lives of our students, we must develop ethical guidelines and standards for how we deal with these and other issues in our classroom. Conversations about the ethical considerations of our teaching work should be part of every gathering of contemplative educators, and I look forward to the emerging body of wisdom on these issues.

NOTES

1. Seats at the first seminar were competitive, with many more applicants than attendees, because participants were awarded stipends and travel funds. For more information on these seminars, see the website for Naropa's Center for the Advancement of Contemplative Education, CACE, http://www.naropa. edu/cace/seminar.cfm.
2. Questions lightly edited for this chapter. "Group-Generated Closing Questions," Naropa University Contemplative Pedagogy Seminar, August 7, 2007. Unpublished.
3. See Harold Roth's chapter (chapter 3) in this book.

4. Alexander W. Astin and Helen S. Astin, Higher Education Research Institute (HERI), *The Spiritual Life of College Students: A National Study of College Students' Search for Meaning and Purpose: Executive Summary* (Los Angeles: University of California, Los Angeles, 2005), 3. The HERI study was funded by a grant from the Templeton Foundation. A copy of the full report is available at www.spirituality.ucla.edu.

5. Ibid., 4.

6. See section 2 of the present volume, "The Contemplative Professor," for these perspectives.

7. Dixie Dennis, "The Biological Basis of Spirituality," in *Searching for Spirituality in Higher Education*, ed. Bruce W. Speck and Sherry L. Hoppe (New York: Peter Lang, 2007), 69–84, quoted in Eugene V. Gallagher, "Spirituality in Higher Education? *Caveat Emptor*," in *Religion and Education* 36, no. 2 (Summer 2009): 71.

8. Monica Byrne, "Yoga and Fundamentalist Christianity," *Sightings: May 2006*, The Martin Marty Center for the Advanced Study of Religion, University of Chicago. http://divinity.uchicago.edu/martycenter/publications/sightings/archive_2006/0518.shtml.

9. http://candst.tripod.com/dawn1.htm.

10. The literature on this is voluminous. For summaries of the issues, see George M. Marsden, *The Soul of the American University: From the Protestant Establishment to Established Nonbelief* (New York: Oxford University Press, 1994); Mark R. Schwehn, *Exiles from Eden: Religion and the Academic Vocation in America* (New York: Oxford University Press, 1993); Mark U. Edwards Jr., *Religion on Our Campuses* (New York: Macmillan Palgrave, 2006); George M. Marsden and Bradley J. Longfield, eds., *The Secularization of the Academy* (New York: Oxford University Press, 1992); C. John Sommerville, *The Decline of the Secular University* (New York: Oxford University Press, 2006).

11. Eugene V. Gallagher, "Spirituality in Higher Education? *Caveat Emptor*," *Religion and Education* 36, no. 2 (Summer 2009): 75–76.

12. Ibid.

13. Barbara Stoler Miller, trans., *Yoga, Discipline of Freedom: The Yoga Sutra Attributed to Patanjali* (London: University of California Press, 1996); Jean Varenne, *Yoga and the Hindu Tradition*, trans. Derek Coltman (Chicago and London: University of Chicago Press, 1976).

14. B. Alan Wallace and his Santa Barbara Institute for Consciousness Studies, in association with Cliff Saron and the University of California, Davis, have been studying the effects of mindfulness meditation on the brain, the mind, and the life experience of a group of subjects. For more information, see http://sbinstitute.com/research_Shamatha.html.

15. Several of our contributors have referenced this statement of James—William James, *The Principles of Psychology* (New York: Henry Holt, 1890), I. 424.

16. St. Gregory of Sinai, "Instructions to the Hesychasts," *Writings from the Philokalia on the Prayer of the Heart* (London: Faber and Faber, 1992), 74–94.

17. Mark U. Edwards Jr., *Religion on Our Campuses: A Professor's Guide to Communities, Conflicts, and Promising Conversations* (New York: Palgrave Macmillan, 2006), 45.

18. Diana Eck, *Encountering God: A Spiritual Journey from Bozeman to Benares* (Boston: Beacon Press, 1993), 168.

19. Diana Eck, *A New Religious America* (New York: Harper One, 2002).

11

INVITATION AND COERCION IN CONTEMPLATIVE PEDAGOGY

SID BROWN

Contemplative pedagogy announces (rather loudly for such a quiet group of practices) that each of us has an interior life and that the interior life is important to learning. When a teacher declares that a part of today's class experience will be ten minutes of silence, during which time a student can engage in this or that practice or training of the mind, the teacher is declaring that learning is not simply dependent on receiving information, playing with information, and conversing with others about information. It is not simply memorization or analysis. Learning is dependent upon some recognition, exploration, and perhaps manipulation of one's interior, private experience. This overt recognition of the interior life throws some issues into relief, including those of coercion and privacy.

My initial concern about contemplative pedagogy and coercion arose out of the awkwardness of asking students to engage in practices that 1) resemble fundamental aspects of my own religiosity (and are therefore unsuitable not only for a class *about* religion but also for a class full of students who did not claim my own religion as theirs); and 2) are not standard in-class practices (and therefore made me feel awkward and demand that I be self-conscious in my decision to include them and how I included them).

When I first began to reflect on these issues, I often wanted to sweep my concerns away by concluding simply that the variety of ways I use contemplative pedagogy in the classroom are not overtly religious in any way—you would have to know a bit about the roots of these practices in order to associate them with a particular religion. Further, I told myself, they really do not take up much in-class time. Also they are always presented as options, not requirements. I felt that they were effective at doing something about learning, and I was often inspired by student responses, but I was uncomfortable with the practices too. I repeatedly told myself that given their lack of overt religiosity, their brevity, their seeming harmlessness, and the students' own choice in the matter, I could abandon my self-conscious reflection on contemplative pedagogical techniques and simply use them as I saw fit. I often found myself in a quick loop of anxious intellectual tail-chasing about the legitimacy of contemplative techniques in the classroom and tried to interrupt that loop by dismissing my concerns.

Examined more deeply, however, I found my awkwardness to be rooted in one question: What is appropriate knowledge for my classroom? Or, what counts as legitimate classroom work? And that question reveals questions of power—who defines what knowledge is in my classes?

Many years ago when I first began teaching Buddhism, and I wanted to teach students about meditation, I would lecture about it and ask students to read primary and secondary texts on meditation, and I would answer their questions. One year one of my students asked about meditation, "Isn't that brainwashing?" I turned the question over to the class and they became toddlers at the seaside, splashing about in messy analysis, delighting in discussing this possibility. They loved to see what they knew about meditation and consider what brainwashing might be, and it was an interesting bit of analysis to invite students to take up. Through years of study I had been trained in what kind of knowledge and what kinds of discussion were appropriate in the classroom; then a student had questioned that, helping me to redefine it. We shared the power in the classroom to define what knowledge was relevant.

It is not easy to discern what appropriate classroom knowledge is. Another professor might consider my including this question in discussion as not only a relinquishing of power but also a lowering of my standards. After all, the students were supposed to be learning what Buddhist meditation is, not what brainwashing is. But I was convinced that the students learned more about Buddhist meditation as they engaged the question—they were forced to analyze it and other things they do (watch TV, recite in church) in light of it, which made the material more relevant to them, so they learned more. Further, I wanted to encourage their asking this kind of question because I want to encourage curiosity in general, and because this kind of question can help students discern what the world around them is like and how they want to live their lives in this world.

As years have passed and increasingly more people have an awareness of the strength of the advertising industry, however, my students now respond utterly differently to the question of brainwashing. They look at me dully, bored. This is a dumb question, even a boring one, because they know that brainwashing is all around them: watching TV or movies, surfing the internet. It is all, obviously, brainwashing. Billions of dollars a year are spent on controlling their minds and behaviors, and they know it.[1] Yet these same students delight in messy analysis after *being given the reflective experience of their own brainwashing.* For this exercise, one that dramatically introduces them to the contents (and lack thereof) of their minds, I show them more than twenty logos of major international companies, asking them to identify the companies as they can.[2] Then I show pictures of local plants and trees and ask them to write their names down. Finally I show them pictures of our governor and our senators and pictures of pop stars such as Angelina Jolie and Brad Pitt. Then I give them a few minutes to reflect silently on what they learned through this exercise; what follows have been conversations as stimulating and incisive as any teacher could imagine.

In short, I use my higher status in the classroom as an authority figure supported by institutional university infrastructures and social norms in the setting of classroom standards to coerce my students into examining the contents of their minds. None of these students would sit down and list the names of corporations based on their logos without my having asked them to do so. Few would identify their local plants unless they were in a botany class. I coerce students into things all the time. As is true, perhaps, for all teachers, I use all kinds of pressure including, most significantly, social pressure to help them learn. I may be uncomfortable with all this power and how overtly, covertly, and seemingly good-naturedly I sometimes use it, but the whole idea of any class is that those in it would not otherwise do what it takes to learn what there is to learn without joining a group to help them do it.

I see the classroom as a space where power is constantly negotiated. How one uses one's power in the classroom and for what purpose is complicated. Some teachers prize obedience and submission, attempting to claim all the power and unilaterally decide what occurs in the space and time they have with their students. They are likely to learn, however, that both teachers and students have power and agendas,[3] and that students resist domination in countless ways: by not doing homework, delaying the start of class, or avoiding eye contact with the professor.[4] My students, for example, seem to use what power they have to transform the situation into what they think they want. (In a sense, I think we all often try to transform any situation we are in into what we think we want!) How students transform the situation can depend on how a professor views and uses the power she has to define what counts as knowledge in the classroom.

A professor who acknowledges that a student's interior life plays a role in learning ideally honors that interiority and helps students honor it themselves. Some professors let that interiority stay interior, but others find that attention to our inner lives invites greater personal honesty in the classroom on the parts of both teacher and students. Students and professors both can share more of their interior lives as they explore the topic of the class. The teacher shapes (or tries to shape!) the classroom and the students, of course, but in this case there is more room than usual for the students to shape the teacher and the classroom. As students share more and notice that in this kind of classroom their interior lives

create legitimate knowledge in the classroom, they can become more embold-
ened. Results, then, of greater attention to interior lives can include greater reciprocity and mutual assertiveness. In such cases a professor watches what counts
as knowledge change depending on who is in the room.

In a day-long workshop on global warming I watched what counts as
knowledge change as one student struggled. After she had engaged in a contemplative exercise—in this case to spend two minutes silently exploring a raisin
with all her senses and reflecting on the inclinations of her mind as she did so—
she told the group that she had begun the exercise angry. She had rolled her eyes
inwardly as she heard the instructions, she said, submitting herself to the activity
because of social pressure: "I would *never* do this were I not in this group."
When she had signed up for that workshop on global warming (which included
presentations by scientists, social scientists, and those from the humanities
including mine on ethics, consumerism, and contemplation), she had not
planned to spend a seemingly inordinate amount of time focusing on a raisin. It
was an unwelcome surprise. What I offered was not knowledge that she considered relevant to her quest. She may have come with the expectation schools often
foster of students sitting passively and receiving knowledge. Perhaps it seemed
overtly religious to her, or "new agey," stupid, or a combination of those—use-
less, but also embarrassing. Part of her interest in coming was to learn about
global warming, and a covert part was to maintain a certain status, reputation,
and self-image—a hidden motivation for many of our actions.

In the discussion that followed, it became clear that this student had engaged
at least for a bit in the contemplative exercise and that she felt she had gained
from it in an unexpected way. As she observed the raisin in all its detail using her
sight, touch, smell, and taste, she got a glimpse, she said, of the inner world of her
son, a painter whose subjects are often magnified images of small objects depicted
in great detail. She understood for the first time, she said, how her son must
spend hours every day as he paints, how he relates to the inanimate objects that
are the subjects of his work. This was not what I was aiming for when I included
this exercise in the workshop that day. I was aiming, rather, at introducing the
participants to different ways of consumption, including this very slow, considered, self-aware consumption of a raisin. But the student offered up this insight,
which is not a bad one to have for her life and quite significant for one of her primary relationships in that life. I am not convinced this story ends as neatly as I
would like to end it here. Frankly, it is difficult to know what she really experienced and learned. The woman revealed her new understanding about her son in
a strained way. It left me wondering if she had responded to nonverbal coercion,
the unspoken social pressure of the group, to put a happier face on her assessment
of the exercise than was really true for her. On the other hand, perhaps stepping
back from her initially angry reaction and hearing the observations from other

participants gave her a larger perspective about the significance of close, mindful attention to something as ordinary as a raisin.

What is the difference between the coercion I use to support students in reading their assignments and the coercion I use to support them in exploring their interiority? That, after all, is what I think is the main difference between contemplative pedagogy and other kinds of pedagogy—the degree to which a student's interior life is made an overt part of a class. Lecturing by a professor is standard and accepted (and in some places even passé, fighting for a comeback) and seems to allow little recognition or involvement of students' interior lives. Increasingly, discussions among students and professors, small group discussions, skits, role play, drawing and diagramming are mainstream in-class practices, at least for the humanities and social sciences. These approaches bring greater spontaneity and more of the students' private lives into the public arena of the classroom and thus result in more communal construction of knowledge. Contemplative pedagogy, or the introduction of contemplative techniques into a class, brings even more opportunities for professors and students to construct knowledge communally, drawing upon the profoundly private aspects of their lives. It can seem to take reciprocity to a new level (or perhaps returns education to an old level, when institutions of higher learning were monasteries, at least in Christian and Buddhist societies[5]).

The communal creation of what counts as knowledge is heightened simply by a professor's calling students' attention to their interiority. (A teacher is saying, "What is important to know in this class is not only what I say as your teacher but also what you find out and create in your own mind.") It is heightened more when a professor chooses to invite more public acknowledgment and discussion of interior lives. This new level is highlighted by the difficulty in assessing it. To ask a student to sit in silence for ten minutes and do a certain exercise with his or her mind is not as easily measurable as to test a student's ability to "take out a pencil and piece of paper," or to ask them to memorize and then write down, upon request, a certain list of words or a quotation. Students may sit there and quietly do something utterly different from what you ask them to do in their silence, and the professor has no way of knowing, no way of testing, no way of assuring himself of student cooperation. The beauty of the elusiveness of assessing a person's interior life highlights some of the central problems in education today: too much of what professors do in the classroom is "to enact rituals of control that [are] about domination and the unjust use of power,"[6] and stress what is measurable and trivial rather than what is immeasurable and profound. Thus contemplative pedagogy can bring a new kind of freedom as well as profundity, spontaneity, intimacy, and excitement.

Yet one can (and people do) measure aspects of contemplative learning. If a professor teaches a class on meditation, she can require a journal of reflections on meditation practice that will be graded and count as a main component of the grade in the class. She can then judge by the contents of the journals what students have learned about themselves, the practice, and the central content of the class. I use journal assignments, yes, and I grade journals, too—but I cannot condone grading journals based on what students have learned about themselves. That kind of attempt at quantifying a person's most personal interior life raises another challenging ethical issue in contemplative pedagogy: privacy. If a student wants to earn a good grade on that meditation journal, he may very well have to open up more of his interior life to public inspection than he wants to, more than he should. (Or, and perhaps worse in the long run for the student, he might just choose to lie.)

The situation reminds me of the mindful dialogues I require of students in Introduction to Asian Religions. In an effort to help them recognize the sensitivity of religion as a topic of conversation, overcome their disinclination to discuss such a sensitive topic, and introduce them to some tools to use to discuss it peacefully and well, I require them to have a careful, reflective conversation with someone whose religious understanding of the world is quite different from their own. They have a careful one-on-one dialogue with someone else that includes such questions as "What's your fondest and oldest memory related to your own religion or secular values?" and "What is your most painful memory related to your own religion or secular values?"[7] The student and her partner each answer each question, taking at least a full three minutes for each person to answer each question. I teach the students how to listen nonjudgmentally, to listen for understanding rather than for other reasons. I ask them to speak honestly when they answer and to slow down and note how they feel as they answer. If I tell the students to go out there and get vulnerable in this exercise, they do—becoming sometimes too vulnerable. (It is no wonder because students spend an inordinate amount of time learning through public sources about what used to be considered private—through Facebook and through "reality" and talk shows on TV.) I caution them too—helping them to learn how to calm down and speak when they feel they know what they want to say. I want students to be honest with others, deeply honest. But I also want them to be calm and know themselves. After all, I am teaching them to have robust inner lives, and to value them. And the thing about an inner life is that it is, in fact, inner. You can make it an overt part of your public life or you can keep it private. Emphasizing that choice is essential. Also important is recognizing that when students and professors share their interior lives in the classroom, discussion may be awkward, lacking the smooth showmanship that some of us prefer. The moments we shared discussing the raisin experience in the climate change workshop were clumsy. We were all uneasy. That lack of ease on all our parts, however, did not seem to indicate a problem so much as a depth—we were realizing how important our conversation was. These are profound issues that can be awkward, but that does not mean they are bad or unhelpful.

As a person who has engaged in contemplative practices for over twenty-three years and has benefited from them, I have come to feel obliged to introduce the practices. I introduce them very carefully, with self-doubt and questioning and simultaneously (or at least alternately) with delight in the spontaneity, intimacy, and profundity that nourishes me as well as my students. I read every day how more and more scientific experiments are proving their usefulness (most particularly in fighting depression), and I think these practices may be one good way to struggle with challenges my students (as learners, as workers, as citizens, as humans engaged in relating to others) face in our fast-changing, information-saturated, consumerism-driven, and unjust world. I never *require* students to engage in these practices; students have the choice of participating or not. You can get an A in any of my classes without contemplating. If you want to explore your inner life more, however, you can.

I will continue to watch carefully how I use the power I have in the classroom and how I respect my students' privacy and help them cultivate a sense of it. Contemplative pedagogical techniques are windows to the interior life, and should be respected as such. I open those windows whenever I assign a reading or activity that excites my students, whenever I ask them to free-write on a topic. In this way, contemplative pedagogy is very much like the kinds of teaching done every day across the nation. As such, it is not necessarily simple and good. One introduces, with care and reflection, motivated by concern for the world and the students, new ways of teaching. One watches how the experiment goes and reflects. And one recognizes that even seemingly harmless and peaceful practices can be used for ill. After all, Buddhism, ideally focused on relieving suffering, played a military role throughout World War II. Meditation was used in officer training; one Soto priest and scholar went so far as to "equate the suicidal spirit of *kamikaze* pilots . . . with the complete enlightenment of Buddhism."8

In a sense, most of us are undergoing some kind of brainwashing all the time—be it from our governments, corporations, media, or our own habitual thought patterns and those of our loved ones. In our world, extraordinary amounts of money, time, and creativity are used to encourage greed, ill-will, and superficiality. Power is used every moment to cause, overtly and covertly, pain and death, and the more we acquiesce to these sorts of worldviews, the more we contribute to ongoing injustice. In the face of this, as a teacher, I am obligated to call my students' attention to their interior worlds and help them recognize how their minds work, how they perceive the world, and how they can use the power they have to alter their minds, their perceptions, and the world. This is no small matter—it is something akin to talking to fish about water. I hope, however, that this greater attention to their minds will help them see clearly the water in which they swim every day and so play a greater role in creating the kind of water more of us can swim in healthfully and happily. It is the least I can do.

NOTES

1. In 1950, annual global spending on advertising was less than $50 billion; in 2002 it reached $446 billion, increasing almost nine times in fifty years. Advertising takes up 25 percent of network television programming time and 66 percent of newspaper space, not to mention on the internet. Gary Gardner, Eric Assadourian, and Radhika Sarin, "The State of Consumption Today," in *State of the World 2004: Special Focus, The Consumer Society*, ed. Brian Halweil, Lisa Mastny, Linda Starke (Washington, D.C.: The World-watch Institute, 2004), 14.
2. Kent Curtis, Assistant Professor of Environmental Studies at Eckerd College, kindly shared with me his version of this exercise. Evidently various versions are in existence.
3. Mary Phillips Manke, *Classroom Power Relations: Understanding Student-Teacher Interaction* (Mahwah: Lawrence Erlbaum Associates, Publishers, 1997), 7.
4. Seth Kreisberg, *Transforming Power: Domination, Empowerment, and Education* (Albany: State University of New York Press, 1992), 17.
5. See especially Robert Thurman's "Meditation and Education: India, Tibet, and Modern America" (chapter 2 in this volume) and Brian Stock's "The Contemplative Life and the Teaching of the Humanities," *Teachers College Record* 108, no. 9 (S 2006): 1765–74 and 1760–64.
6. bell hooks, *Teaching to Transgress: Education as the Practice of Freedom* (New York: Routledge, 1994), 5.
7. I am still searching for a better, less awkward phrase than "secular values" to use for students who have had little contact with institutional religion. Suggestions welcome.
8. Brian Daizen Victoria, *Zen at War* (Lanham: Rowman & Littlefield, 2006), 139.

12

INTERIORITY AND EDUCATION

The Neurophenomenology of Contemplation

TOBIN HART

At a conference I attended recently, a presenter explained that he was involved with contemplative architecture. I think most of us in the audience were trying to imagine what this work was about. Did it mean building meditation halls or religious buildings? Were the construction workers hammering nails in unison with eyes closed? He went on to explain that for him contemplative architecture was designing a building with more space on the inside than there was on the outside. This image hints at a key aspect of education—developing spaciousness within us in order that we may meet and take in the world that is before us.

Interiority not only points toward the learner but also at the process of learning itself, looking not only at the outer data but also opening into our selves, and cultivating such qualities as: nondefensive openness, flexibility of thought, curiosity and questioning, a sense of wonder, suspension of disbelief, leading with appreciation over judgment, an emphasis on contact over categorization, accommodating rather than merely assimilating, a willingness to really meet and therefore be changed by the object of inquiry whether a new idea or a new person. This is like a two-headed key opening a series of locks that lead simultaneously into our selves and into the data. In this sense we recognize that *what* we know is bound to *how* we know.

This chapter is excerpted from Tobin Hart, "Interiority and Education: Exploring the Neurophenomenology of Contemplation and Its Potential Role in Learning," *Journal of Transformative Education* 6, no. 4 (2008): 235–50.

Contemporary education is dominated by an approach to knowing that emphasizes both the rational, which involves calculation, explanation, and logical analysis, and the sensory, characterized by observation and measurement. Together these two form the rational-empirical approach that has set the standard for knowing across most disciplines. Contemplation adds a third way of knowing—a missing link—that both complements and enhances the rational and sensory. The contemplative mind is opened and activated through a wide range of approaches—from pondering to poetry to meditation—that are designed to shift states of mind in order to cultivate such capacities as deepened awareness, concentration, and insight.[1]

NEUROPHENOMENOLOGY OF LEARNING: FOUR ASPECTS

One hundred years ago William James, the reputed "father" of American psychology, recognized two complementary approaches to exploring human consciousness.[2] One looks directly at human experience through the tools of introspection and reflection unearthed by subjective questions such as: "Where are you now? What are you thinking, feeling, sensing?" The second approach is essentially neurobiology—the neurophysiological correlates of experience. One hundred years later we have reached a point where these two streams of inquiry are coming together in an unprecedented fashion. Subtle subjective phenomenological descriptions alongside data from brain measurement and imagining devices such as fMRI and EEG bridge these two domains. Terms such as "contemplative neuroscience"[3] or neurophenomenology[4] mark this "green zone" of mingling inner and outer technologies.[5]

Applying a neurophenomenology lens, I would now like to explore four aspects of interiority and contemplation especially as they relate to learning: Presence, Clarity, Detachment, and Resilience. I am certain that we are really not ready to have any kind of definitive conversation on this evidence. There is simply not adequate data of this kind directly on education and learning. However, I think there is enough evidence to piece together some of the practical possibilities, logical connections, and relevant questions as they relate to learning and the inner life and in so doing to extend an exploration of what these inner technologies have to offer learning.

1. Presence, Attention, Focus, Flow. If you have ever found yourself having just read several pages in a book only to pause and realize that you have no idea what you just read, you know the importance of focus and attention on learning. Through such experience we understand that in learning the *quantity* of time-on-task is subordinate to the *quality* of attention one brings to the task. If we are distracted, lost in our thoughts, or shut off in some way it is very difficult to absorb or learn well. An ability to focus, concentrate, and deploy attention is basic and essential to learning. Nearly all contemplative practices train concentration—whether through such injunctions as repeating a mantra, focusing on love, watching the breath—in order to train the mind and quiet habitual internal chatter.

Attention, memory, learning, and performance are largely state-dependent—that is, the state of body, mind, and emotions are central to learning. One of the most well established effects of contemplation is a change in physiological state, which in turn cascades into shifts in affect and cognition. This state change, especially as it relates to the autonomic nervous system, has been well documented for more than forty years. For example, if we ring a bell, close eyes, and focus on our breath or a sense of love, we send a signal throughout the body-brain system that decreases blood pressure, lowers heart rate, and reduces cortisol levels.[6] Such an immediate shift can have a powerful influence on the ability to focus or be present in the classroom by reducing anxiety and helping to quiet the habitual chatter of the mind. This shift in turn allows us to either lock on to material or consolidate freshly learned material thereby avoiding retroactive interference to memory (muddling up memory with the next material). In this sense much of education may benefit from simultaneous training in both the right *skill* set and the right *mind* set.

In addition to this basic physiological response, some recent data suggest that the more an individual focuses attention, the more likely there is to be an increase in frontal lobe activity in the brain.[7] The frontal lobes are most often associated with higher cognitive function. With respect to contemplative practice, Newberg and colleagues found that meditation practitioners focusing on a visualized image increased regional cerebral blood flow significantly during a practice involving visualization.[8]

Maintaining focus often leads to a sense of absorption and is frequently the natural state of a small child filled with wonder. Learning is joyful and deeply nourishing in such states. For learners at any age deeply pleasurable encounters involving focused concentration have come to be known as *flow*.[9] Whether working on a math problem, building a chair, or running rapids in a kayak, *flow* is characterized by high concentration on a particular activity, merging of action and awareness as we lose a sense of our self and along with it our usual sense of time. This immersion is deeply satisfying and the effort seems almost effortless— we and it are flowing. By deepening one's capacity for sustained concentration, contemplative practices may help engender flow states.

2. Silence, Imagination, Creativity, Clarity. Problem solving requires creativity and imagination that extend beyond the information given. Creativity involves flexibility, originality, synthesis, insight, and divergence of thought. Imagination and creativity have a central place at the table of education alongside knowledge and logic. In a 1929 interview published in the Philadelphia *Saturday Evening Post*, Einstein, when asked about his own process of discovery, responded: "I'm enough of an artist to draw freely on my imagination, which I think is more important than knowledge. Knowledge is limited. Imagination encircles the world."

In addition to developing the ability to hold and deploy attention, some contemplative practices invite a kind of opening and receptivity that may result in a flow of new ideas, breakthrough insight, or clarity. Clarity and insight come unbidden, but they can be wooed and welcomed and this often involves a kind of interior emptying, a sense of surrender, openness, and receptivity. Silence and stillness may set the stage for the process. Silence can invite the chattering mind to settle down and recede a bit, in turn opening awareness of more subtle currents of consciousness. There is no need to get into a metaphysical conundrum as to the source of these currents (e.g., God, our own mind, higher self) in order to recognize their functional value. Especially as it relates to education, the value lies in the quality of the material or insight as well as the more enduring shifts in being, rather than in an attribution of source. And again, sometimes there is silence with no content whatsoever. In some instances a subtle transformation of consciousness is claimed to take place out of immediate awareness and without any identifiable form.

In Persian poetry the poet often refers to himself or herself by name at the end of the poem as a sort of signature. In five hundred odes, Rumi concludes with the word *khamush*, silence. In silence, in emptiness, in stillness, we open to some deep place and become its conduit. Rumi said it this way:

> There is a way between voice and presence where information flows.
> In disciplined silence it opens.
> With wandering talk it closes.[10]

The "disciplined silence" requires, as Rollo May said, "hold[ing] . . . [oneself] alive to hear what being may speak. [This] requires a nimbleness, a fine-honed sensitivity in order to let one's self be the vehicle of whatever vision may emerge."[11] Gowan makes the point this way, "When Michelangelo did the Sistine Chapel he painted both the major and the minor prophets. They can be told apart because, though there are cherubim at the ears of all, only the major prophets are *listening*."[12]

At least two different kinds of neuroscience data may correspond to experiences of silence, breakthrough, and clarity. The first is a change in EEG alpha and theta brain wave rhythms. Increased alpha activity (8–12 hertz) is associated with deep, relaxed alertness—silence and stillness—that also seems to be a gateway into theta (4–7 hertz) states, which have been associated with the experience of creative breakthroughs.[13] A variety of studies found increases in alpha and theta activity over the frontal regions of the brain during meditation.[14] These studies mainly investigated different forms of voluntary concentrative meditation on an "object" (e.g., mantra or breath).

Along with descriptions of breakthrough, sometimes we may experience moments of extraordinary clarity when it feels like our whole mind seems to be wide awake. This experience of clarity may be related to neural synchrony. In addition to alpha and theta activity, large-scale brain coordination appears in recent studies on gamma wave (25–42+ hertz) synchrony. Long-distance (throughout the brain) synchrony is thought to reflect large-scale neuro-coordination and occurs when two or more distant electrodes oscillate with a precise phase relationship that remains constant over time.[15] Lutz and colleagues found that large-scale brain coordination increases during mental practice (in this case loving-kindness and compassion meditation in which participants were asked to generate feelings of love and compassion toward all sentient beings without focusing on anyone in particular) and that the size of synchrony patterns increased more for long-term practitioners than for the controls when participants shifted from neutral to meditation states.[16] It appears that the baseline or "resting" state of the brain may be altered by long-term contemplative practice resulting in a generalization of state benefit to our general presence, that is, greater ongoing clarity. While these studies are very preliminary and we do not know the functional consequences of sustained gamma activity, it may indeed relate to a state of clarity and "fine-honed sensitivity."

3. Detachment, Witnessing, Metacognition. William James made a distinction between the "I" and the "me." The "me" represents the contents of our consciousness—the thoughts, feelings, and sensations that rise and fall throughout our waking life. The "I" is that part of us that can watch or witness those contents. What are you aware of right now? What thoughts, feelings, and sensations do you notice? If you were able to notice, then some aspect of you was doing the noticing—what James called the "I" and others have referred to as the witness or observer.

A practice of mindfully watching what arises in the stream of consciousness—thoughts, feelings, sensations—without either pushing them away or clinging to them, develops a capacity for detachment.[17] This detachment is most often described not as a distant objectivism but instead as a nondefensive attitude of interest and curiosity. For example, rather than just feeling angry, such witnessing allows us to step back and notice ("I see that this is really upsetting me") and perhaps inquire about it while in the midst of it: "I wonder why I'm so upset?" This not only develops the potential for emotional regulation and impulse control, but also develops interior "muscles" of reflection leading to metacognition. Emerson hints at this developmental arc: "Our thoughts first possess us. Later, if we have good heads, we come to possess them."[18]

In this witnessing or watching what occurs is "a mindful reflection that includes in the reflection on a question the asker of the question and the process of asking itself."[19] This process "begin[s] to sense and interrupt automatic patterns of conditioned thinking, sensation and behavior" opening one to see in fresh ways.[20] Such openness, curiosity, and flexibility toward what we are observing are characteristic of great learners and deep learning. In addition, as we simply and honestly observe and tolerate our own reactions, we may also gain a tolerance for others. Such tolerance is central to understanding multiple points of view, which is a characteristic of higher order cognitive functioning and empathic understanding. Self-observation and reflection help to expose and deconstruct positions of role, belief, culture, and so forth in order to see more deeply or from multiple perspectives. This allows students the conceptual flexibility to see beyond the information given and beyond their own presuppositions.

Contemplative practices are traditionally designed not only for short-term state shifts but also as a way to cultivate more generalized long-term traits, such as compassion or detachment that, if successful, should be reflected in neurobiological data. Aftanas and Golosheykin tested twenty-five Sahaja yoga meditators, whose practice involves "thoughtless awareness" or "mental silence."[21] They did demonstrate increased alpha and theta activity during meditation but there was also another effect while not meditating. The two groups were shown four brief video clips; three clips were "emotionally neutral" and one "emotionally negative" (an except from Michael Haneke's film *Funny Games* in which two young people are abusing a family). In the study, EEG data reflected lower "tonic arousal" and greater proneness to sustain "internal locus of attention." Essentially the data suggested that the meditation group did not get carried away in a reactive state so easily, did not lose their "center," and were able to maintain a degree of openness and witnessing detachment. Impulse control problems, distractibility, road rage, low frustration tolerance, and distractibility are all affected by this capacity. In this sense such practice seems to provide, as T. S. Eliot wrote, a kind of "stillpoint in a turning world."[22]

4. Resilience, Emotional Balance, Well-Being. Education has become increasingly involved in teaching for character, health, and civility, reflecting contemporary societal needs. The greater the complexity and demands—the external stressors—the greater the need for psychological and emotional balance and resilience. In a state of chronic stimulation or low-grade anxiety it is difficult to concentrate, step back and watch ourselves, be still and silent, and maintain sensitivity toward one another. In other words, our emotional state is significant not only for our well-being but also for our capacity to learn.

Contemplative practices appear to help the individual return from and modulate a state of arousal and therefore may be valuable for balance and resilience. During stress the HPA axis (hypothalamus, pituitary, adrenal cortext) coordinates an autonomic nervous system response that gets us ready for fight or flight in part by increasing levels of cortisol. But in an age of constant stimulation designed to grab our attention, shock or arouse us, not to mention the accelerated pace of the day, we may not return to an optimal baseline state, that is, to calm back down. The hyper-arousal of the HPA axis and elevated levels of cortisol have been related to obesity, memory deficit,[23] even the neurobiology of suicide.[24] Chronic stress or corticosterone treatment induces pathological alterations in brain function including cognitive deficits. The good news is that contemplative practice has been shown to reduce the level of cortisol during nonstressful events, increase response during stress, and quicken the return to baseline levels.[25]

In addition to these biochemical changes, another line of affective neuroscience research has uncovered a difference in the activity of the prefrontal cortex that may have something to tell us about well-being and resilience. A difference in relative activation of the left versus the right prefrontal cortex reflects differences in emotional responsiveness. Greater relative activity on the left side seems to correspond to "positive" emotional states (joy, empathy, caring) as opposed to anxiety, depression, and greater emotional resilience. High relative activation in the left versus the right prefrontal cortex marks either a fleeting positive mood or a positive affective style.[26]

Davidson's research with Buddhist monks reveals that their ratio of left to right activation was greater than any of the nonmeditating participants previously tested. When the monks and the nontrained subjects were asked to meditate on compassion, the monks showed a greater shift toward the left-prefrontal cortex than control subjects. Focus on virtuous or positive mental states, such as compassion, empathy, joy as opposed to anxiety and depression, may engender a more resilient affective style including a greater modulation of and faster recovery from stressful events.

It should be clarified that experiencing a variety of emotions is not intrinsically maladaptive, and neither is just promoting positive feelings entirely adaptive. Beyond the obvious richness that a full range of emotions brings to human existence, emotional expression and processing difficult emotional material enhances immune system response, for just one example from the scientific data.[27]

But what may be even more immediately significant for learning is a study in which participants were trained in an eight-week program in their work place centered on mindfulness meditation.[28] Two measures were employed: 1) brain electrical activity was measured before, immediately after, and four months following the training program; 2) an influenza vaccine was given to both the experimental group and the control. Those trained in the eight-week program showed a greater relative activation of left prefrontal cortex (associated with "positive" affect). Additionally, there was a significantly increased immune response (antibody titers) to the vaccine among the meditation group compared with the control group.

In combination, these studies point to the potential value of contemplation in engendering emotional resilience, which in turn may impact one's capacity to learn.

CONCLUSION

This preliminary review suggests that capacities for presence and attention, breakthrough and clarity, detachment and metacognition, and emotional resilience and balance are significant components of interiority that may be valuable for enhancing the process of learning and living. Further, these dimensions have neurological substrates that are affected by a wide range of contemplative practices. While current research is hardly conclusive, neurophenomenological data does appear to demonstrate that significant changes are indeed occurring in the mind (experience) and the brain as a result of contemplative practice. The effects on the neurophysiological changes range from immediate state shifts to long-term trait patterns to changes in brain structure.

Developing interiority may be most valuable not simply as an adjunct to knowledge acquisition but as central and essential to the process of deep and life-long learning. Learning more and more deeply is tied to the way and to the degree that we meet information. Contemplation as a way of knowing complements and enhances rational and sensory epistemic modes and may enrich capacities to meet oneself, one another, and tends to approach information non-defensively, pregnant with depth.

Can the architecture of education engender more spaciousness and graciousness to welcome in the world? When educational practice recognizes that the internal and external are bound to one another and also transformed by one another in a kind of reciprocal revelation, then education moves toward becoming a wisdom tradition itself.

NOTES

1. Tobin Hart, "Opening the Contemplative Mind in the Classroom," *Journal of Transformative Education* 2, no. 1 (2004): 28–46.
2. William James, *The Principles of Psychology* (Cambridge: Harvard University Press, 1981).
3. B. Alan Wallace, *Contemplative Science: Where Buddhism and Neuroscience Converge* (New York: Columbia University Press, 2007).
4. Francisco J. Varela, "Neurophenomenology: A Methodological Remedy for the Hard Problem," *Journal of Consciousness Studies* 3, no. 4 (1996): 330–49; Evan Thompson, "Neurophenomenology and Francisco Varela," *The Dalai Lama at M.I.T*, ed. Anne Harrington and Arthur Zajonic (Cambridge: Harvard University Press, 2006).
5. One note of clarification may be in order. This blended approach does not merely reduce experience to its neurological-biochemical substrates, as has been the pattern in a modernist biomedical paradigm. Rather than the brain

operating in one-directional linear causality, current understanding recognizes that experience and brain/body activity are correlates of one another. Experience both affects and is affected by the brain/body.

6. Michael Murphy, Steven Donovan, and Eugene Taylor, *The Physical and Psychological Effects of Meditation: A Review of Contemplative Research 1991–1996*, second edition (Petaluma: Institute of Noetic Sciences, 1997).

7. C. D. R. Friston Frith, P. F. Liddle, and R. P. J. Frachowiak, "Willed Action and the Prefrontal Cortex in Man: A Study with PET," *Proceedings, Biological Sciences of the Royal Society of London* 244 (June 1991): 241–46. Jose Pardo, Peter T. Fox, and Marcus E. Raichle, "Localization of a Human System for Sustained Attention by Position Emission Tomography," *Nature* 349 (January 1991): 61–64.

8. Andrew B. Newberg et al., "The Measurement of Regional Cerebral Blood Flow During the Complex Cognitive Task of Meditation: A Preliminary SPECT Study," *Psychiatry Research: Neuroimaging* 106, no. 2 (April 2001): 113–22.

9. Mihalyi Csíkszentmihályi, *Flow: The Psychology of Optimal Experience* (New York: Harper Perennial, 1991).

10. Jalal-al Din Rumi, *The Essential Rumi*, trans. C. Barks, A. Moyne, J. Arberry, R. Nicholson (San Francisco: Harper San Francisco, 1995), 109.

11. Rollo May, *The Courage to Create* (New York: Bantam Books, 1975), 91.

12. John Curtis Gowan, "Creative Inspiration in Composers," *The Journal of Creative Behavior* 11, no. 4 (1977): 250.

13. Elmer E. Green and Alyce M. Green, "Biofeedback and States of Consciousness," in *Handbook of States of Consciousness*, ed. Benjamin B. Wolman and Montague Ullman (New York: Van Nostrand Reinhold Co., 1986).

14. H. Benson et al., "Three Case Reports of the Metabolic and Electroencephalographic Changes During Advanced Buddhist Meditation Techniques," *Behavioral Medicine* 16, no. 2 (Summer 1990): 90–95.

15. Francis Varela et al., "The Brainweb: Phase Synchronization and Large-Scale Integration," *National Review of Neuroscience* 2 (2001): 229–39.

16. Antoine Lutz et al., "Long-Term Meditators Self-Induce High Amplitude Gamma Synchrony During Mental Practice," *Proceedings from the National Academy of Science* 101, no. 46 (November 2004): 16369–73.

17. Meister Eckhart, *Meister Eckhart: Selected Treatises and Sermons*, trans. J. M. Clark and J. V. Skinner (London: Faber and Faber, 1958).

18. Merton M. Sealts, *Emerson on the Scholar* (Columbia: University of Missouri Press, 1992), 257.

19. Francisco Varela, Evan Thompson, and Eleanor Rosch, *The Embodied Mind: Cognitive Science and Human Experience* (Cambridge: MIT Press, 1993), 30.

20. Ibid., 122.

21. Ljubomir Aftanas and Semen Golosheykin, "Impact of Regular Meditation Practice on EEG Activity at Rest and During Evoked Negative Emotions," *International Journal of Neuroscience* 115 (2005): 895.

22. "Burnt Norton" (the first quartet), IV.10, in T. S. Eliot, *Four Quartets* (New York: Harcourt, Brace, and World, 1971).

23. Jacob Raber, "Detrimental Effects of Chronic Hypothalamic-Pituitary-Adrenal Axis Activation from Obesity to Memory Deficits," *Molecular Neurobiology* 18, no. 1 (August 1998): 1–22.

24. J. F. Lopez et al., "Regulation of the 5-HT Receptors and the Hypothalamic-Pituitary-Adrenal Axis: Implications for the Neurobiology of Suicide," *Annals of the New York Academy of Science* 29, no. 836 (1997): 106–34.

25. Christopher R. K. MacLean et al., "Effects of the Transcendental Meditation Program on Adaptive Mechanisms: Changes in Hormone Levels after Four Months of Practice," *Psychoneuroendocrinology* 22, no. 4 (May 1997): 277–95.

26. Richard J. Davidson, "Affective Style, Psychopathology, Resilience: Brain Mechanism and Plasticity," *American Psychologist* 55 (November 2000), 1196–1214; Richard J. Davidson, "Well-Being and Affective Style: Neural Substrates and Bio-Behavioral Correlates," *Philosophical Transactions of the Royal Society (London)* 359 (2004): 1395–1411.

27. Henry Dreher, *Mind-Body Unity: A New Vision for Mind-Body Science and Medicine* (Baltimore: Johns Hopkins University Press, 2003).

28. Richard J. Davidson et al., "Alterations in Brain and Immune Function Produced by Mindfulness Meditation," *Psychosomatic Medicine* 65 (2003): 564–70.

IV

CONTEMPLATIVE-BASED
COURSES

13

EMBODIED CONTEMPLATIVE LEARNING

Aikido as a Case Study

MICHELLE M. LELWICA

EMBODIED CONTEMPLATIVE LEARNING

This chapter explores the embodied dimension of contemplative knowing by discussing a course that combines the study of Aikido (a Japanese martial art) with seminar-style discussions of diverse religious and cultural texts that deal with "the body."[1] Aikido's emphasis on developing mindfulness through non-competitive partner training makes it an interesting case study of "embodied contemplative learning." The mindfulness cultivated through Aikido practice requires students temporarily to suspend their analytic-rational capacities and to be fully present *in* their bodies. In conjunction with course readings and discussions, these aspects of Aikido open up a whole new dimension of learning for students—both about religion and about themselves.

The course is entitled Religion and the Body, but Aikido is more aptly described as a spiritual path (a *do*, or "way") than a religion. Thus, the very title of the course exposes students to some of the problems with how religions are defined.[2] The intense physicality of Aikido training creates a kind of "lab" for students to explore the ideas they encounter in the academic part of the class. The aim of this physical training, then, is not simply to teach students how to do Aikido, but also to give them a "hands-on" experience that serves as a resource for intellectual reflection.

CULTIVATING "BEGINNER'S MIND"

Students enroll in this course knowing that they are required to attend a one-hour Aikido class twice a week at the *dojo* (training hall), in addition to regular classroom time. But few of them have any idea what they are really getting into. The surprise begins almost immediately as they enter the *dojo* for the first time. The wood-framed space is large and unencumbered; its silence is audibly peaceful.

When students enter this quiet, spacious, unfamiliar environment, they may also enter an interior space of *not-knowing*. Later in the semester, they will encounter and discuss the concept and practice of "beginner's mind" to help them recognize and appreciate this internal place of not-knowing. The Zen master Shunryu Suzuki, whose book we read, explains: "If your mind is empty, it is always ready for anything; it is open to everything. In the beginner's mind there are many possibilities; in the expert's mind there are few."[3] Bernie Glassman Roshi, whose book is also assigned, describes this mode of knowing as "unknowing, or letting go of fixed ideas."[4]

Students are invited further into this place of "unknowing" as they are asked to remove parts of their unique personality (such as clothing, jewelry) and suit up in homogenous-looking training uniforms called *gis*. Then they are shown how to bow before stepping on the mat and before the start and end of class. As a gesture of humility, the practice of bowing simultaneously fosters "beginner's mind" while expressing gratitude for the opportunity to learn.

At the beginning of the class, students learn how to fall down ("take *ukeme*"). Falling down is not only a necessary practical skill in Aikido, but it also serves to deepen their sense of "unknowing" by reinforcing a sense of humility. No one tells them this directly—at least not during the first few weeks of training. Instead, their *sensei* (professional Aikido instructor) demonstrates the art of falling and nonverbally invites the students to try it. They quickly discover that falling down is much harder than it looks.

The predominantly nonverbal mode of instruction in Aikido tends to baffle the students. They are accustomed to the dominant protocols of academia, in which professors verbally convey information through a lecture format to students who may or may not be listening. By contrast, Aikido students are encouraged to "steal" the knowledge from their *sensei*. This presumes that they are hungry for it as they proactively study their teacher's example. Given the difficulty of the Aikido techniques, the silent instruction can frustrate even the most earnest students. In our classroom "debriefings," students often ask: "How am I supposed to learn when the teacher doesn't *tell* me what to do?" This question is revealing, and we explore its assumptions through questions like: "What is the 'knowledge' we are seeking?" "Who is responsible for our learning?" "What can the experience of 'not knowing' teach us?"

BECOMING MORE MINDFUL

Investigating these questions makes students more mindful about their educational experience. With the help of their readings, they begin to see how different modes of apprehension produce different kinds of knowledge. In conventional, Cartesian education, *knowing* something means *mastering* it through rational analysis. But with the embodied contemplative pedagogy of Aikido, not-knowing is a fertile starting point since education is seen to be an ongoing *process* of training the mind, body, and spirit.[5] When students practice a technique over and over again, they are not only developing a physical skill, but they are also building their *ki* ("energy") through focused concentration, studying spiritual qualities such as harmony (blending with their partners), humility (repeatedly falling down or bowing), and compassion (showing sensitivity to each other's different shapes and sizes). One can read a book on the art of such training (and we do), but this kind of knowledge is relatively superficial compared to the understanding that comes through sincere and repeated practice. In the end, a purely conceptual understanding of Aikido is not only insufficient but potentially distorted.

The embodied contemplative epistemology of Aikido also makes students more mindful of their own mental habits. To facilitate this growing awareness of their inner experience, I ask students to consider: "What happens internally when you have a hard time executing a particular Aikido technique?" "What ideas or feelings arise when you don't understand what you're supposed to be doing?" By investigating these questions, students learn to observe their thoughts, feelings, and bodily sensations as they arise from moment to moment, without judging or getting attached to them. Many students are surprised to learn just how much chatter their minds generate, even in an environment like Aikido where the process of learning is largely nonverbal. Becoming mindful of this mental chatter—for example, "I'm no good at this technique" or "If my partner were more flexible, I could do this move better"—makes them more conscious of their habitual thought patterns (e.g., self-criticism, blaming others). This awareness not only frees them to be more intentional about their thinking, but it also enables them to see that they are more than their thoughts.

This freedom from the trappings of the "mind" (Descartes' rational thinking self) also comes from the experience of *being present* that embodied contemplative learning fosters. In Aikido, mindful presence is cultivated through the one-pointed concentration (*nen*) that the physical training requires.[6] Such concentration is necessary, not just because the techniques are difficult, but also because they are potentially dangerous. Students have to be present in their bodies and pay close attention to what they are doing to avoid getting hurt or inadvertently injuring their partner. As a result of their single-minded effort, they often leave the *dojo* feeling both physically and mentally relaxed. They say things like "an hour of training cleans my mind," or "practicing Aikido gets me out of my normal mode of planning or worrying about what's going to happen next and allows me to just be where I am and do what I'm doing." The capacity to be fully present in the moment is a valuable, transferable skill since the process of learning in any area depends on the ability to focus attention on the subject of study.

PROMOTING SELF-DISCOVERY, PERSONAL WELL-BEING, AND SOCIAL RESPONSIBILITY

Cultivating mindfulness and learning from a place of "unknowing" are just some of the ways in which embodied contemplative pedagogies can enhance a student's academic experience by promoting self-discovery and well-being. These educational benefits are particularly significant given the high levels of psychological duress and disengagement students are reporting today, together with their widespread interest in spirituality and developing ethical values.[7]

Because students are whole persons and not just walking brains, pedagogies that engage their contemplative minds and physical bodies are more likely to captivate their attention. Students in the Religion and the Body course are notably more engaged in their learning than students in my more conventional courses because the Aikido "labs" give them a tangible way to understand the ideas we discuss in class. The training provides a touchstone for contemplating their own spiritual practices and beliefs, as well as the other embodied spiritual practices studied in the course, such as Zazen meditation, shamanic trance, and the whirling of Sufi dervishes. Students' papers frequently reveal how the course pedagogy keeps them invested in the process of learning. "I was more committed to my education than ever," one student wrote, "because I could see a direct connection between what I was learning and how it applied to my life."[8]

Regardless of how devoted we are to the academic methods of our discipline, sooner or later we have to reconcile with the reality that (to paraphrase bell hooks), our students need more than good analysis and information.[9] They need knowledge that is meaningful to them, and knowledge that helps them know how to make responsible choices, how to cope with difficulty, and how to do their part to make a positive difference in the world. The beauty of embodied contemplative pedagogy is that it has the potential to help students make meaningful connections between what they learn in our classes, the issues they face in their own lives, and the problems in the world around them.

BENEFITS FOR THE ACADEMIC STUDY OF RELIGION

Do pedagogies that promote students' self-discovery, personal well-being, and sense of social responsibility compromise the academic endeavor? Learning that activates different ways of knowing by engaging students' bodies need not shut down their critical faculties. On the contrary, it can enhance their analytic and critical thinking skills.

The experience of "not-knowing," for example, teaches students to tolerate ambiguity and relish the questions rather than rush for clear, easy answers. Similarly, the skill of mindfulness helps students hone their capacity for nonjudgmental observation, enabling them to examine and appreciate diverse religious and cultural phenomena on their own terms, rather than imposing their preconceived notions. Moreover, engaging contemplative ways of knowing moves students beyond a "logocentric" view of religion that overemphasizes its cognitive dimensions and neglects both the physical practices through which religious ideas are cultivated and reinforced and the aesthetic and emotional resonances that make them compelling.[10]

The epistemological diversity that embodied contemplative pedagogies introduce can also increase students' awareness of the diverse *sources* of knowledge that permeate religions in both pre- and postcolonial contexts. Engaging the body in the process of learning about religion helps dismantle what Vasudha Narayanan calls "the authority paradigms based on texts alone," while it valorizes complementary ways of knowing and sources of knowledge that have been marginalized by dominant, hegemonic cultures.[11] Thus embodied contemplative learning can introduce students to categories and questions that are well suited for studying the spiritual lives of people in nondominant religious traditions or in pre- or postcolonial situations.

CONCLUSION

In her book *Centering*, the potter, professor, and poet M. C. Richards defines education as "the process of waking up to life." This quote points to the connection between education and religion: both are means for transforming consciousness, and both have the ambiguous potential to wake us up or put us to sleep. Whether the process of teaching and learning enlivens and enlightens us, or dulls and depletes us, may depend on the extent to which our search for understanding engages not only our heads but our whole being. For, to quote M. C. Richards again, "It is in our bodies that redemption takes place. It is the physicality of the crafts that pleases me: I learn through my hands and my eyes and my skin what I could never learn through my brain."[12]

NOTES

1. I am grateful to the Bringing Theory to Practice Project, an independent project in partnership with the American Association of Colleges and Universities and funded by the Charles Engelhard Foundation, for providing initial funding for this course in the form of a Start-Up grant. I would also like to thank the Dovre Center of Concordia College, which provided additional funds for research related to the course.

2. Kwok Pui-lan discusses the problematic character of the term "religion" in *Postcolonial Imagination and Feminist Theology* (Westminster: John Knox Press, 2005), 202–205.

3. Shunryu Suzuki, *Zen Mind, Beginner's Mind* (Boston: Weatherhill, 2005), 21.

4. Bernie Glassman, *Bearing Witness: A Zen Master's Lessons in Making Peace* (New York: Bell Tower, 1998), 43, 67.

5. This triad of mind, body, and spirit (or *ki*) is integral to the philosophy of Aikido, its view of human beings, and the purpose of the training. See Kisshomaru Ueshiba's classic text: *The Spirit of Aikido*, trans. Taitetsu Unno (New York: Kodansha International, 1984).

6. Ueshiba, *The Spirit of Aikido*, 36–37.

7. On students' psychological duress, see: Richard Kadison, *College of the Overwhelmed: The Campus Mental Health Crisis and What to Do About It* (San Francisco: Jossey-Bass, 2004); Donald Harward, "Engaged Learning and the Core Purposes of Liberal Education: Bringing Theory to Practice," *Liberal Education* (Winter 2007): 8–10. For students' interest in spirituality, see: Higher Education Research Institute (HERI), *The Spiritual Life of College Students: A National Study of College Students' Search for Meaning and Purpose: Executive Summary* (Los Angeles: University of California, Los Angeles, 2005), 3.

8. Quoted with student's permission.

9. bell hooks, *Teaching to Transgress: Education as the Practice of Freedom* (New York: Routledge, 1994), 19.

10. See Stephen Marini, "Sacred Music in the Religious Studies Classroom," *Spotlight on Teaching/Religious Studies News* 16, no. 2 (2001): 3; and Guy Beck, "Hearing the Sacred: Introducing Religious Chant and Music into Religious Studies Teaching," *Spotlight on Teaching/Religious Studies News* 16, no. 2 (2001): 2.

11. Vasudha Narayanan, "Embodied Cosmologies: Sights of Piety, Sites of Power," *Journal of the American Academy of Religion* 71, no. 3 (September 2003): 499, 516.

12. Mary Caroline Richards, *Centering in Pottery, Poetry, and the Person* (Hanover: Wesleyan University Press, 1989), 15.

14

REFLECTIONS ON THEORY AND PRACTICE

The Case of Modern Yoga

STUART RAY SARBACKER

PEDAGOGICAL APPROACH

Over the past three years, I have had the opportunity to develop and teach a course entitled Theory and Practice of Modern Yoga at Northwestern University. In teaching this course, I have drawn upon my formal training as a certified yoga teacher and years of study and training in various Hindu and Buddhist traditions of yoga and meditation. What is exciting and arguably groundbreaking about this course is that it has not been simply an uncritical introduction to contemporary practices of yoga, but rather a mediation of academic (critical-historical) and practitioner representations of the history, theory, and practice of yoga. Pedagogically, the students and I enter into a "liminal" place in which we engage intellectually and experimentally with yoga—simultaneously. This integration brings about a paradoxical process of "demystification" of the history of yoga and, at the same time, an immersion in the experience of yoga that many students find powerful and transformative in its own right.[1] The pedagogy for the course is rooted in an integration of readings on the history of modern yoga, representations of yoga by key modern formulators, and in-class practice sessions that involve both the mental and physical disciplines of yoga. Students emerge from the class with a foundational understanding of the development of modern yoga in its historical contexts and the various factors behind its immense appeal to contemporary practitioners on an international scale. They also, ideally, leave the course with the tools necessary to establish a personal practice of yoga, if they so choose, that can be a basis for further deliberate and informed exploration of its techniques and methods. The conversations and experiments in this course have consistently pushed my own boundaries as a scholar and practitioner of yoga. The course has demonstrated time and again the virtue of a scholar-practitioner approach to the topic, and it has provided me with insights into yoga that have led to new academic theories and topics for classroom discussion. Moreover, it has motivated and inspired my own continued development as a teacher and practitioner of yoga.

Individual class sessions are structured to reflect the theory and practice dynamic of the course. The first part of class is dedicated to discussion of weekly readings, and the second half to in-class practice. When possible, the theory aspect of the class and the practice aspect revolve around the same tradition, teacher, or set of practices; this approach creates a sense of parity and allows for the exploration of the contrast of intellectual study and contemplative practice. The practice component typically starts off with basic and simple practices and advances over the course of the quarter to accommodate the students' level of preparation and progress. This adaptability coincides with the larger pedagogical issue of working with students at their level of intellectual engagement in the classroom. I draw here from my academic pedagogy, which is influenced by current dialogic educational models and by Buddhist notions of "skillful means" (*upaya kaushalya*), in addition to drawing upon my formal training as a yoga teacher.[2] Students bring a great variety of dispositions and qualities of mind and body into the classroom, and courses (whether contemplative or conventional) have to be adapted significantly if they are to be successful. Background knowledge, previous training (in dance, athletics, yoga, or other disciplines), physical, mental, and emotional dispositions, and many other factors make each student and each class distinctive. I have offered this course three times, and each class has had a different dynamic and unique ethos. One class was highly populated by dance students, another with older students, and another was a large class with numerous athletes and a significant population of students from a South Asian cultural background. Students have also brought varied expectations to the class, some viewing it as a potential answer to various problems in their life, some as an opportunity to get back "in shape," and some as an "easy" or "fun" class to balance science classes. Some students enroll with few expectations and a high degree of curiosity.

With respect to the logistics of the course, one of the challenges is finding appropriate spaces for the discussion of theory on the one hand, and for practice on the other. In some cases, I have had to reserve one room for the theory component and another for the practice. An oversized room with non-plush carpeting and unattached desks that can be moved (as yoga "service" by a team of students) served well as a space in two cases. In another, I had the opportunity to use a formal dance space on campus that was helpful in some ways but challenging in others. I also have students sign an injury waiver in which they take responsibility for listening to their bodies and avoiding injury. Trying to help students avoid injury is one of the most challenging and stressful aspects of the course, and I spend considerable time discussing strategies for avoiding injury and in adjusting and instructing students in ways to limit the possibility that they will hurt themselves.[3]

SEQUENCE OF THE COURSE

The initial phase of the class covers two primary topics—developing a broad definition of yoga (including a sense of its history and development), and getting a historical perspective on the development of modern yoga and its unique set of parameters. The form of yoga that I introduce on a practical basis is a modified (adapted for beginners) form of the Ashtanga yoga of K. Pattabhi Jois, a prominent yoga teacher from Southern India (Mysore in Karnataka). This particular yoga tradition is highly systematized and thus makes for a coherent and orderly (yet still quite challenging) introduction to yoga. Jois is also a disciple of Tirumalai Krishnamacharya, the so-called father of modern yoga. A first class session is dedicated to reading about and discussing the history of yoga, drawing upon a chapter from Gavin Flood's *An Introduction to Hinduism* that gives a useful introduction to yoga concepts. Students volunteer their ideas about what yoga is, based on their experience.[4] We augment the opening session with an introduction to a form of yogic breathing, or *pranayama* (lit., "breath control"), entitled *ujjayi pranayama* (lit., "victorious control of breath"), and basic concepts of developing internal muscular locks (*bandha*) that are utilized in the Ashtanga system. This is all done in a seated posture (*asana*), and gives students an initial "experience" of yoga that often ends the class session on a positive note, with the students highly motivated to learn more.

The second class session explores one of the most "modern" of all yoga practices—and most ubiquitous—the so-called Sun Salutation (*Surya Namaskara*). Students are exposed to modern representations of this practice as the *sine qua non* of the yogic enterprise and its physical and spiritual benefits through readings of Jois and other teachers. Drawing from the work of Joseph Alter and Elliott Goldberg, students are introduced, via this practice, to the "modern" history of yoga, most notably the integration of European physical culturalist thought and bodily culture (including fitness culture and gymnastics) with Indian traditions of physical culture, yoga, and Hindu ritualism.[6] Students also have an opportunity to explore the connections between physical discipline and ideology, especially the relationships between physical culture, colonialism, and nationalism. This study leads to interesting discussions about the social implications of "practice." In practice, to learn the flowing movements (*vinyasa*) and postures (*asana*) of the Sun

Salutation often serves as a touchstone and gateway into the range of modern and contemporary yoga traditions that are explored over the course of the quarter.

Subsequent class sessions are dedicated to building upon this foundation through readings (and allied writing assignments) on the formation of modern yoga in the Krishnamacharya lineage, through looking at Krishnamacharya's work and that of his son Desikachar and Krishnamacharya's most prominent disciples, K. Pattabhi Jois and B. K. S. Iyengar. The academic foundation for this study is an examination of Norman Sjoman's *The Yoga Tradition of the Mysore Palace*, a groundbreaking study that delineates the development of Krishnamacharya's yoga from threads of premodern Hatha yoga traditions, Indian wrestling, and European gymnastics and military training, among other sources.[7] Theoretical and methodological sophistication is brought to the discussion through reading Benjamin Smith's essay on contemporary Ashtanga yoga, entitled "Adjusting the Quotidian: Ashtanga Yoga as Everyday Practice." Smith discusses the social and ideological implications of the practice of modern yoga, and integrates the theories of Bourdieu and others into the discussion.[8] Presentations of the works of Krishnamacharya, Desikachar, Jois, and Iyengar are complemented by the use of a variety of audiovisual materials (slides, video footage, and institutional website representations) that give further substance to the images and ideas of these teachers.[9]

In the practice sessions, students move toward developing a sequence of yoga postures that exemplifies the modern yoga rubric as found in the Krishnamacharya lineage and embodied in the practice of Ashtanga yoga and in the tradition of Iyengar yoga. One of the most important dynamics that emerges in practicing Ashtanga and Iyengar modalities is the stark contrast between the styles developed by the two disciples of Krishnamacharya. One provides a moving, dynamic practice, and the other a static, alignment-oriented practice. This dynamic often elicits strong responses from students, who tend to gravitate toward one model or the other. And the percentage breakdown of preferences for one model or the other varies considerably from class to class.

Out of the confluence of theory and practice emerges a conversation about the various components that make up "modern yoga." Students are able to contribute experiences and perspectives by mastering this repertoire through postural and breathing practice and the development of awareness and concentration. Students express their intellectual and physical development and struggles in weekly journal assignments that ask them to reflect on the "experiment" of bringing together theory and practice. Over the latter part of the quarter, we explore other modalities of yoga, including Sivananda yoga, popular "Vinyasa" traditions, and meditative yoga traditions, and we look more broadly at the spectrum of contemporary practice and its relationship to modern yoga. The course ends either with an instruction by visiting teachers from various schools of yoga, or a visit to a local yoga studio as a "fieldwork" experience. The most recent course offering ended with a visit to a studio where the class was introduced to "hot yoga," that is, yoga in a room with the thermostat set around 100° F. Although not all of the students enjoyed that session—it felt like "yoga boot camp" for many of us—it was an unforgettable experience.

OUTCOMES

One of the most exciting and challenging issues of teaching such a class is the sheer range of valuable directions in which intellectual discussion and correspondent practice can go. My strategy overall has been to balance the structure of the progression of ideas and practices with an openness to the issues that resonate with students. One key discussion that has extended through all of the class sessions is that of "authority" and "authenticity" in modern yoga. This is often developed in the form of questions as to whether yoga in its modern forms is "authentic," given its hybrid nature, and whether the proponents of modern yoga are to be viewed as creative geniuses, as disingenuous, or as something in between.

Another discussion has revolved around the idea of juxtaposing religion and spirituality, and the degree to which yoga can be seen as separate from its religious moorings. This issue is particularly of interest to students that feel a strong attraction to yoga but are wary of commitment to a religious tradition. Students also often express that their understanding of their own bodies, or their embodiment, has been transformed both by the theory and the practice of the course. Discussions often emerge regarding the nature of the "brain-centered" academic model, and the degree to which they as students feel out of touch with their bodies. Athletes, dancers, and others often express a sense of having, for the first time, an intellectual understanding of experiences and practices they have learned over time but have not reflected upon.

Out of these and other issues come a range of discussions that have implications in the students' lives and in broader cultural studies—stress and health, gender, body image, diet and eating disorders, tattoos and piercings, athletics and physical culture, consumerism and commodification, and the mind-body relationship, among others. Along with many of these important and interesting discussions, the course provides an opportunity for students and teachers to get to know each other on a different level, arguably as more of a "whole person" through practices that engage mind and body in a direct way.[10] This holistic model of education introduces a degree of enthusiasm and engagement in the classroom that is unique, in my experience.

The results of the class have been manifold. The great majority of the students come out of the course being able to define yoga broadly in an intelligent way and to speak knowledgeably about representative factors and traditions of modern and contemporary yoga. Beyond this, students report to me a range of personally meaningful results from the course; such positive feedback encourages me to continue developing this experiment. Among other results, students communicate that they have found significant release from stress and considerably more peace in their life; they have come to radical shifts in self-perception, including body image; they have found a method that seems to ease the pain of various diseases and physical conditions; they have deepened their understanding of their own religious or spiritual practice; they have found themselves performing beyond previous limits in their athletic activities; they have found a medium for growing friendships and romantic relationships; they have exceeded the boundaries of their own self-perception; they have come to look differently on the physical culture that surrounds them; and they have found a connection or reconnection to their family and ancestry.

The final assignment for the class is an "integrative paper" in which the students work to apply one or more of the key theories discussed in class to the development of their own intellectual and practical understanding of the practice of yoga. In these papers, I often see what I find lacking in the academic writing of students in other classes—a coherent bridging of issues that are relevant to the student with history and theory. In many respects, this is just a beginning, but nevertheless a potentially important one. It is ultimately the responsibility of the students to pursue their continued intellectual development and their practice, if they choose to do so, following the course. It is my hope that the course provides a solid foundation for them to continue their study of yoga in whatever ways they desire.

NOTES

1. Turner's term "liminality," the in-between state, is of course tied strongly to another one, "*communitas*," or community formation. Liminality in this context is an excellent conceptual touchstone for working in the sphere of the theory-practice dynamic, and certainly the unique and thus liminal qualities of these courses lend to a community-forming and bonding process among students and between students and teacher.
2. Stuart Sarbacker, "Skillful Means: What Can Buddhism Teach Us About Teaching Buddhism?" *Method and Theory in the Study of Religion* 17, no. 5 (2005): 264–73; Ira Shor, *Empowering Education: Critical Teaching for Social Change* (Chicago: University of Chicago Press, 1992).
3. As a part of this process, I also request that they inform me of any health conditions that should be taken into consideration. Both mental and physical factors are clearly important in the context of a contemplative pedagogy. In some cases, I have asked for a physician's approval to be given. I have had a significant number of students enroll in the class either at a doctor's

recommendation or because of some particular health problem the student is suffering from and hoping to resolve. Yoga can cause a range of injuries and exacerbate existing conditions (physical, mental, and emotional), and I make it clear to them that practicing yoga is not without risks. In one offering of the course, I was joined by another teacher, Joseph Mills from Northwestern University's Dance Department, who helped me considerably in developing the confidence to work with students on a physical level. His contributions extended far beyond this, well into the more theoretical issues of embodiment and performance as well.

4. Gavin Flood, *An Introduction to Hinduism* (Cambridge: Cambridge University Press, 1996), 75–102.

5. The students in this course have told me consistently how much they actually *enjoy* coming to class every week. This speaks volumes, in my opinion, to the desire, if not need, for students to have experiential learning opportunities that combine physical movement and contemplative awareness along with the more conventional course components.

6. Critical-historical readings are drawn from Joseph Alter, *Gandhi's Body: Sex, Diet, and the Politics of Nationalism* (Philadelphia: University of Philadelphia Press, 2000), 83–112, and Elliott Goldberg, "Worshipping the Sun Indoors: Surya Namaskar Mixed Up with Muscle Cult and Hatha-Yoga Cult," in *Radiant Bodies: How Modern Hatha Yoga Was Created* (unpublished book manuscript, 2006). The description of the practice of the Sun Salutation is drawn from K. Pattabhi Jois, *Yoga Mala* (New York: North Point Press, 2002), 34–47, and K. Pattabhi Jois *Sūrya Namaskāra* (New York: Ashtanga Yoga New York, 2005).

7. Norman Sjoman, *The Yoga Tradition of the Mysore Palace* (New Delhi: Abhinav, 1996).

8. Benjamin Smith, "Adjusting the Quotidian: Ashtanga Yoga as Everyday Practice" (paper presented at Cultural Studies Association of Australasia [CSAA] Conference, Murdoch University, December 2004).

9. These include T. K. V. Desikachar, *The Heart of Yoga: Developing a Personal Practice* (Rochester: Inner Traditions International, 1995); Jois's aforementioned *Yoga Mala*; and B. K .S. Iyengar's *Light on Yoga: Yoga Dipika* (New York: Schocken, 1994). Desikachar's text discusses the legacy of Krishnamacharya at length; Iyengar's work, known by many as the "bible" of modern yoga, represents a coherent crystallization of many of the principles of modern yoga, and is an excellent text to work with in the classroom.

10. One important element of this is physical touch. The fact that I have a responsibility to adjust and accommodate students through physical touch in the yoga classroom sets it apart in a significant way from the conventional classroom where touching is implicitly, if not explicitly, prohibited. This is not necessarily an easy thing to do, as it takes a degree of courage to shift paradigms that are deeply ensconced in our academic culture.

15

SUSTAINING LIFE

Contemplative Pedagogies in a Religion and Ecology Class

BARBARA PATTERSON

We stand in a circle, twenty-five students and me, their teacher. The class is Religion and Ecology and today's lesson happens within our 135-acre campus green space, Lullwater Park. Some students scope out the landscape around us—invasive privet and indigenous white oaks. Others shift from right foot to left, shuffling in the sandy soil deposited by storm surges through the South Fork of Peachtree Creek beside us. My eyes meet the few looking directly at me. We exchange tentative anticipation over the contemplative practice we are about to begin. Even after six years of teaching this class, my gut knots as we take a more complicated practice into our repertoire. We are moving again from theory to practice in order to return to theory; so goes the cycle.

We have prepared for this sequence by reading and discussing selections from *The Miracle of Mindfulness* by Thich Nhat Hanh, along with texts from the early Christian desert Mothers and Fathers, and texts by Philip Sheldrake and Burton Christie-Ward. Contemplative principles evolve into practices that culti-vate individual and communal awareness of thought, feelings, and environment. The practices draw our attention to the present moment, to analysis, and some insight. In a particular way, we will notice how we think and feel what we are doing. We will keep our minds, hearts, and bodies alive to present realities in this particular place.[1]

When our class begins our contemplative practice, students quiet their minds by paying close attention to the breath. In this laboratory, we consciously watch our minds and note its interplay with our emotions in relation with this place. We investigate what marks a place, who gets to be in it, and how we can

155

claim relationship to or with it. Here we explore our experiences, asking what powers sustain or attempt to control all this life? The point of this exercise is to train and mature our capacities to notice, to self-consciously *examine* ourselves and others in a natural setting. Using our senses as gentle guides to bring us back to the present, we are doing the mindful work of "interbeing" (meditation teacher Thich Nhat Hanh's word for interdependence), the reality that nothing exists separately from anything else.

Our place-based class requires pedagogies capable of holistic acquisitions of knowledge. Using a multidisciplinary approach, we work in locations that present webs of aesthetic, scientific, empathetic, competitive, and individual as well as collective dynamics at the cellular and system levels. One way a colleague and I assessed the effectiveness of contemplative pedagogies was to implement a pilot study of the students in my class. As a preliminary stage in our research, Ashli Owen-Smith (PhD, Emory's Rollins School of Public Health) devised a simple pre- and post-test survey for the class. We built our questionnaire from existent instruments already tested and validated that matched an initial coding of over thirty student portfolios, chosen from four semesters of this class. [2] Using a Grounded Theory approach, we read through these portfolios several times, initially identifying areas of intellectual, ethical, and personal growth named by the students.[3] We fine-tuned these key categories, consolidating them into four ways in which contemplative pedagogies affect learning. These four are: interpersonal empathy, self-concept (including academic performance), interpersonal support, and levels of gratitude. With their permission, students took the survey at the beginning and end of the course. The initial results are promising in that students demonstrated higher mean scores in each of the four areas by the end of the semester. We have improved our questionnaire and are in the process of developing additional implicit methods, including focus-group interviews and coding portfolio entries.

This very initial quantitative information confirms that learning with reflective consciousness across intellectual and personal boundaries increases students' analytical capacities and understanding. Learning in a community that values interdependence and raises questions of compassion and justice aids their intellectual confidence. Our early research suggests that contemplative pedagogies prepare students to resist quickly applied assumptions and overly individualistic approaches. They slow down, pay more critical and compassionate attention, and problem-solve ethical dilemmas. One senior reflected on this different approach:

> When will I know meditation's calm . . . avoiding the "raging blaze" [*sic*]. Although these verses were written thousands of years ago by a Theravadin monk, they apply even more so to us today. Life in the United States moves at a dangerous pace and the stimulations we

submit our bodies to are intense if not overkill. Discouraging is the little emphasis we put on rest and care. . . . We cannot do it alone.[4]

A first step in contemplative pedagogies is to pause, to closely notice what is actually arising.[5] By stretching open the spaces that might prematurely fill with conclusions, contemplative pedagogies make room for discipline-based content that also raises questions of ethics for sustainability. As their intellectual confidence grows individually and in community, students link textual analysis with community-based research posing ethical challenges. Recognizing their privileged and less privileged backgrounds in dialogue with dynamics of race and ethnicity, they seize this class as an opportunity to examine their own evolving intellectual work. That work remains reflective, attuned to the questions: "How do I make it through today well and whole enough to wake up tomorrow and want to do it again? How do I do that alone and with others?" Our preliminary pre- and post-class data for the most recent class as well as existent academic developmental research[6] indicates that students want to increase their capacities to answer this question.[7] Their portfolios also bear this out through three entries a week over the semester. One senior male writes:

> My thirst for knowledge and getting a true liberal arts degree . . . makes me actually become narrow-minded because I never take the opportunity to take a second, take a deep breath, and meditate or reflect about my life and my involvement with Emory as a place.

In the first class, we challenge students' conceptions about the importance of integrating existential and environmental realities of place with their academic lives. Using a structured observation exercise in a campus ravine, students work in teams of five following given instructions. That information begins with a brief history of the wooded ravine named for Dr. Baker, a biology professor who, with his students, planted most of the campus. It then asks students to locate and describe a single boundary anywhere within the ravine using only their five senses. Using a phenomenological approach, this exercise requires paying full attention to the "richly textured field[s]" of phenomena and experience "in which we are corporeally immersed."[8] Once the instructions are clear, we stand silently looking into the woodlands. Many stare at the damaged creek bed severely eroded by runoff from our nonporous campus surfaces. Their attention falls on invasive species. How do we live—how do we learn? They dive into the assignment.

They begin writing down their individual, sensorial explorations. No talking. After five minutes, they share their findings with their team. Focused on boundaries in themselves, students discover how hard it is to know if logs, rocks, or streams have boundaries. Where do they start and stop? Moss grows from the

ground across a log. Water overflows the stream's banks. Human-based definitions fail to describe what they see, smell, hear, and touch. The effects of multiple factors, wind, weather, plant growth, and human/creature interventions defy
stable definitions. Discussion of why and how we live in and with boundaries
follows, including a first look at current theories of "place."[9] Beginning with
living beings in Baker Woodlands, students reconsider how definitions of places
are used to mediate particular perspectives on natural and unnatural boundaries;
when and why they exist or fade. Soon our conversation turns to developmental
issues about human-to-human perceptions of boundaries.[10] Issues of self-other
identity, agency, and meaning-making interrelate with questions about sustainability and how we live.[11] A junior asks why upper-class students wear sorority
and fraternity t-shirts during the first few days of the semester. What boundaries
do they establish, keeping whom out and in?

Research indicates that contemplative pedagogies work best through
sequenced exercises beginning with skills for focused attention. Students then
collect data, analyze it, create hypotheses and test them, in order to retheorize
what they have learned.[12] Weekly during the last two months of class, students
examine the same twelve-by-twelve-inch square in a location they choose. Each
time, they silently observe for twenty minutes, write down field notes, and only
later craft analyses and responses in their portfolio entries. Over time, the
boundaries of their habitual conceptions break down, decolonizing their usual
labels and categories.[13] Realizing the effects of nature-driven cycles bringing
change over two months, students stretch their own cognitive frames toward
new cycles of understanding and insight. One male physics major challenges his
habitual reductionism:

> Descriptive language is a means of reconciliation . . . the incongruity of
> experiences . . . concessions have to be made . . . try to recreate it or
> describe it. Begin with a smooth whoosh, baahaahaaaaaaa . . . of scent.
> Bum, BoomBOOMBOom, tat ratatatatatatttaaa as the green serrated
> discs begin to shuffle. Feehee, feehee, rrr waaa FEEhee of the brown
> curved rays.

> Silence . . .

Integrating self-other consciousness into descriptive and analytical work is difficult. It reinhabits and reforms student learning toward holistic epistemologies.
Another male writes:

> This repeated phenomenological exercise challenges the core of my
> being. It challenges me to look and act objectively, but ultimately leads
> me to feel an emptiness as I open and close myself off, even for just
> twenty minutes, from the rest of my environment . . .

Part of the reinhabitation work of this class draws us beyond the campus into the diverse communities of Atlanta facing sustainability challenges. Visiting the West Atlanta Water Alliance (WAWA), an educational and advocacy group for green spaces and sustainable development, students see firsthand the intersecting realities of race, class, economic limits and opportunity, and political power.[14] As one rising senior woman wrote:

> Learning how the sewage pollution of upstream North Atlanta negatively affects those who live in South and Southwest Atlanta makes us grapple with socioeconomic barriers . . . the environmental burdens that African Americans face (around) hazards of (polluting) air, water, and waste.

Whether in urban forests, historical places, or community green spaces, students using contemplative pedagogies develop skills to learn from counter-instances of preconceived theories and conclusions.[15] From our preliminary research, we observe increased curiosity about interdependent learning through multidisciplined approaches and training for increased empathetic responses to ordinary life. Decision-making intellectually and morally crosses boundaries using academic and contemplative practices as students mindfully "mix it up a little with others" in the places they live.[16]

How can we live well today, together and alone, so that we want to wake up tomorrow and live again? This question is a core tenet of liberal arts education awakened in substantive ways through contemplative analysis and reflection. A graduating senior writes:

> Keeping "practices of breathing" . . . releases more space for struggle involving real choices for living. Keeping a portfolio over the fifteen weeks students track how their integrative learning starts, builds, circles back, repeats, get performed, amended and re-performed . . .

Through contemplative frameworks and practices, we pursue that key question, how do we live and find sustainable answers?

NOTES

1. See Thich Nhat Hanh, *The Miracle of Mindfulness* (Boston: Beacon Press, 1976), 11; and *Being Peace* (Berkeley: Parallax Press, 1987), on interbeing, 83–102.
2. The instruments from which we drew questions include: Interpersonal Reactivity Index (Davis 1983), Academic Self-Concept Scale (Zorich and Reynolds 1988), Interpersonal Support Evaluation List (Cohen and

Hoberman 1983), The Self-Liking/Self-Competence Scale (SLCS) (Tafarodi and Swann 1995), and The Gratitude Questionnaire (GQ-6) (McCullough, Emmons, and Tsang 2002).

3. See P. L. Rice and D. Ezzy, *Qualitative Research Methods: A Health Focus* (New York: Oxford University Press, 2002).

4. All portfolio citations in this chapter are provided with the students' permission. Their names and identities are protected.

5. See Simone Weil, *Waiting for God*, trans. Emma Craufurd (New York: Perennial, 1992), 105–16.

6. See Robert Kegan and Ray Danowski's *In Over Our Heads: The Mental Demands of Modern Life* (Cambridge: Harvard University Press, 1994), and Sharon Park's work, *The Critical Years: The Young Adult Search for a Faith to Live By* (San Francisco: Harper & Row, 1986).

7. See Arthur Zajonc's article, "Spirituality in Higher Education," in *Liberal Education* 89 (Winter 2003): 55–56.

8. See David Abram's *Spell of the Sensuous: Perception and Language in a More-Than-Human World* (New York: Vintage Press, 1996), especially 214–16.

9. Thanks to Brian Campbell for the following: Doreen Massey, "A Global Sense of Place," in *Marxism Today* (June 1991): 24–29; and Karen Halttunen, "Groundwork: American Studies in Place—Presidential Address to the American Studies Association November 4, 2005," *American Quarterly* 58, no. 1 (2006). See also David Harvey, *Justice, Nature, and the Geography of Difference* (Cambridge: Blackwell Publishers, 1996).

10. See William G. Perry's work, especially *Forms of Ethical and Intellectual Development in the College Years: A Scheme* (San Francisco: Jossey-Bass, 1999). Also John Dewey's *Democracy and Education* (New York: Free Press, 1996).

11. See Mary Taylor Huber and Molly Breen, *Integrative Learning: Putting the Pieces Together Again*, © 2006 The Carnegie Foundation for the Advancement of Teaching website; also see Sharon Parks, *Big Questions, Worthy Dreams: Mentoring Young Adults in Their Search for Meaning, Purpose, and Faith* (San Francisco: Jossey-Bass, 2000) and *Leadership Can Be Taught: A Bold Approach for a Complex World* (Boston: Harvard Business School Press, 2005).

12. See David Kolb, *Experiential Learning: Experience as the Source of Learning and Development* (Englewood Cliffs: Prentice-Hall, 1984).

13. See Raymond Williams, *Problems in Materialism and Culture* (London: Verso, 1980), 67–85.

14. See Doreen Massey, "Power-Geometry and a Progressive Sense of Place," in *Mapping Futures: Local Cultures, Global Change*, ed. Barry Curtis Jon Bird, Tim Putnam, George Robertson, and Lisa Tickner (London: Routledge, 1993).

15. See Michael Burawoy et al., *Ethnography Unbound: Power and Resistance in the Modern Metropolis* (Berkeley: University of California Press, 1991).

16. See Renato Rosaldo, *Culture and Truth: The Remaking of Social Analysis: With a New Introduction* (Boston: Beacon Press, 1993), 224.

16

ADAB

Courteous Behavior in the Classroom

BRIDGET BLOMFIELD

The first thing I teach in all of my Islam courses is the concept of *adab*, which is central to classical Sufism. Sufism, often called *tasawwuf*, is the mystical dimension of Islam. It is a spiritual approach "directed towards the transformation of man's being and the attainment of the spiritual virtues; ultimately it leads to the vision of God."[1] Sufis are concerned with developing spiritual virtue, an ethical lifestyle, and an intimate relationship with God and all of God's creations. It is the esoteric method of the Prophet Muhammad's teachings that calls for the transformation of one's being through work on *nafs*.[2] This contemplative approach includes a code of ethics and virtuous behavior called *adab*, or good manners, which develops the practitioner spiritually, emotionally, physically, and intellectually. I teach this concept by asking students to observe their everyday behavior and witness their egos. They are asked to question their motives and actions and to try to develop patience and compassion.

As the starting point of Islamic spirituality, Sufism is not only based on the intellect but also the heart, which is the resting place for love and knowledge. Within Sufism, there are specific virtues to which one must adhere so that spiritual states develop. States of consciousness, which are acquired through years of spiritual practice, become "stations of being." Among these stations are contemplation, intimacy, endurance, contentment, and most importantly, courteous behavior and a code of ethics. Love, then, manifests as kind and courteous behavior and becomes one of the crucial motivating factors for the Sufi, because "the true man attaches his heart to none but love."[3]

As part of their study of Islam, students focus on these attributes and are taught a code of ethics that includes gracious behavior. The practice of *adab* is used in the learning environment to initiate the students into a new understanding of themselves and a way to relate to others with attentive compassion. On a daily basis students pose questions to themselves to develop a relationship with the authentic self that ultimately gives rise to a kindness toward others. Among these questions are:

- What am I giving my life to?
- What am I saying yes to?
- Who is it in me that needs to be right, perfect, or angry?

By pondering questions like these, students develop an understanding of their own humanness and the humanity of others. They are able to see life in a larger framework than immediate reactions of like and dislike.

As a code of behavior, *adab* exemplifies goodness and fairness similar to the concept of loving-kindness in Buddhism. Students are the judges of their own inner development in my classes; I ask them to be their own "guardian" through a series of exercises and self-reflection. In this way, education of the soul becomes a choice and a commitment alongside the challenging readings of great Islamic scholars. Just like the Sufi masters, students are encouraged to pay attention to their efforts, for it is their *niyyat* (intention) that is most important.

The pursuit of education sometimes comes from a desire to fill an inner emptiness, a means to answer existential questions. If anxiety is attenuated through information, life feels safer, more definable. Students can be challenged academically, but they can also take what they learn spiritually and apply it in their daily lives. Through contemplative practice and self-reflection, education makes students more intelligent, open-minded, compassionate, and understanding.

Educational environments often value the putting forth of more information, not the personal meaning underneath that information. I believe that intellect and spirituality are complementary, permitting students to write in a scholarly fashion while maintaining a personal and heartfelt understanding. Often too much importance is put on third-person writing styles where the writer is distanced from the experience. I believe that it is important to encourage students to write and speak from their personal experience. I agree with bell hooks, that the real job of an educator is to empower the student:

Fundamentally rooted in a love for ideas we are able to inspire, the classroom becomes a place where transformations in social relations are concretely actualized and the false dichotomy between the world outside and the inside world of the academy disappears.[4]

Education, then, is not an elite function within the ivory tower, but a system where "critical consciousness is rooted in the assumption that knowledge and critical thought done in the classroom should inform our habits of being and ways of living outside the classroom."[5]

By adapting spiritual exercises that are pertinent to the subject, students begin to understand the difference between *knowing* and *knowing about*. Through the intentional practice of *adab*, students learn conscious listening and speaking skills, learning that develops them as humanitarians. They become balanced intellectually, spiritually, and psychologically, through the immediate experience where education is epistemology. I ask students to participate in the contemplative exercises as fully as possible and frame them in order to catalyze human compassion and personal well-being in the practitioner. I explain to students that they do not need to give up personal religious convictions or convert to Islam. The approach to the exercises is seen as experimentation, a tender curiosity into one's behavior.

I do not assume that students are religious just because they want to study religion. The classes include Buddhists, Christians, Muslims, Jews, atheists, and the nonreligious. Religious or not, students study religion inquisitively, and many are interested in the cultural and political aspects of religious tenets. Atheist students benefit from the study of *adab* as much as anyone else, because the emphasis of this Sufi practice is on the search for meaning through truth, love, and beauty—not a belief in a deity or higher power. For example, one student in the Sufism class wrote:

> I really like the message of *adab*. I think everyone needs to live by it and our world would be a better place. I just love it because that's how I basically live without being a religious person. I am not a perfect person but I try to make good decisions and be what is considered a good person. *Adab* reminds me to do that.

Adab, then, is not just how one behaves or acts. It is a way of being. *Adab* is graciousness and courtesy, a way of listening, seeing, and acting. It is based on the ability to read a situation intimately, almost intuitively, and then act appropriately. Students traveling in cultures other than their own, where they do not know the appropriate customs, learn to be acutely aware of their surroundings, to watch carefully and follow their hosts. During one visit to a well-known and admired Bektashi Baba in Turkey, the Baba said the students had the best manners he had ever seen. All they were doing was mimicking his graciousness. One student wrote:

> In the presence of the Baba I felt holiness. He was so kind and he treated us with the utmost respect. He was the one who deserved the

respect. I realized that this was his *adab*, the concept we had repeatedly discussed in class. I tried to show him that even though I am not religious, I too, knew *adab*. I watched every move the dervishes made and followed their cues. I tried to be attentive and listen from a deep place. I tried to observe from "my inmost heart."

Through his courteous behavior, the Baba helped the students to understand the saying of the Prophet Muhammad, "The person with the best faith is he who is the best mannered. . . . "[6] Another student from the study-abroad program in Turkey was also moved by the Baba's actions at a dinner held to break the fast of Ramadan:

At first, I didn't see why we kept stopping while we were eating. But soon I began to get an idea, which the Baba later confirmed— it was in order to teach us patience. I could understand this— I tried to be patient, and when we would start eating again after a pause, the food tasted as good as it had when I took my first bite, and I felt grateful. After all, just becoming a Sufi takes a lot of time and patience.

Religious studies students were able to compare different religions while studying Sufism. Some students felt that *adab* was very similar to the Buddhist concept of loving-kindness. Christian students were able to see respect, gratitude, and humility in both Sufism and Christianity. They quickly shared quotes from the Bible in the same way that Muslim students quoted the Qur'an. A student from the World Religions class wrote in her reflection paper:

I was surprised that all Muslims, not just Sufis, practice *adab*. I personally believe that Jesus tells us to love our enemies and to not seek revenge and yet we, meaning the Christian population as a whole, continue to do so. We continue to hate our enemies as well as our neighbors rather than trusting in love, another crucial part of being a Christian. The concept of *adab* reminds me of the Bible passage "Love your enemies, do good to those who hate you, bless those who curse you, and pray for those who mistreat you. If anyone hits you on one cheek, let him hit the other one too; if someone takes your coat, let him have your shirt as well . . . do for others just what you want them to do for you" (Matthew 5:39–41, 43).

In this way, practicing *adab* brought students to a greater understanding of their own worldview and helped them in their everyday life, in ordinary situations. *Adab* is not only our ability to act graciously, but to speak consciously as well.

Students were able to incorporate the concept of *adab* into their daily lives, adding meaning to a variety of situations. One student from the class on Sufism reported:

> I was driving home when a woman cut me off. I started to get really angry and started to yell at her and cuss her out. Then, for some strange reason, I remembered about what we learned about taking a deep breath and reentering into the moment. I took a few breaths and thought, "Yes, I have practiced *adab*." I did not yell unkindly. I felt relaxed and happy because I had practiced the way of a Sufi. I felt like I was a better person for not losing my temper. The rest of my day was great!

Direct knowledge can be supported by another person's experience, but when something is personally experienced more deeply, it becomes a way of being, linking the body, mind, and heart. Education, then, becomes a direct, body-felt awareness. It is an embodied presence brought about by an inner awareness rather than an externalized theory or concept. With *adab*, "attention turns inward to its own physiological and psychological processes."[7] It affords "the goal-less enterprise of pure being, where non-attainment, non-grasping, non-doing and non-achievement shape the course of our experience."[8]

Focusing on *adab* while working on one's *nafs* allows one to return to the essential self, as students are asked to examine themselves and their behavior. A student from the Introduction to Islam course wrote:

> It never really occurred to me that I could really learn how to *be* in a situation. I had always studied for an exam to pass the test and then move on. The practice of *adab* changed that for me. I realized that doing the reading, writing and participating in class showed respect for the teacher and my fellow students. I learned a lot about Sufism but I learned a lot about myself, some things not so good that I want to change. I kept thinking about *adab* all semester and asked myself "What kind of person do I want to be?" It [*adab*] became really important to me.

Muslim students were more familiar with the concept of *adab*, but not necessarily with the importance of it to most Sufis. One student from Saudi Arabia, brought up in a more conservative Wahhabi environment, was initially critical of many Sufi practices like music and movement. As the course progressed, he quit saying that Sufism was *bida* (innovation), and he started to soften and see the positive teachings. He wrote:

At first when our teacher talked about Sufis I didn't like it. In my country [Saudi Arabia] we don't know about Sufis but as I learned I started to understand the importance of *adab* and why the Sufis like it. Then I could say to my classmates, "Yes, this is Islam, this is my religion." I felt proud of my religion because the American students wanted to [practice] *adab*.

Because Muslim students had grown up understanding *adab*, they had already incorporated it into their lives. Another Muslim student said:

First, ethics is the most important thing in a person's life. We have a nice proverb in Arabic, which is "if you want to know a person ask about his friends." The second one is *adab*. In our religion Allah asks us to put *adab* in the front of our eyes all the time. *Adab* teaches us forgiveness, of course it's a beautiful thing to forgive anyone who did something wrong to you or broke your heart.

Students felt that they learned patience, trust, respect, and humility through the practice of *adab*. Teaching to cultivate inner listening and conscious speaking requires commitment to recognizing and expressing beauty in thoughts, words, and deeds. A student from the Islam class in Turkey said:

what I have tried to do lately is to remember to take a deep breath and think about the beauty each person has. Each person is a miracle, and each person has extraordinary qualities. So, I try to focus on the beauty in the person rather than what is annoying me, try to remind myself of the aspects I really love about them. I have found that when I do this, my annoyance is mitigated. I feel like it has really helped me to become more patient with others and helped me avoid saying something or acting in a way that I would only regret later.

Therefore, regardless of one's religious beliefs, the concept of *adab* makes lives richer and more meaningful. It gives practitioners the ability to live ethical lives and be conscious and respectful of others and of themselves. One need not be a Sufi to practice *adab*, but for all practitioners there is more peace and less anger. It requires a surrendering of the ego, as one student noted:

For me, *adab* is in all the religions and is common sense. It reminds me of what I believe in as a Christian. "Love is patient, love is kind. It does not envy, it does not boast, it is not proud. It is not rude, it is not self-seeking, it is not easily angered, and it keeps no record of wrongs. Love does not delight in evil but rejoices with the truth. It always protects, always trusts, always hopes, always perseveres" (1 Corinthians 13: 4–7). In this way I feel that Sufis and Christians are the same.

The practice of *adab* is a reminder to act in a compassionate, thoughtful, and loving manner in every situation. It teaches one to think before speaking and consider the needs of the other. *Adab* leads to the desire to serve humanity in gratitude and humility, for "whatever venture you are engaged in, let love, harmony and civility be your guiding star."[9]

NOTES

1. William Chittick, *The Sufi Doctrine of Rumi* (Bloomington: World Wisdom, 2005), 9.
2. Loosely translated in the West as "ego."
3. Abu Yazid Bastami as quoted in Nasrollah Saifpour Fatemi, Faramarz S. Fatemi, and Fariborz S. Fatemi, *Love, Beauty, and Harmony in Sufism* (South Brunswick, NJ: A. S. Barnes and Co., 1978), 47.
4. bell hooks, *Teaching to Transgress: Education as the Practice to Freedom* (New York: Routledge, 1994), 195.
5. Ibid., 194.
6. Shaykh Fadhlalla Haeri, *Prophetic Traditions in Islam*, p. 203 (Mishkat, 190–92) in *The Book of Character*, ed. Camille Helminski (Watsonville: The Book Foundation, 2004), 364.
7. Eugene Taylor, *A Psychology of Spiritual Healing* (Westchester: Chrysalis Books, 1997), 61.
8. Ibid., 28.
9. N. S. Fatemi, F. S. Fatemi, and F. S. Fatemi, *Love, Beauty, and Harmony in Sufism*, 207.

17

EXPERIENCING MEDIEVAL CHRISTIAN SPIRITUALITY

KRISTINE T. UTTERBACK

BACKGROUND TO THE COURSE

As a teacher of medieval history, I struggle to help my students get a "feel" for a world very different from their own. The problem that creates for twenty-first-century Americans is obvious, since I can neither bring a medieval peasant to class nor take field trips to medieval sites. When I saw a call for proposals from Contemplative Mind in Society in 1999 (Contemplative Practice in Teaching Fellowships), I realized that contemplation could offer my students first-person experience of an important dimension of medieval life. At that time, I had never heard of contemplative pedagogy, so I viewed my endeavor as experiential learning, but as I have taught the course, the contemplative focus has subsumed the experiential.

I had practiced the Christian Centering Prayer for several years, and I was intrigued by the challenge of developing a course that combined the history of medieval Christian contemplative practice with experiential learning. Since receiving the grant, I have offered the course Medieval Christian Contemplation in History and Practice three times, cross-listed in religious studies and history. Pedagogically I want to allow the students to experience the Middle Ages in some small but real way. I have a personal hope, shared with the students, that they might find these practices rewarding enough to continue to use them, now or later in life.

I employ a simple methodology. I teach medieval Christian practices that illustrate three approaches to contemplation—body, mind, and heart: the Jesus Prayer (body), *lectio divina* (mind), and centering prayer, based on the

171

fourteenth-century classic *The Cloud of Unknowing* (heart). Since the University of Wyoming operates on a fifteen-week semester, I devote about one month to each practice, with a week for introduction and one for wrap-up. Each student must commit to practicing the method we are studying, for about twenty minutes each day (Monday through Friday). Since I see the individual practice as central to their learning, discussions of their practice account for a substantial portion of their grade (60 percent), based on an essay drawn from their experience of the particular practice. In the following discussion, I use standard Christian terminology; however, in class, I can take a more nuanced approach, helping students find descriptions of ideas that they find meaningful, if the Christian ones are disquieting to them. The students must be willing to open themselves to the practices, but they need not accept any particular theology.

COURSE CONTENT

I begin with the desert Fathers and the development of both eremitical and coenobitic practices in early Christianity. We read and discuss some sayings of the desert Fathers and Mothers.[1] This leads naturally into the development of the Jesus Prayer, a mantric prayer form, which has a physical prostration practice as well, though it is rarely used in Western (Latin) Christian practice.[2] The students read *The Way of a Pilgrim and The Pilgrim Continues His Way*, a book that relates the story of a nineteenth-century Russian who took seriously the Pauline injunction to "pray without ceasing" and who, over time, learned to pray the Jesus Prayer constantly. While not a medieval text, it is highly readable and shows how the Jesus Prayer transformed the life of the man who practiced it.[3] I teach them the Prayer,[4] and we practice it in class. I describe the development of Jesus beads, which they either purchase or make themselves.

Second, we turn to *lectio divina*, a contemplative method for reading holy texts, generally, though not exclusively, biblical texts. This practice developed when people lacked commentaries on scripture, and often even scripture itself, so they would read and memorize vast portions of the Bible. *Lectio* played an important role in Benedictine monasticism from the sixth century, remained preeminent throughout the Middle Ages, and is still in use today. The practice of *lectio* involves reading a passage contemplatively. When a word, phrase, or idea catches the individual's attention, he stops and spends time with the portion of text until it has yielded its nourishment. Then he continues until he finds another such portion of text and does the same thing until the end of the allotted time. The focus is not on the quantity read, but on the insights offered through the Holy Spirit's guidance during the reading.[5]

In its taught form, *lectio divina* has four parts: *lectio*, the reading of the text; *meditatio*, listening to what the text has to say; *oratio*, offering the text as a prayer to God; and *contemplatio*, where the individual simply sits and rests in God and/or the text. These stages allow for the discussion of the process, but it does not necessarily happen that way, since any stage can occur at any time.[6]

Students often find this slow, intentional reading to be difficult, with its purpose of acquiring deep understanding, not information. This approach, so at variance with the way students must study for most classes, is very challenging for most students. To assist them, a nun from the Abbey of St. Walburga, a contemplative Benedictine community thirty miles away from Laramie, comes to discuss the process with the students. We also usually go visit the abbey, which helps give the students a context for the practice.

Third, I introduce Centering Prayer, based on the fourteenth-century English contemplative classic, *The Cloud of Unknowing*. In this practice, the individual chooses a sacred word to express her intention of being in God's presence.[7] Sitting comfortably, usually on a chair, she introduces the sacred word silently. Then she simply sits quietly. When she notices thoughts (which can include mental, physical, or emotional sensations), she repeats the sacred word to reintroduce her intention of, and assent to, being in God's presence. At the end of the allotted time, she sits quietly, peacefully allowing her thoughts to return to normal, adding the Lord's Prayer, if desired.[8]

Each week we discuss assigned readings and the previous week's practice and do the practice ourselves, which gives each student at least some experience of it, even if they fall short outside of class time. This provides a chance to answer questions that the students might have and encourages them to keep trying, reminding them that everyone, including me, has similar difficulties. As the semester progresses and trust develops, some may share experiences or difficulties. Students find it easier to discuss difficulties than deep inner experiences. They are more likely to discuss those latter experiences with me in private, if at all. I work to provide an atmosphere of expansiveness and confidentiality, where the students feel safe enough to open themselves to contemplative experiences. I have to have sufficient trust in myself and contemplative practice to allow the process without demanding any particular result. I can require that they practice, but the results are beyond me.

ASSESSMENT IN A CONTEMPLATIVE CLASS

When I began teaching this class, I spent a lot of time trying to decide how to evaluate and assign a grade to the students, especially regarding the learning from their practice. Obviously I could have had them journal after their practice, but this seemed likely to defeat my purpose. Knowing they had to describe their experiences, they would evaluate their practice throughout, or else "look for" things to say about a given session, exactly what I do not want them to do. I wanted them to experience the practice, not think about words to describe it. I decided to allow the students to "self-assess" their practice later.

I assign a written paper, due about a week after we finish each method, in which they describe their experiences, including how faithfully they practiced. They seem to be quite frank about the extent of their practice, and the challenges and benefits from each one. For instance, they might flatly say that they found the practice difficult and only did it occasionally, or alternatively that they enjoyed it but were so busy that they had trouble finding time to do it as they would have liked. In assessing these assignments, I do not consider what the students experienced, but 1) whether they fulfilled their practice commitment; 2) how much they reflected on their experience of the practice, and 3) the quality of their essay writing.

Many students are pleased to learn that Christianity has a contemplative tradition within it, since it is very different from much of what they hear about Christianity. Even when they have trouble with some of the practices, they find the experience worthwhile, and they often call it the most unusual course of their academic career. It is certainly one of the most satisfying for me to teach.

One question might be raised about teaching religious practices in a state school like the University of Wyoming. This course has brought neither negative feedback nor questions of its propriety. Although the libertarian ethos in Wyoming may be part of the reason, I think two other factors contribute. First the course is derived from documented historical practices, making it a legitimate source for academic inquiry. Second, since the course is elective, students self-select. Not all the class members are Christians, but they are generally individuals open to spiritual aspects of their lives. Given recent studies indicating a strong desire among students to develop spiritually as well as intellectually during their college careers, such student interest is not surprising.[9] The course gives them the opportunity to explore spirituality within an academic environment, yet another safety measure for them.

NOTES

1. The following are just a few examples. Athanasius the Great, *The Life of St. Anthony* (Willits: Eastern Orthodox Books, n.d.); Laura Swan, *The Forgotten Desert Mothers: Sayings, Lives and Stories of Early Christian Women* (New York: Paulist Press, 2001); Thomas Merton, *The Wisdom of the Desert: Sayings from the Desert Fathers of the Fourth Century* (Boston: Shambhala, 2004).

2. Christianity does not have a truly physical prayer form, due perhaps to its ambivalence to the body, especially in early Christianity. Cistercians may

have practiced walking meditation around their enclosure, but walking meditation has never formed a major part of Christian prayer.

3. Helen Bacovcin, trans., *The Way of a Pilgrim and The Pilgrim Continues His Way* (New York: Image Books, 1978). See also Monk of the Eastern Church, Kallistos Ware, ed., *Jesus Prayer* (Crestwood: St. Vladimir's Seminary Press, 1987).

4. "Lord Jesus Christ, [Son of God,] Have mercy on me [a sinner]." People vary this mantra, such as leaving out the bracketed portions, but this forms the basic prayer.

5. Numerous books describe *lectio divina*, including Michael Casey, *Sacred Reading: The Ancient Art of Lectio Divina* (Liguori: Liguori Publications, 1996); Thelma Hall, RSC, *Too Deep for Words: Rediscovering Lectio Divina* (Mahwah: Paulist Press, 1988); and M. Basil Pennington, OCSO, *Lectio Divina: Renewing the Ancient Practice of Praying the Scriptures* (New York: Crossroads, 1998).

6. In Christian tradition, the term *contemplation* generally refers to wordless, imageless practice (apophatic), while *meditation* refers to discursive practice, frequently using images (kataphatic).

7. The sacred word has no intrinsic meaning, and is not sacred except as it carries out the expression of intention to open oneself to the movement of the Holy Spirit. It differs from a mantra, since it is only introduced when the individual finds herself distracted. In this form, distractions are not a problem to be solved, but actually an opportunity to reaffirm the desire for God.

8. William Johnston, ed., *The Cloud of Unknowing and the Book of Privy Counseling* (New York: Image Books, 1973); Thomas Keating, OCSO, *Open Mind, Open Heart* (New York: Continuum International, 2006); Thomas Merton, *Contemplative Prayer* (New York: Image Books, 1969).

9. See, for instance, the 2005 University of California (Los Angeles) study, "Understanding the Role of Religion and Spirituality in the UCLA Undergraduate Experience," part of a broad study conducted by the Higher Education Research Institute. This was part of a project funded by the Templeton Foundation, entitled *Spirituality in Higher Education: A National Study of College Students' Search for Meaning and Purpose* (http://www.spirituality.ucla.edu/index.html).

V

CONTEMPLATIVE EXERCISES
FOR THE CLASSROOM

18

AWARENESS PRACTICES IN AN UNDERGRADUATE BUDDHISM COURSE

ANDREW O. FORT

This essay describes two contemplative exercises assigned in my course, Buddhism: Thought and Practice. The course is an upper-level, undergraduate seminar enrolling between eighteen and twenty-five students. It is primarily a lecture and discussion-based historical survey of Buddhist traditions. However, since a theme in the course is the Buddha's emphasis on meditative and ethical practices for the cessation of suffering (*nirvana*), I incorporated the two contemplative exercises as an attempt to give students a flavor of this dimension of Buddhist teaching and practices in a liberal arts university setting. The exercises are meant to provide an alternative, perhaps more "Buddhist," mode of inquiry to catalyze a better realization of two goals of liberal education: a more accurate understanding of others' worldviews and increased reflective "self"-awareness.[1]

To begin, I would like to state my debt to Mackenzie Brown and Randall Nadeau of Trinity University in San Antonio, who were the original sources of the exercises in this form. They generously shared their versions with me, and I then reworked them to fit with Texas Christian University students. They have given their approval for me to publish this work under my name alone, but it is a shared product, as is true for teaching in general.

MEDITATION EXERCISE

In this exercise, I ask students to do a week-long practice that introduces basic Theravada *vipassana* (noticing) meditation, and to keep a daily journal that serves as a resource for the reflective essay they turn in afterward. The project is mandatory, but grading is optional (which allays some student concern about academic evaluation of an experiential exercise). When I last taught the course (spring 2008), about half chose to be graded. I evaluate them on quality of presentation (clean copy, proofreading, following directions), clarity and thoroughness of their description, and degree of self-reflection and insight.

The meditation directions state: "You need not accept any Buddhist doctrines to do this exercise; all you need is the capacity to notice your thoughts. The aim is twofold: for you to better understand a basic Buddhist practice and to become more aware of your thoughts and feelings. Understanding other worldviews accurately and attaining increased reflective self-awareness are two important goals of liberal arts inquiry. The exercise of observing your experience is not intended to conflict with any religious convictions, but if you feel it does, you will be given an alternative assignment. I urge you to talk with me about any questions that arise."

The instructions include:

1) Write down what you expect to get out of this project.

2) Find an object of meditation that matches your personality, following a typology provided by Buddhaghosa, author of the *Path of Purification*.[2] Buddhaghosa outlines six personality types or temperaments, how to recognize these types, and the meditation subjects suitable for each type. Choose the personality type and meditation subject that most closely resemble you.

3) For a week, spend ten to fifteen minutes each morning and evening practicing "noticing" meditation. The instruction sheet shows you how to sit comfortably in meditation posture. Each morning, follow your breath for ten or fifteen minutes as shown in the reading and in class. Simply follow the breath and notice what you notice.

4) For the first four evenings, meditate on the chosen meditation object in a simple form; for example, you might meditate on the body or on friendliness, simply being aware of the object and your thoughts and feelings about it. For the last three evenings, contemplate its deeper aspects, such as: Where am "I" in my body? What is permanent in my body? Or, to whom am I truly friendly? Why? To whom am I harsh or angry? Why?

I tell the students to keep a journal handy after each meditation and to write down what they noticed in their body, feelings, and thoughts, yet not to be distracted by rehearsing what to write during the meditation. I point out that they should let go of specific, especially exaggerated, expectations or notions of "progress." I also tell them to expect distractions such as roommates and loud music, since they are at a university, not a meditation center.

Finally, they are to write an essay (five to seven pages) about their experience of meditation practice that reflects upon their expectations, the type of person they decided they were (and why), and the meditation subject they chose (and why). They are to include a daily journal (preferably typed) of thoughts and feelings, any problems (such as excitement, fear, strange images or sensations, sleepiness), and a comparison of morning and evening meditations, including possible development or regression during the week. They are to conclude with a reflection on what they learned from meditation practice, examining in particular the difference between their expectations and their actual experiences.

What is the feedback? Most are deeply struck by the difficulty of following even the most basic meditation practice. They struggle to count up to ten breaths without losing focus. Many gain some increased bodily awareness while practicing, and a few express real pleasure: "I envisioned my lungs expanding and contracting with each breath, sending oxygen throughout my body as the blood pumps within me . . . I started to appreciate each breath as a gift that keeps on giving, a life-giving action that we often forget about."[3] While a few find the exercise easy to follow, most express impatience and frustration with themselves, and many directly experience their own "drunken monkey mind." Although I tell them to stop if they have pain, some students experience a bit of physical suffering and discover that sickness (colds, allergies) interferes with their practice.

While some students see themselves as a mix of Buddhaghosa's greed, hate, or delusion types, many are unpleasantly surprised to see how well they fit one of these categories. They see how driven they are by their own expectations (including the achievement of enlightenment in a week!), their intense desire to "do it right," and the extremely fast pace of modern American life.

There is an interesting mix of imagery: kinesthetic (floating, swimming), visual (people or presences, psychedelic visions), and aural (voices and music). On occasion, the imagery is quite evocative, as in the case of a student who saw himself in a river: "I was actually surprised by how much more at peace I felt when flowing through the river rather than resisting it. As I continued, the river opened into an ocean, through which I sank deeper and deeper. When I sank to the very depths of this ocean, I fell into a vast space both empty and non-empty." A few students report unusual sensations or disturbing images.

Some students make a significant shift from seeing dorm life as a "distraction" to accepting, even embracing, their surroundings. One student was upset with his roommates for their noisiness over the week but then asked himself, "What am I doing? Am I trying to blame someone else to get away from the fact that I cannot concentrate?" He reflected, "I am living and there are living beings around me. I realized that those noises were the sound of life. I should be grateful for being alive and living in such a lively world."

Still, few of them describe much experiential crossover between meditation time and the rest of their lives. Neither is there much ongoing philosophical reflection on Buddhist ideas, though a few students begin an insightful inquiry into the nature of their selves. Frequently, students battle sleepiness or the anxiety that they should be doing something "productive." While students reveal much about their mental process in the reports, they expose little of their personal struggles, except for occasional comments about such things as an eating disorder, money pressure, and tension with parents. Over the years, I have found virtually no mention of sexual thoughts, and none of bedmates interrupting meditation. Perhaps this finding illustrates a point I make a number of times in the course: meditation (or Buddhism itself) is not therapy, though it can be therapeutic.

PRECEPTS EXERCISE

The second exercise is an opportunity to reflect on what it would be like to follow the first five ethical precepts of the Buddhist tradition. Again, I tell students that they need not accept Buddhist doctrine in order to do this exercise; they simply need to be aware of their thoughts and actions. The aim is twofold: to understand basic Buddhist ethical practice and to become more aware of their thoughts, feelings, and actions, and how these affect other beings. Readers may note that students are not required to keep the precepts; again, the point is increased awareness as part of liberal arts inquiry, which they can gain whether or not they practice various restraints.

Students keep a daily journal for five days; the first entry is a short statement of what they expect from the exercise. Then, they choose a different precept for each day (in any order) and write a journal entry on the series of questions under the precept. I recommend that each journal entry be one-half to one typewritten page in length, and they need to write at least one more page on reflections and insights about themselves and Buddhism after doing the exercise. The precept instructions follow.

1. Avoid harming sentient beings. In the past twenty-four hours have you: Eaten anything? What? How did it get on your plate—who planted or nurtured it, harvested or butchered it, cleaned and cooked it?

Harmed anyone or anything? By aggressive behavior or avoidance? By speech or facial expression, intentional or unintentional? By laughter?

2. Avoid taking what is not offered. In the past twenty-four hours have you: Bought anything? How? Was it "freely given"? Where did you get the money? Did you really need the item? Why? What would you do if you didn't have it?

Borrowed anything? Why? Was it really given freely? Will your use diminish its value, or cause hardship to the loaner?

3. Avoid false speech. In the past twenty-four hours have you: Lied? Said something not strictly true? Equivocated? Exaggerated? Hidden the truth from another? Why? Have you thought about the effect of your words before you spoke?

Have you actively sought the truth in your studies? Out of class? Do you honor your teachers and the knowledge they share?

4. *Avoid lust.* In the past twenty-four hours have you: Had or acted on a sexual fantasy? Why did you desire your partner? Was your partner a willing participant? What are the implications of your actions? Were you mindful of the consequences, psychological or physical/medical?

Wanted something you can or should not have? Why? Why can't or shouldn't you have it? Would it harm others to have it? Would it harm you?

5. *Avoid intoxicants.* In the past twenty-four hours, have you: Taken alcohol or other consciousness-altering substances? What was the impact on your senses and awareness? Were there later physical or mental consequences?

Have you intoxicated your consciousness by going on the Internet (checking email, Facebook, gaming), listening to music, or watching TV or a movie?

Did your use of such intoxicants cause you to violate any other precept (harming, taking, lusting, speaking falsely)? Did it take time away from your studies and the pursuit of wisdom?

Many students engage seriously with this exercise, wrestling with whether to follow the precepts or indulge in "forbidden" behavior. They come to uncomfortable realizations about their "self"ishness when trying to follow even one precept a day. They often gain a greater respect for the difficulty of Buddhist practice; such respect is a major goal of this exercise. There is little revelation of behavior outside of social norms, and most students are realistic and accurate about what they will learn. For example, one student wrote: "By observing the five precepts, I am going to uncover some things that I probably would rather not see, some things I probably should work on and correct, but probably never will and just end up accepting them as flaws." Another student noted how challenging mindfulness was: "I was afraid of losing mindfulness throughout the day and falling back into my regular daily routine without any thought. Because [this happened], I often became frustrated at myself when I forgot and did not practice the precept of the day. Frustration also [occurred] when I *would* follow the precept of the day, for I know that in my daily life I do not practice and embrace the Buddhist lifestyle; I am no monk."

Perhaps unsurprisingly in our highly individualistic culture, this exercise brings many students new insights about our fundamental interdependence and interrelatedness; for example, they have to consider how food gets on their plates in the dining hall, from farm to cafeteria worker. Many students are dismayed by how often they harm others by speech, and they see more clearly the nature of "false speech" as incomplete or absent speech rather than outright lying. Students also understand in more subtle ways what it means for something to be "freely given." When considering this precept, a number of students recognize how privileged they are, an insight that causes them to express gratitude to parents for the opportunity to be at college.

When contemplating lust, most students avoid talking about sexual matters, aside from many male students admitting to lustful thoughts. But, some students wrestle with their understanding of love versus lust. They perceptively speak of their lust for more time to sleep or even to study. They write comments such as: "I realized I don't 'take time' to be in the present [which is] ironic since it is the only place we can be," along with references to "wasting," "saving," or having "free" time. They (and I) also learn about the extent of their intoxication with technology (one called it a "spell"), including iPods, email, and web surfing, especially Facebook. Many students admit to spending three or four hours a day on the latter. One student wrote: "Just writing this paper I've checked Facebook no less than 47 times over five hours—now 48. Through close observation I realize just how often I'll do something, often anything, to avoid sitting with my thoughts." Another student added, "I learned that I can be more attached to things than I am to people, which is horrible. I spend more hours on my computer than with my friends." (Sometimes I learn more than I want to know about their selfishness and unkindness, especially during relationship breakups.)

To conclude, students report that these exercises are very valuable in gaining a more practical or "lived" understanding of the Buddhist tradition. Many of their course reviews at the end of the semester mention the contemplative practices as one of the most valuable and memorable elements of the course. Remarks express, for example, the students' respect for the rigors of Buddhist practice: "I learned that getting rid of stress isn't free. I feel the meditation put me in a much better mood and I felt less stress. After a few days I started to want to meditate more often. But the most important thing I learned is that meditation and getting in the 'zone' was pretty difficult. I finally can put in perspective how much better the Buddha must have been at this than I am." Students also appreciate how the exercises enliven honest self-examination: "The precepts project gave me another perspective on my daily activities. Do we live up to our standards? Not really. We always complain about attitudes of other people, and do not notice our own reactions. Also, it was interesting how being aware of the precept changed / did not change how we act. This project was very insightful. It helped me stop and analyze how I lead my life."

Over the years, I have continually found it revealing and at times moving to observe students honestly share about their experiences, sometimes with disarming sincerity and other times with sparkling insight. I am convinced that the exercises provide more insight into a mode of inquiry revealing a Buddhist understanding than do lecture and discussion. Again, these contemplative exercises offer a concrete opportunity for the realization of two goals of liberal education: a more accurate understanding of others' worldviews and increased reflective "self"-awareness.

NOTES

1. This is not the place to discuss the problematic notion of "self" in Buddhism, but I could not resist framing this word with quotation marks.
2. From *The Six Types of Persons by Buddhaghosa*, found in Edward Conze, trans., *Buddhist Scriptures* (New York: Penguin Books, 1959), 116–21.
3. All quotations are included with permission from the respective students.

19

CONTEMPLATIVE INQUIRY

Beyond the Disembodied Subject

ANNE CAROLYN KLEIN AND ANN GLEIG

The maid ran for love. The wife ran out of fear
And jealousy. There is a great difference.
The mystic flies moment to moment
The fearful ascetic drags along month to month. . . .
You can't understand this with your mind.
You must burst open!

—Rumi[1]

This charming narrative by a legendary contemplative touches on three themes important for us. Contemplative approaches to study take nuanced interest in first-person experience, and shaping relationships with oneself and with others, and with the kinds of bodily energies that come forth or are suppressed in the process.

Rumi touches on all this in just a few lines. His poem tells of a jealous wife who is careful that, for seven years, her husband is never alone with their attractive maid. Then one day at the baths, she realizes she has left her silver washbasin at home and sends the maid to fetch it. The maid eagerly runs to her task. No sooner is she gone than the wife, realizing what is at stake, takes off for home herself.

Rumi takes the occasion to contrast the burning love of the maid with the calculated and fear-based motivation of the wife. He is suggesting that in order for spiritual work to be effective it must burn with love and longing rather than fear and jealousy. This is the path of the mystic. Most of us are, if not ascetics, nonetheless burdened by the structures—psychological, energetic, and conceptual—that keep us at a distance from the fire in our own lives. Contemplative pedagogies help us examine the nature and source of this fire by calling attention to ways of knowing our culture often ignores.

These pedagogies expand on the objective, third-person disembodied paradigms of knowing. Within a contemplative perspective, the knowing subject herself, her mind and its depths, her body and its subtle energies, becomes a focus of interest. What are the capacities and functions of such a knowing subject? They are not just the accumulation of data, but an ability to recognize the various states that arise at different times—whether of quiescence, agitation, insight, or a subtle recognition of colors, images and energy flows—that seem to present themselves to awareness, potentially bringing information about self, other, and environment with them.

Contemplative practices come in many forms, from traditional Buddhist mindfulness to chanting-with-visualization, to the more recently introduced practice of inquiry. All involve trajectories of learning that contemplative studies can and should identify and clarify. Doing so makes clear that the academy can expand its understanding of what learning means. Increasing the depth, strength, and clarity of attention, channeling or smoothing out the energy flows through the body, and receptivity to internal imagery—these are all things that can be learned. In this chapter we note how such learning is associated with Buddhist meditation and with the practice of inquiry central to A. H. Almaas's Diamond Approach, a contemporary Western contemplative tradition. We consider these in terms of two intertwined aspects of first-person inquiry: the relevance of contemplative practice to the body and its energies, and to the kind of relationship one has with oneself, with others, and with knowledge.

BODY AWARENESS

Classic Buddhist mindfulness training can intensify awareness of sensory objects as well as the internal senses themselves. It also can increase the depth and stability of awareness. These traits have to do with the "verticality" or depths of mind, in contrast to its horizontal reach for more information. Practices of simple chanting, or of focusing on a glowing letter at one's heart whose light expands as one sounds that letter, also enrich such verticality. Deepening awareness of the mind in this way is also to deepen awareness of the body and also to enter more deeply into bodily experience. In our class, after an initial training in classic mindfulness of breathing, we introduced a simple one-vowel chant. Several students commented that using sound helped to anchor the attention and the energies that support attention. That is, when the mind is distracted, it is not only that one's mental focus is shifting, or that various images are appearing, but the energy of one's body is also moving in ways it does not when attention settles. A shift in either affects the other.

Such practices suggest a mind-body reciprocity quite different from the Cartesian model upon which most learning of information is based. Contemplative experience offers students an opportunity to reflect on that model—to read Descartes, for example—with critical curiosity born of such experience—*I think therefore I am.* But should the body be excluded from the kind of knowing that constructs identity? Can everything be understood through the horizontal and information-laden mind alone?

To observe breath is to observe the most obvious energy flow of the body. Focusing on the breath generally leads to greater awareness of more subtle energies as well. Sometimes, closely attending to the body yields imagery that expresses or impacts *one's feelings* at the time. One student, after observing his breath, reported a surge of yellow energy-light that seemed to him to hold the quality of happiness. He remarked, "I don't know how you can feel a color, but I did." Just as in dreams, in contemplative practice boundaries of the senses are porous. In this way, students learn that training attention inward can reveal worlds of imagery, energetic patterning, and insight that become food for further reflection. These images can be understood through the lens of religious, artistic, or psychological resources. A new channel of discovery opens. At a more advanced stage one could point out that yellow or gold is associated with an enriched consciousness in Buddhism, and with essential joy and curiosity in the Diamond Approach. The student could inquire whether, given specific circumstances, this arising seemed random or addressed some current issue. Most classroom situations will not be suitable for this level of discussion; it is delicate work and one would need a specific contract with students to brook such inquiry, especially in the presence of other class members. We did not construct such a contract in our class and it would likely not be advisable to press forward even privately unless one is a psychotherapist or a trained teacher in a particular tradition. Likewise the instructor did not mention that only hours before she had had an extremely powerful experience very similar to what the student described before, and had even used the words "how can I feel color" in her own reflections.

As we consider the limits and possibilities of contemplative studies, we must also acknowledge the power of this material to self-consciously challenge the "objective scholar" or "talking head" paradigm. Still, joining the personal and pedagogical is not without risks. Contemplative pedagogy touches students and teachers in deeply personal and unpredictable ways. Becoming aware of one's own thoughts, emotions, and body with fresh clarity can be a painful and disconcerting process as well as an empowering and transformative one. For the teacher, preparing students for the transformation contemplative practices engender, holding a space for these transformations, and providing support inside and outside the classroom become pressing issues. Similarly, teachers must negotiate between their traditional professorial role and counseling students through what might be the beginnings of a transformative process. Also to be navigated is how much teachers share of their own first-person experiences. Some criteria are needed to help us understand when this is inappropriate, even self-indulgent, and when pedagogically meaningful.[2] We must make clear that beyond a basic level of self-awareness and transformative learning, the broad arc of deep personal transformation or the addressing of deep-seated psychological issues are outside the realm of responsible contemplative education. Where that delicate line is drawn must be negotiated carefully.

RELATIONSHIP WITH SELF, OTHERS, AND TEXT

Like rivers to the ocean, practices such as breath observation, chanting, or inquiry yield increased appreciation of how we clutter our mental space, and of the dynamism available when clutter is reduced. When students recognize that different techniques can, in this sense, have similar outcomes, they can begin to look past differences in rhetoric, theology, or worldview to the similar behaviors they support.

For example, Buddhism emphasizes compassion as a driving motivation for practice—impelling one to know oneself well enough to realize fully one's dynamic potential, and then show others how to do the same. Almaas emphasizes the force of curiosity, fueled by a love for the truth that itself readily opens to compassion. Incorporating these two approaches into the classroom helped to give students a holographic perspective on elements common to many contemplative traditions. Observing breath, cultivating compassion, or engaging in inquiry as described further on all help students see more clearly how they habitually relate to themselves, to each other, and to the objects of their learning, ideally gaining a fresher relationship with self, other, and text.

Inquiry is the main method of the Diamond Approach. Inquiry is an open-ended investigation into whatever is arising in one's present experience, whether thoughts, emotions, images, body sensations, or energetic qualities. Unlike the simple witnessing of classic mindfulness, inquiry directly engages personal content; it brings keen discrimination to what was once beyond personal awareness. According to Almaas, following the thread of present experience allows access to more immediate and fundamental dimensions of self and reality. This is because in his view the psychophysical and the spiritual inform and mirror each other, thus one does not try to transcend the psychological, but probe it more deeply.

Inquiry engages the relational on a number of levels. Most obviously, the actual practice involves two or three people speaking in turn and listening closely to each other. It uncovers past conditioning—most specifically self-images and object relations—revealing how these shape and distort our relationships in and to the present. While psychology aims for the replacement of rigid self-images with more flexible ones, this inquiry can ultimately lead to the dissolving of all images into the nondual spaciousness of what Almaas calls Being. This liberation from past conditioning allows for a true intimacy and immediacy: as one gradually divests oneself of such structures, many entirely new types of energetic feelings, accompanied by visions of colors, are experienced in the body. This bears directly on our ability to relate. Unless we can respond to what is actually occurring rather than what we imagine,

> there will be no real relating. There will be only mental interaction, one image interacting with another. There will be no real human being relating to another human being; there will be your past interacting with someone else's past.[3]

Inquiry also fosters a new relationship to knowledge. It cultivates a curious, fresh openness that embraces not-knowing as necessary for discovery. "Openness means that you are not stuck in 'I know this, and that's it.' Openness means that no knowledge is final knowledge . . . it is the expression of a spaciousness in the mind, a spaciousness and awareness in the knowing capacity."[4]

After introducing the practice of Almaas's *Spacecruiser Inquiry*, students were instructed to take ten minutes each for an open-ended inquiry into their present experience while their participant partners listened. As a guideline, we suggested that students approach the practice as a type of spoken mindfulness practice. They could do this either as a silent journaling process or in spoken monologues in triads. Initially, three students out of twelve opted for the solo journaling process; in the last exercise all participated in the triads. These students wrote about the difference, and how powerful it was to listen and be listened to by a real person. This was an opportunity to learn about the impact of another's presence on oneself.

In utilizing inquiry to explore contemplative approaches to relationality, we had three interrelated aspects in mind: relationship to self, to other, and to knowledge. In this context, many students reported a new recognition of how habitually self-critical they were and how restrictive this was, inside and outside the classroom. As one reflected:

> it [inquiry] helped me to uncover the manner in which I constantly have what I would associate as "super-ego" tendencies of thought. Things I personally admonish myself for, am worried about, etc. This exercise helped me to become aware of that, and try to change deeply embedded thinking patterns.

Another student wrote:

> With the Diamond Heart, I was challenged to listen from a centered and empathetic state and also challenged to share with the external world my internal processes. I noticed that a lot of my barriers have to do with my relationships and this approach helped make many of those clear. I started to realize how much I try to manipulate my environment to my liking, presenting my body and my sentiments in a style that I think will be most favorable instead of just being straightforward and authentic.

One of the primary gifts of contemplative pedagogy is an invitation to a new relationship to the objects of our study. Our class touched upon this with Paul Griffith's *Religious Reading*, which differentiates between "religious reading" in which the reader has a dialogically introspective relationship with the text, and "consumerist reading" which is oriented toward the acquisition of information and modeled on metaphors of production, consumption, use, and control. It is a relationship of participation rather than separation with our texts that contemplative approaches offer. In order for such an inter- and intrasubjective dialogue to be feasible, however, we need to transform deeply entrenched patterns of approaching texts as objects to be controlled and contained. Like Rumi's maid, we need to run, read, and relate from love and not from fear. Contemplative pedagogy is of much value here.

CONCLUSION

We begin to see that the contemplative is not beholden to the idea that emotions and reasons are two distinctly different states or that rationality rules in the strictly Kantian sense. Through reflecting on why compassion, for example, is a reasonable response in a world where everyone equally wants happiness, we can open into actual feelings of compassion. Likewise, by tapping deeply into our own feelings and the kinds of images, memories, or associations linked with them, we can gain clearer insight into the causes, or reasons, for them. When jealousy feels like a punch in the stomach, for example, we slowly remember that our sibling seemed favored at the dinner table. Second, most contemplative practices have a fundamentally nondualistic orientation. For example, both the Buddhist and Diamond Approach systems hold that when these practices bring their full fruition, the ordinary dualistic way of approaching self and world will be challenged and finally dissolve. At the same time, both make clear that a collapse of ordinary dualistic processes is not disruptive to one's ability to be in the world. Third, the contemplative practitioner understands herself as a being whose mind, body, feelings, and energies are inextricably intertwined. She learns that simple attention can open to insight or to vision, and can settle the body's energies or refine them. Any of these shifts, brought to some modest level of maturity, can begin to reveal and break up the kind of self-habituations that dull us to the fire of our own curiosity and learning, and to the aliveness of our own consciousness.

NOTES

1. Jalal al-Din Rumi, *The Essential Rumi*, trans. Coleman Barks with John Moyne (New York: Harper San Francisco, 1995), 178–80.
2. These questions are discussed in the concluding section of the report from Piper Murray, "Meeting on Contemplative Pedagogy in the Disciplines: Philosophy, Religious Studies, Psychology," Amherst College, Amherst, Massachusetts (March 28–30, 2008) at the Center for Contemplative Mind in Society.
3. A. H. Almaas, *Diamond Heart Book Four: Indestructible Innocence* (Boston and London: Shambhala, 2001), 187.
4. A. H. Almaas, *Spacecruiser Inquiry: True Guidance for the Inner Journey Home* (Boston and London: Shambhala, 2002), 17.

20

LOVE OF WISDOM
PUTS YOU ON THE SPOT

The Warrior Exam

DALE ASRAEL

"What is fearlessness?"

The question hangs in the air.

Two students, one the Questioner and the other the Respondent, sit face to face, engaged in the most ancient form of inquiry: asking and answering questions. Around them, similarly seated on low cushions, is a circle of their peers. Their instructor sits as a member of the circle, where both students can see her.

Questioner: "What is fearlessness?"

Respondent: "In the book we studied, the author said, 'Fearlessness is knowing the nature of fear.' That means being willing to face fear and experience it directly. It doesn't mean not having any fear."[1]

Questioner: "What is your own experience of fearlessness?"

The Respondent looks down, a furrow deepening between her brows. "I don't really know what fearlessness means in my own experience. I always retreat when I'm scared."

The Questioner regards at her silently. After a few moments, the Respondent raises her eyes and meets the Questioner's gaze.

Questioner: "What are you experiencing right now?"

Respondent: "I'm afraid I'm making a mess of this exam, like I always do when I get scared."

This chapter has been excerpted and adapted from "The Love of Wisdom Puts You on the Spot: The Warrior Exchange as Contemplative Pedagogy," MA in Contemplative Education thesis, Naropa University, June 2008.

Holding her gaze, the Questioner gently asks, "What are you experiencing right now? Start with your physical sensations."

The Respondent closes her eyes and sits up straight. "My stomach is in a knot. My hands are cold, but I feel like I'm sweating. My jaw is tight. I can feel a headache starting."

Questioner: "Can you feel your breathing right now?"

Respondent: "I think I'm failing. Everyone must be thinking I'm stupid."

Questioner: "Can you open your eyes and look at us, and just feel your sensations? Even if you feel very uncomfortable, will you look at us? Don't believe what your thoughts are telling you."

The Respondent looks first at the Questioner, and then at each person in the circle around her.

Questioner: "What are you feeling right now?"

Respondent: "Shaky. Warm. Not knowing anything, but I'm connected; I'm here."

Questioner: "What is the nature of fear for you in this moment? What is your direct experience of this moment in your body and mind?"

Respondent: "Mmmm . . . Big energy. Shaky and surging, like a huge wave."

Questioner: "What is fearlessness?"

Respondent: "Leaping into the unknown! If I don't freeze up when I feel fear, the energy of the fear carries me!"

Questioner: "I accept your answer. Thank you."

The students bow to one another.

This is the Warrior Examination, a form of dyadic inquiry used in many Naropa University courses as a midterm or final examination.[2] Whatever the subject matter, the form of the Warrior Examination remains essentially the same.

The classroom is arranged with chairs or cushions in a circle, and two seats in the center. The instructor has prepared three bowls, each containing small pieces of paper, each folded so that no one can see what is written on them. One bowl contains the questions, which she has composed and given to the class a week or two in advance, so that the students can prepare their answers individually. Each student has prepared answers for all questions, since there is no way to know in advance which question he or she will select from the bowl. The other two bowls contain the names of all of the students. The instructor draws one piece of paper from the Respondent's bowl, opens it, and announces the name of the student who will answer the first question. The chosen student sits on one of the central seats. The Respondent selects a piece of paper from the Questioner's bowl, opens it, and announces the name of the student who will be her partner in the Examination. The Questioner sits in the other central seat, facing the

Respondent. The students bow to one another in the Naropa tradition, a gesture of mutual respect.

The Respondent draws a piece of paper from the third bowl, containing the questions the instructor has prepared. The Respondent opens the slip of paper, reads the question silently, and hands it to the Questioner. The Questioner reads the question aloud, so that everyone in the circle can hear it.

The Respondent takes a few moments to consider, and then begins to speak, answering the question. The Questioner asks follow-up questions to help the Respondent clarify or complete what he or she has answered. Some questions may help the Respondent identify an error in the answer. Some of the follow-up questions help the Respondent articulate a fuller explanation coming from her own contemplation of the topic.

When the Questioner assesses that the answer is complete, he or she states in the traditional manner, "I accept your answer." The examination ends with a closing bow.

The process is then repeated, until each student has had an opportunity to both question and respond. When everyone has done so, all bow together to conclude.

The essence of the Warrior Examination is the use of a series of open-ended questions to draw out increasingly subtle levels of understanding of the subject matter. When it works well, the Respondent will hear herself articulate elements of the subject matter she did not previously realize she understands. This happens when the right question is asked at the right time, provoking a direct experience of the answer, which is then put into words. In the example described at the beginning of this chapter, the Questioner's skill supported and provoked the Respondent into an embodied understanding of fearlessness that was more immediate than the theoretical definition of "fearlessness" she had memorized. In such moments, the true purpose of the Warrior Examination is revealed— beyond being a method of examining and evaluating students' understanding of subject matter, it is a vehicle of further learning that can challenge Questioner and Respondent simultaneously and spontaneously into fresh levels of understanding. The Warrior Examination, with its origins in traditional Tibetan Buddhist scholastic debate, is a practical application of a central theme of contemplative education as it has developed at Naropa University, articulated in the statement by Naropa's founder, "The love of wisdom puts you on the spot all the time."[3]

The Warrior Examination is, of course, only one of the evaluation tools used at Naropa University, which employs all the customary measures such as research papers, reflection papers, objective and essay examinations, class presentations, and other classroom project assignments. This examination form is especially useful in demonstrating the students' inner development of reflection and personal insight stemming from contemplative practice and academic study joined together.

The questions that compose the Warrior Examination are designed uniquely, to cover the material studied; to encourage students to examine the implications of the topics independently, including investigating how the topic applies to their own personal life situations; and to provoke a fresh nonconceptual glimpse of the essential meaning of the topic. Examples of exam questions in my Naropa meditation courses (taken for academic credit) include:

- Explain the author's statement that "meditation is the 'Great Teacher'" giving specific examples from the reading.[4] What is meditation teaching you?
- How does inquisitiveness deepen meditative experience? How can a practitioner cultivate inquisitiveness in the midst of physical or psychological struggles?

These questions require that the students know what they have studied, and that they have considered the implications of the material. Such questions also ask the student to discover further levels of meaning by investigating direct personal experience in the moment of being questioned. The follow-up questions provided by the Questioner, which arise naturally in the midst of the encounter, are open-ended; and the Questioner has to put aside any tendencies to look for answers he or she would have given.

One of the most widely used follow-up questions in Warrior Examinations is some variation of "What have you observed about this topic from your own personal experience?" This requires more honesty and bravery in the form of personal contemplation than merely articulating what has been studied.

After a series of follow-up questions, the Questioner might conclude with an unplanned and unexpected question such as: "What, in one brief sentence, is the essence of this topic?" Such a question, if truly spontaneous, can spark the Respondent into mentally leaping beyond scripts and concepts into a fresh utterance, a new discovery of meaning found right in that "on-the-spot" moment.

One Naropa instructor gives students the final Warrior Examination questions at the very beginning of the semester, to provide an overview and inspiration to the students right from the start of the course. Another instructor does not give the students any questions in advance; she relies on the element of surprise to stimulate the students to fresh, on-the-spot contemplation. Some instructors write specific questions for specific individual students. These questions focus on themes in the course curriculum that have been especially meaningful or confounding to the individual student for whom they have been written. An example of a personalized question is "How might a practitioner use meditation as a way to hide from the challenges of life?"

The role of the instructor during the Warrior Examination is to "hold the container," often completely silently. The instructor's presence models the quality of attentive listening that the circle of peers offers to the two in the center. The instructor will tell the students in advance how many minutes they will have; usually, ten minutes per question is more than enough. The instructor may provide a signal, perhaps by ringing a small bell, when there is only one minute remaining. Only if the students get stuck might the instructor intervene, suggesting a direction for questioning. When a Warrior Examination is used as an evaluation tool, the instructor will provide written anecdotal feedback the following week, commenting on such elements as: theoretical understanding of subject matter; personal contemplation of the material; ability to articulate thoroughly and clearly; experiential understanding; presence; skill in listening; skill in questioning; any specific moments of clarity that occurred. Points are given to each area for grading purposes.

Students' written responses to the question, "What was your experience of the Warrior Examination?" reveal that different kinds of learning occur in the process.

The following excerpts were selected from hundreds of samples citing their experiences, collected in my courses over many years.

> I spent hours and hours preparing for the exam. . . . I saw it as a great opportunity to review all that we've been studying. It was refreshing to go back to the earliest readings from the first couple of weeks in the course. . . . During the exam, I felt I had a decent handle on most of the questions but definitely learned more listening to the other members of my group. (11/06)[5]

> I was especially motivated to know the material, not for my own sake, but for the sake of the person who would have me as their questioner. I felt that I was responsible for someone else's well-being, not just my own. (10/06)

> I had studied for the question I got and thought I understood it pretty well. But when K. started asking me questions—he was very kind, and his questions were totally relevant, but I didn't have answers prepared about any of them—I was suddenly in a place of not knowing instead of knowing. It threw me for a minute, but then I remembered that this kind of exam is about "warriorship" which in that moment meant "showing up completely" whether or not I knew what to say. So I trusted the situation, and by the end, just answering his questions, I heard myself saying things—real things I meant and understood as I said them—that I hadn't realized I knew. It was mind-blowing. (12/05).

It was beautiful, teaching me about staying in the moment with difficult emotions and the importance of having the support of another's
presence while doing that. From my own experience of being held in
attention, I also learned how to sit with another person who is dealing
with difficult feelings. (10/06)

My typical fashion is to hang back, thinking, thinking, thinking. But
this experience pulled me right into the present moment. There was
nowhere else to be. (7/05)

It's scary to put myself right out there, but it also feels present and
authentic. I found that in the middle of all that energy, I couldn't con-
ceptualize. It didn't work to hide in familiar words about the question I
drew—what I'd read and heard and thought before about this topic. I
was out there, living the question at that moment. (7/05)

My experience of observing students is that the moments of "gap" in the conceptual mind do naturally occur; but they can only be permitted to have their full
effect—the direct experience of the open space of mind beyond concept—if the
teacher, as well as the student, is adequately trained to relax in this openness.
Open space is unpredictable, groundless, capable of giving rise to anything.
During Warrior Examinations, I have observed that when the instructor or the
students are uncomfortable with the utter fluidity and shiftiness of open space,
there is a strong tendency to try to manipulate it by filling it up with concepts or
discursiveness in an attempt to get that openness under control. Meditation practice is one of the primary ways to train in relaxing with the unpredictability of the
mind. Practices such as mindful breathing meditation can train instructors and
students alike to become familiar with the mind and all that it produces. We can
learn to relax, with precision and gentleness, observing the play of thoughts and
emotions, rather than trying to control the mind. In this process, one discovers
there is freshness in our awareness, which allows us to be, very simply, with each
moment of experience as it is arising, occurring, and dissolving on its own.

I have observed some instructors panicking at the moments during a Warrior Examination when the space opens, beginning to talk in a speedy and discursive way, or moving on to the next dyad quickly, as if the encounter were
finished (when it is actually at its most fertile moment). When this happens, the
openness and potency are lost. The teacher's capacity to remain present—silent,
relaxed, alert—in the nonconceptual instant invites everyone to share in the
depth of that moment, and demonstrates to the students how they, too, might
pause and open at such a moment.

I continue to receive feedback from students about the long-term positive
effects the training in the Warrior Examination has provided. One student com-

plained to me often, during her years in an MA in Counseling program at Naropa University, how much she hated being put on the spot in these examinations. I was surprised to receive a telephone call from her several years after her graduation. She told me that she was working as a high school counselor. She described the way students daily asked her for help with a range of situations she had not encountered herself. "Although I'm well trained in counseling," she said, "I have never personally had to go through what these young people have to deal with. At first, I felt I had nothing to offer, and would dread it each time a student came into my office to ask me for help. Then I remembered the Warrior Exam. And now, I tell myself, 'I can do this. It's just like one more Warrior Exam!'" She thanked me for training her to "relax with the unknown" in the Warrior Examination.

Other graduates have reported that they attribute to a large extent their ability to "ride the energy of fear" and "leap into fearlessness," their ability to articulate clearly and ask open-ended questions, and their familiarity with the "gaps" in their linear thinking and ability to appreciate them as opportunities for creative responses to situations to what they learned from Warrior Examinations.

NOTES

1. Chögyam Trungpa, *Shambhala: The Sacred Path of the Warrior* (Boston: Shambhala, 1988), 47.

2. "Warrior" is based on the Tibetan word *pawo* defined as "one who is brave" (rather than one who makes war). In this sense, "warrior" redefines the notion of bravery to include the quality of gentleness. The warrior is courageous enough to act in whatever way a situation requires, while remaining open-hearted and compassionate to oneself and others simultaneously. Trungpa, *Sacred Path of the Warrior*, 63.

3. Faculty meeting with Chögyam Trungpa, Rinpoche, unpublished transcript, July 18, 1975.

4. H. Gunaratana, *Mindfulness in Plain English* (Boston: Wisdom Publications, 1993).

5. Excerpts that have only a date are anonymous excerpts from students taken from post-Warrior Examination written reflections.

21

A MEETING OF MINDS IN CYBERSPACE

Eco-Contemplative Methods for Online Teaching

JANE COMPSON

I have never met at least two-thirds of the students I teach every semester. This is because I am one of the ever-swelling ranks of teachers whose classrooms are increasingly held in cyberspace. What peculiar challenges to contemplative pedagogy are posed by the fully online modality, and how best to respond to them? This essay will address such questions and describe some practical exercises that encourage students to reflect upon their interconnectedness with other forms of life.

I have never been one to plan and script my classes too closely, and it was only when I began teaching online that I realized how much I rely on my own presence in the classroom. By "presence," I am referring to those elements of the teaching experience that cannot be predicted or planned for until I step into a room full of students. Even those of us who predate the iPod generation are probably familiar with computer games where the players or their avatars attain special abilities or "power-ups" to boost their progress through the levels. Sometimes these power-ups expire, and the avatar is left vulnerable and relatively impotent. Moving from the traditional classroom to the online modality is, for me, something akin to losing all the pedagogical power-ups associated with physical presence. Body language, visual feedback, humor, repartee, even my bafflingly beloved British accent—all of these tools are decommissioned in the online pedagogical kit.

How am I to be "present" in the contemplative sense—alive to, radically accepting of, and fully inhabiting the present moment—when that "present moment" is not shared with the students? Learning in the online classroom is for the most part "asynchronous," meaning that neither our moments nor our physical locations are shared.

One of the classes I most regularly teach online is called Philosophy, Religion and the Environment.[1] An aim in the class is to encourage students to think "ecologically"—to recognize and reflect upon the interdependence and interconnectedness of all forms of life. I use contemplative methods in the hope that students will internalize this interdependence, in addition to understanding it intellectually. This is especially challenging when most students are accessing the class material from a context that underscores our disconnection from the natural environment and from each other—indoors and alone with their computers, likely in air-conditioned rooms.

For me, a key aspect of contemplative pedagogy is authenticity.[2] I understand pedagogical authenticity as a refusal to "fake it," a willingness to be honest about my hopes, fears, and vulnerabilities. When paired with a sense of fully inhabiting and accepting the present moment, this authenticity tends, in my experience, to create an atmosphere of openness and willingness in the classroom. The challenge is how to translate this authenticity into an online format. I try to do this by being as transparent as possible about my teaching methods and rationale.

My class begins with a module on the concept of worldviews, and this starting point provides an excellent platform from which to introduce contemplative learning in the context of different ways of knowing. I also explain *why* I am using these techniques in terms of students' own learning experiences and the course learning objectives. I explain that contemplative exercises may enhance their overall attention and study skills, in addition to increasing their engagement and intimacy with the course material. I also try to address students' concerns about contemplative methods, particularly about religious affiliations. I assign Tobin Hart's article "Opening the Contemplative Mind in the Classroom," which eloquently and succinctly addresses most of their concerns.[3] It is particularly helpful because it briefly introduces a variety of contemplative exercises. Alongside the Hart reading assignment, I ask the students to note some "whats, whys, and hows" of contemplative education, and to identify a few specific practices that they would be interested to explore and apply.

My first step, then, is to explain to students the rationale of using contemplative methods in the course. My second step is to provide them with instructions for a variety of contemplative practices by referring them to articles or online resources, including audio files, which guide students through short mindfulness or contemplative exercises.

The third step is to establish how the contemplative component of the class will be woven in with the "conventional" content and, importantly, how it will be evaluated. For each module, students engage in a content-related contemplative exercise and then write a reflective discussion posting on their experience. For the culmination of the class, students write a reflective paper that interweaves their contemplative experiences and their critical engagement with course materials.

The first exercise of the semester is a seed-planting exercise, adapted from an exercise introduced to me by Arthur Zajonc.[4] Students are invited first to prepare themselves by engaging in a contemplative practice of their choice that involves relaxation, silence, and introspection. Once the mind is calm, they are invited to hold a seed in their hand and to spend a few minutes closely examining the physical qualities of the seed before closing their eyes and becoming aware of its potential, where it has come from and how it has come to be in their hands at this moment. Finally, students are invited to let go of their focus on the seed and to allow their minds into a more relaxed, open awareness, expanding their attention to whatever thoughts and feelings arise with what Zajonc describes as the "afterimage" of the seed. Then they are invited to plant the seed mindfully, and, as time goes on, to nurture it as it grows. I encourage them to reflect on all the causes and conditions that make the seed grow, and also to see its growth as a metaphor for their learning process for the semester. They are then invited to write their experiences of this exercise in a reflective discussion posting.

This exercise seems to work particularly well for an online class focused on environmental issues, because it—temporarily at least—brings students into thoughtful contact and relationship with the processes of the natural world. Additionally, it creates a sense of community among the students who, throughout the semester, share with each other the highs ("Wow! My seed has a shoot!") and lows ("Oh no, it seems to be withering") of seed-nurturing. Even this simple task seems spontaneously to prompt reflection about wider issues of relationship. One student, for example, chose to plant a seed that came from flowers grown by her Guatemalan grandmother, and the exercise prompted a moving reflection on the student's connectedness with earlier generations and ancestral places. Another student bought her seed and soil from Walmart, and this prompted reflections on the commodification and industrialization of nature. Such responses provide a treasure trove of "teachable moments" through which I can help students to draw connections with course content. It allows some spontaneity into my online teaching. In addition, the personal nature of some of the reflections fosters a sense of trust and interconnectedness that counteracts the potential insularity of cyberspace.

Throughout the semester, the seed becomes a contemplative theme to which we repeatedly return in the context of course topics. For example, in one module, students read articles from aboriginal and non-Western perspectives that critique, among other things, Western individualism, materialism, and alienation from nature. For the contemplative exercise, students read a delightful story by Satish Kumar explaining the transition from individual self-centeredness to community awareness by using an analogy of a seed that sheds its casing and merges with the earth around it in order to thrive.[5] Students are invited to read the essay using Hart's "deep listening" technique, then to reflect on how the story relates to their own experiences and how assigned readings tie into the analogy of the seed. [6]

In the next module, students read about Buddhist perspectives on environmental issues. For contemplative reflection, I assign a reading by Thich Nhat Hanh that contains the following passage: "What we call a self is made only of nonself elements. When we look at a flower, for example, we may think that it is different from 'nonflower' things. But when we look more deeply, we see that everything in the cosmos is in that flower. Without all of the nonflower elements—sunshine, clouds, earth, minerals, heat, rivers, and consciousness—a flower cannot be."[7] Particularly thoughtful students are able to make the transition from awareness of the contingency of their growing seeds to their own contingency as individuals. In a related exercise, I invite students to become aware of what they are doing in the present moment and then to ask themselves: What are all of the conditions and factors that make this state of affairs possible? Both of these exercises give the students an experiential sense of their connectedness not only with the physical, nonhuman universe, but with an almost infinite regress of teachers, inventors, designers, builders, workers, ancestors, and other beings. Students begin to get a visceral understanding of how their self is dependent upon myriad not-self elements.

Various readings in the module on Buddhism focus on the concept of craving. The power of craving is excellently described by Pema Chödrön, who talks about being "hooked" by various thoughts and desires.[8] In order to observe this psychological phenomenon in their own experience, students first watch an online interview with Chödrön in which she explains the dynamic.[9] I then invite them to walk through a store or look through a magazine and note the number of times their attention is "hooked" by a desire for something, and to reflect on the felt quality of that experience.

The intent behind these contemplative exercises is to "live" a concept *experientially* and *interiorly*, so that students recognize its relevance in their own lives. Students are generally very enthusiastic about these exercises, and their papers at the end of the semester testify to levels of insight and engagement that can make for encouraging—sometimes even thrilling—reading. Most of the ideas for these exercises arise out of my own contemplative engagement with the course materials. I experience both gratitude and humility when I see that students so readily share their contemplative insights with me and with each other. It gives me the sense that, while we may have never met in person, we have shared a meeting of our minds across cyberspace.

NOTES

1. The anthology I use for this course is Richard C. Foltz, ed., *Worldviews, Religion, and the Environment: A Global Anthology* (Belmont: Wadsworth Thomson, 2003).
2. See Parker J. Palmer, *The Courage to Teach: Exploring the Inner Landscape of a Teacher's Life*, second edition (San Francisco: Jossey-Bass, 2007), 9–34.
3. Tobin Hart, "Opening the Contemplative Mind in the Classroom," *Journal of Transformative Education* 2, no. 1 (2004): 28–46. See also Arthur Zajonc, "Cognitive-Affective Connections in Teaching and Learning: The Relationship between Love and Knowledge," *Journal of Cognitive-Affective Learning* 3, no. 1 (2006): 1–9, as well as the multiple resources at www.contemplative mind.org/programs/academic.
4. At the Center for Contemplative Mind in Society Retreat for Academics, Phoenicia, New York, March 6–9, 2008.
5. Satish Kumar, *You Are Therefore I Am: A Declaration of Interdependence* (Dartington: Green Books, 2006), 18–19.
6. Hart, "Opening the Contemplative Mind," 9. In this exercise, students first center themselves, then listen to a reading, allowing an openness to the reading without trying to analyze it or "figure it out." They observe without judgment their own reactions to this experience.
7. Thich Nhat Hanh, "The Sun My Heart," in *Dharma Rain: Sources of Buddhist Environmentalism*, ed. Stephanie Kaza and Kenneth Kraft (Boston: Shambhala, 2000), 87.
8. Pema Chödrön, "How We Get Hooked, How We Get Unhooked," in *Hooked! Buddhist Writings on Greed, Desire, and the Urge to Consume*, ed. Stephanie Kaza (Boston: Shambhala, 2005), 27–33.
9. http://www.pbs.org/moyers/faithandreason/media_players/chodron_full. html.

22

MINDFULNESS IN THE HISTORY CLASSROOM

Teaching as Interbeing

SHU-CHIN WU

All social movements involve conflicts which are reflected intellectually in controversies. It would not be a sign of health if such an important social interest as education were not also an arena of struggles, practical and theoretical.

—John Dewey, *Experience and Education*

When I attend mindfulness or contemplative education workshops and seminars, I am frequently asked by fellow participants: "History? How do you teach history by using contemplative pedagogy?"[1] Occasionally, a few participants will jump to my defense and attest that "contemplative pedagogy can be used in *all* courses, regardless of the academic discipline." The doubting question and the resounding retort, with their conflicting views, evoke the new field of contemplative education as a wild place: uncharted, challenging, full of abundant opportunities. As a new and serious devotee of contemplative education, I set out on the journey into the wilderness by experimenting with contemplative pedagogy in the Asian history courses that I teach at my college. As I continue on this exploration, I have learned to think beyond conventional categories, be playful, respect what it *is* and let go of expectations, and, above all, transform obstacles into opportunities. Teaching, in this approach, is a *lived practice*.

MINDFULNESS AND INTERBEING

Mindfulness centers me in the lived practice of teaching. In the classroom, mindfulness provides a means of integrating what we learn with who we are. When colleagues who are passionate about contemplative teaching argue that contemplative pedagogy can be used in all courses, they often refer to mindfulness in its role as a tool to reduce stress and cultivate attention. This tool can be applied in classrooms of all grade levels and all disciplines. Those who doubt the validity of applying contemplative practice to history as a discipline are aware of the reality that contemporary historical thinking is neither meditative in its practice nor in its aim. History as a discipline has played a very minor role in the discourse of contemplative pedagogy. So, is there a specific historical insight that contemplative practice can help cultivate? How can mindfulness help students learn about history?

A powerful answer comes from the Vietnamese Zen teacher Thich Nhat Hanh. He suggests the term "interbeing" to elucidate that all phenomena are interdependent and endlessly interwoven. This understanding has guided my exploration between mindfulness and history as a discipline. According to Thich Nhat Hanh, to practice mindfulness and to look deeply into the nature of things is to discover the true nature of interbeing. "If you are a poet, you will see clearly that there is a cloud floating in this sheet of paper. . . . And if you continue to look, we can see the logger who cut the tree and brought it to the mill to transform into paper."[2] I have learned from teaching that not only the poet, but also the good historian should be able to see "the logger who cut the tree and brought it into the mill to transform into paper," because to understand history is to understand "the infinite extent of our relations," as Thoreau so eloquently put it.[3]

As a history teacher, with *whom* and with *what* do we have the interrelationship? First is the relationship between teachers and students. As the Dalai Lama reminds us, "There are no subjects without objects by which they are defined, there are no objects without subjects to apprehend them, there are no doers without things done."[4]

Without teachers, there are no students, and vice versa. Using interbeing as a contemplative mode of inquiry, I cease to be judgmental about students' pasts or their habitual ways of thinking, all of which have been influenced by their parents, previous educational experiences, and the culture. To "interbe" with them requires me to meet them *where they are*, to take into account the level of their familiarity with the activity or reactivity of their own minds, and then to introduce appropriate forms and methods of mindfulness practices to them. As a result, I stop being a solo, authoritative lecturer and become a co-traveler in the classroom.

The second relationship is between historians (or history students) and the texts. Historical texts can be understood more deeply when applying interbeing; that is, we understand that historical events only come into being as a result of the interaction of causes and conditions. The elements that make up what we call history are patterns of dependency and interweaving. There are no fixed ways of understanding them because history entails examining previously held beliefs. Contrary to conventional wisdom, texts rarely speak for themselves. To appreciate a historical text, we must dwell in the context of the text, and the result of this process will depend on the historian or history student who enters into the indwelling. The study of history therefore is a process of history, and how we view history varies greatly with the time of writing and with the assumptions of the individual historians.

Many schools nationwide, in all grade levels and in many disciplines, have been using contemplative techniques such as silence, meditation, and yoga in their classrooms with the purpose of quieting the mind and reducing stress.[5] Many anecdotal reports suggest that a few minutes of silent sitting at the beginning of a class benefit the students with increased concentration, inner calm, and mental clarity. Whatever the subject being studied, contemplative moments improve the students' performance of the task at hand.[6] Higher education, however, has been slow to integrate contemplative teaching techniques into classroom practice. Moreover, when it is used as a pedagogical approach, mindfulness is often limited to a handful of departments.

One of the chief obstacles facing contemplative education is the move into an area of study that is traditionally unfriendly to contemplative pedagogy. My own field, history, is an example. The emphasis of historical studies traditionally has been analytical, not contemplative. As a result, the teaching and learning of history in today's universities deal almost exclusively with analysis of historical texts and seem closed off to the possibility of incorporating contemplative inquiry.

Since there is no preexisting model for teaching history by using contemplative pedagogy, my initial attempts at applying contemplative method in my classes were filled with caution and anticipation of obstacles. I wondered if the conditions were ripe for using contemplation in teaching history. I also tried to be sensitive to the professional, institutional, and student cultures, looking for appropriate ways to bring the contemplative dimension into the classroom. I asked a lot of questions in contemplative workshops and seminars about the validity and appropriateness of incorporating contemplative pedagogy into different disciplines, especially in the field of history.

In my own classroom, at first I only planted the contemplative "seed" spontaneously when students seemed to be receptive to its message. It is only now, after several years of exploration, questioning, and contemplation and with the support of like-minded colleagues, that I have developed a clearer idea of teaching history by using contemplative pedagogy.

With a contemplative perspective, I come to understand that adopting a solely analytical approach to history is problematic in that the knower does not fully dwell in that which he or she knows. It is when we put ourselves in another person's shoes—through empathic understanding of the historical circumstances in which historical actors encounter and respond to their environment—that we can fully dwell in what we know and gain a more accurate and rounded understanding of history. Rather than detached observation alone, what develops student awareness is meaningful "encounter."

CONTEMPLATIVE EXERCISES IN THE CLASSROOM

What are some ways we can introduce "encountering" as contemplative practice in the history classroom? Since 2007, in my history course The Vietnam Wars, I have used different mindfulness exercises to invite students to encounter and experience history, instead of remaining indifferent, outside spectators of history. After previous semesters of piecemeal introduction of contemplative pedagogy, this time I made systematic efforts to further a contemplative orientation. The course's mindfulness exercises include: formal sitting meditation, focused attention, stopping, free writes, reflection papers, deep listening, and mindful speech. The emphasis is placed not so much on formal meditation but instead on bringing awareness to the present moment and into the study of history. These exercises are designed to help students to see what happens in their conscious and unconscious mind and to invite them to experience the clear, open, vast, and alert state of mind when they are at ease.

Exercise 1: Stopping

One exercise I have used is to show a documentary film about the Vietnam War at the beginning of the course, before students learn anything substantive about the war. Right after viewing, before students have had time to reflect analytically on the film, I give them one minute to write down an immediate response. Then, I ask them to stop, cease all activities, and create a reflective space in which they observe whatever is going on in their own mind. After that, I ask them to write a reflection paper about the film as well as examine their initial reaction to it.

What makes this exercise contemplative is that it gives students the opportunity to see where they are, open to (and accept) their inner dialogue, explore new ways of knowing themselves, and read historical texts (including films) in a contemplative manner. One student wrote in her first reaction to the film: "I am suddenly very tense—I have gone all rigid at the images of death and war. Oddly enough, confusion fills my head." After the stopping exercise, she reflected,

> I must admit that after watching the film, I couldn't seem to formulate any clear thought or opinion. After my emotions had time to settle and my mind was once again able to focus, I came to the realization that "pointless" was perhaps the best way to sum up my opinion of American involvement in Vietnam. In sum, I was frustrated by the knowledge gained from the film.

Another student also testified to the usefulness of stopping. She wrote,

> After the film when we practiced stopping, I felt the urge to write more and to let my emotions take over. I kept on thinking of the subject and the different scenes and recordings. Even while writing I kept on thinking. It was just hard not to think and to stop everything. I wanted to criticize and debate the issues, but after awhile I felt myself calming down. Stopping was a different practice for me. Others support us to think further and to keep on going but it does make a student overwhelmed and tired. Stopping gave me a chance to take a break and to come back to the subject when I was calm and taking control of myself, which helped me to be open and to be willing to let others speak.

Ah, "To be open and to be willing to let others speak"! When I read students' reflections, I smile at the way in which they encounter their emotions, their judgment, and subsequently the historical texts—in this instance, a film. It is not simply that a particular student is affected by a particular contemplative practice. Rather, the whole classroom environment opens up. The spirit of letting others speak creates a new environment— an open space— for the class. Did Parker Palmer not once remark, "To teach is to create space"?[7] After the stopping exercise, a multiplicity of voices begins to be heard; disagreements, arguments, debates become doors to understanding, not conflict.

Exercise 2: Contemplative "Debate"—Mindful Speech and Deep Listening

A particularly powerful contemplative exercise in the Vietnam War course is to apply deep listening and mindful speech to a class "debate." For the debate, I divide the students into two groups to recreate the debate that took place during the critical meeting of the National Security Council at the White House on July 27, 1965. One group of students argues in favor of escalating the United States' military role in Vietnam, while the other takes the position of asking for disengagement of the United States' involvement in Vietnam. In the past, I have employed traditional rules of debate, and the debates have yielded mixed results. Then I decided to introduce listening and speaking as dimensions of contemplation. I explain that these are based on the deep listening and mindful speech teachings of the Vietnamese Buddhist peace activist and writer Thich Nhat Hanh. I lay out a simple formula: during the debate, students are encouraged to be open, nonjudgmental, and unassuming and to have the intent to understand rather than to criticize. The students are required to reiterate their opponents' arguments to demonstrate that they truly understand the entirety of the other side's perspectives before they articulate their disagreements.

At the outset of the first debate, a student commented uneasily that she had never done anything like this before. "Neither have I," I said. I did not know what to expect. This might be a complete disaster, I thought to myself. What if it failed? Do I need a backup plan? What was going to happen next? Then I realized that a classroom of silent, puzzled faces was staring at me. I returned to the present and managed to say: "If you do it mindfully, you cannot do it wrong. There is no right or wrong in this debate. Just be aware—aware of what you hear and what you say." The students sat quietly for a while. Some hesitated before they uttered their first words. Then there was a long silence and more hesitation. Discomfort filled the room.

Slowly, the debate happened. I do not really know what prompted the change, but something shifted. The act of contemplation began. Students began to debate their assigned points of view and rebutted others' views by using deep listening and mindful speech, not only with their usual eloquence but also with compassion and understanding, clarity, and tranquility. It was one of the most joyful moments in my teaching career. Mindfulness created a contemplative space that invited students to encounter their own emotions and reactions, to understand both sides of the conflict, and thereby to gain a fuller understanding of history.

FINAL REFLECTION

At the end of the semester, I ask the students to write a reflection paper on the reflection they wrote at the beginning of the semester. The idea is for them to see their own progress during one semester, to see how much they have learned and changed. One student made this comment about the stopping exercise at the beginning of the semester: "This 'stopping' might be needed for the war managers. I wonder if they stopped and thought about what was really happening . . . would they have still continued the war." It is a great delight to read how mindfulness teaches students insights about history. Another student wrote,

"This course not only increased my knowledge about the history of Vietnam and the American War in Vietnam, it also encouraged me to think deeply and critically examine my assumptions about history and the logic used to justify war."

The examples of students who take naturally to mindfulness, however, should not lead us to underestimate the challenges and obstacles facing contemplative educators. In the process of teaching mindfulness in the history classroom, I have been surprised, angered, amused, and disappointed. I was sometimes encouraged, sometimes discouraged. Some students welcome mindfulness exercises in the classroom. Some resist it. Some who welcome mindfulness are not prepared for the kind of encounters that it brings. The experience of incorporating mindfulness in my classroom enriches my experience as a teacher, helps me foster a greater awareness of the difficulties that are facing contemplative educators, and gives me strength and courage to open up dialogues and develop methods to respond to these challenges. The practice of interbeing serves as my anchor to navigate through the obstacles that arise on the path. To interbe with my students, I have to meet them wherever they are. Through practicing and teaching mindfulness, I experience more moments of deep joy. I connect with my students in a new, profound way. Mindfulness not only transforms my students. It also transforms me.

NOTES

1. In this chapter, the terms mindfulness, meditation, and contemplation are used broadly and interchangeably to refer to methods of training the mind.
2. Thich Nhat Hanh, *Peace Is Every Step* (New York: Bantam Books, 1991), 95.
3. Henry David Thoreau, *Walden*, chapter 8.
4. His Holiness the Dalai Lama, *The Universe in a Single Atom* (New York: Morgan Road Books, 2006), 64.
5. Barry Boyce, "Please Help Me Learn Who I Am," *Shambhala Sun* 15, no. 3 (January 2007): 66–73, 119–20; Patricia Leigh Brown, "In the Classroom, a New Focus on Quieting the Mind," *New York Times* (June 16, 2007); Charles Burack, "Returning Meditation to Education," *Tikkun* 14, no. 5 (September/October 1999): 41–46.
6. Piper Murray, "Meeting on Contemplative Pedagogy in the Disciplines: Philosophy, Religious Studies, Psychology," Center for Contemplative Mind in Society, Amherst College, March 28–30, 2008; M. Duerr, A. Zajonc, and D. Dana, "Survey of Transformative and Spiritual Dimensions of Higher Education," *Journal of Transformative Education* 1, no. 3 (2003): 177–211.
7. Parker J. Palmer, *The Courage to Teach: Exploring the Inner Landscape of a Teacher's Life* (San Francisco: Jossey-Bass, 1995), 95.

23

TWO CONTEMPLATIVE PRACTICES THAT ANIMATE THE STUDY OF RELIGION

JOHN D. COPENHAVER

Many languages use the same word to designate breath and spirit: in Hebrew *ruah*; in Greek *pneuma*; in Latin *spiritus*; in Sanskrit *prana*; in Chinese *chi*. Like spirit, breath is mysterious, invisible, inspiring, and animating. In short, breath/spirit is essential to life. This thought is alarming with the realization that one of the defining characteristics of our technological age is its breathlessness. We now possess a dizzying array of gadgets that enable us to multitask and to carry our networking into our leisure and vacations. For many of our students, this is the only world they know. They have few occasions to catch their breath and contemporary academic life only seems to exacerbate the problem.

Consider this portion of a student response to a Skyscape/Mindscape assignment (to be described further on):

> Running, Running,
> I have to go,
> Running, Running,
> I don't have time for that,
> Running, Running,
> I need to eat,
> Running, Running,
> I have rehearsal in 10 minutes,
> Running, Running
> I have to go practice now,
> Running, Running
> STOP, STOP,
> CALM DOWN AND STOP RUNNING!!!!!
> —Feleighta Green

217

When she finally slowed down to contemplate the sky, she realized that she was always running and "never stopping to breathe."

The Greek feminine word for scholar, transliterated *schole*, means rest or leisure, literally, "a pause." Why then is contemporary academic life so frenetic? Certainly the legitimate drive for accountability in higher education plays a role. We are expected to develop "learning outcomes" for our courses and demonstrate that we have met those outcomes through rigorous assessment. Class time set aside for contemplative exercises appears to run counter to this academic ethos. My argument here is that limited, strategically planned contemplative exercises (in and out of the classroom) are not a hindrance to learning but, in fact, enrich and enliven the learning environment and enable students to better grasp key ideas.

In teaching my classes on world religions, I ordinarily employ the phenomenological method. But, in some of my classes I also include an experiential component because I want students to taste, however momentarily, religious experience from the inside. These experiential exercises have the capacity to breathe life into religious studies and expose the beating heart of faith. Slowing students down, quieting them, does not force religious experience on them, but creates the conditions where the apprehension of something "more"[1] can occur. In each class, the something "more" is directly related to the ideas/practices we are studying. Drawing on spiritual exercises I learned during graduate studies at the Shalem Institute in Washington, D.C., I have found ways to incorporate short Sabbaths into the classroom that refresh and enrich the learning experience.

SKYSCAPE/MINDSCAPE EXERCISE

I have space to describe briefly only two of the contemplative practices I use. The first is the Skyscape/Mindscape writing assignment I mentioned earlier in the chapter. This is the only reflective writing assignment I do in my introductory philosophy and religion classes. Typically they have five or six other analytical writing assignments closely related to assigned readings. This assignment does not count much in their final grade (the same as the other assignments), but I do expect them to do it. Sometimes I describe it as a break (a sort of Sabbath) in their educational journey. I do not grade it on content, but rather on their writing, creativity, and, to be honest, a rather intangible quality of authenticity.

In making the assignment, I note that Tom Robbins advised writers to spend a half hour a day doing each of four things: reading poetry (to keep the mind limber); doing yoga or running (to stay physically grounded); thinking about sex ('nuff said); observing the sky (because this is the origin of many religious and philosophical insights). To introduce the assignment, I also use "sky quotes" from poems, the Bible, Shakespeare, and "even concentration camp survivors who cherished their view of the sky as one of the few things the Nazis could not take away."[2]

Assignment

1. Spend one half hour (in solitude) observing the night sky. Describe in some detail the date, time, and weather. This section should include a detailed *skyscape*. By skyscape I mean painting a verbal description of the sky. [I started asking this when I suspected that some students never even went outside; they just started writing the mindscape. Of course, there is no guarantee that they do not invent the skyscape.]

2. Do a *mindscape*. When you get back to your computer, write about what was going on in your mind (only what you are comfortable sharing) during the half hour set aside for observing the sky. It can be in the form of a dialogue, a soliloquy, a poem, a series of questions, or random observations.

When these are due, I have students discuss their papers (two to three pages) in small groups. As we reconvene as a larger class I ask groups to nominate someone from their group to present her or his Skyscape/Mindscape. The nominee can decline, but usually does not. Sometimes I also ask for volunteers. Here is another example of a poetic portion of a Skyscape/Mindscape exercise entitled "Why?"

> Where is your friendly little smile tonight?
> Do you choose to show your teeth only when
> You want to? The grey clouds float like a kite
> Through the abyss of darkness. Many men
> Have tried to unlock the secret of your
> Mysteries. Unfortunately, they find
> You to be leading them on a false tour.
> What is it that you will not let unwind?
> Is the day the root of your selfishness?
> Why doesn't the moon come out to play tonight?
> Is it envious of the sun's long bliss?
> Instead of teaching wrong and right,
> You condone this bad type of behavior;
> While all along, it was your light we savored.
> —Brian Jones

Although students do not learn anything specific about religion or philosophy in this exercise, it does make them more self-aware. They often find their problems, which seem so overwhelming, brought into perspective as they observe the vastness of the heavens. Sometimes they express renewed gratitude for life, for family, and friends. And, occasionally old wounds are reopened. It also functions well as a creative, reflective writing exercise in the midst of the welter of analytical writing they must do. And, without knowing it, they are practicing a rudimentary form of awareness practice, akin to *vipassana* meditation from the Buddhist tradition.

TEACHING A STONE TO TALK[3]

In my courses Religion and Ecology and Asian Religion and Philosophy, we discuss Japanese Shinto and its profound attention to nature. Usually, we have also discussed Zen Buddhism and the concept on nonduality, along with the various art forms that are designed to express/cultivate nondual perception. When we discuss the Shinto shrine (or *honden*), I mention that each inner sanctum contains an object, *shintai*, in which a god, *kami*, is discovered. The *kami* might be discovered in a stone, a mountain, or a bronze mirror. For this exercise I use a stone. I do not pretend we are practicing Shinto, but I do want them, however briefly, to enter imaginatively into Shinto sacred space. For a moment we leave our "objective" examination of religion, and enter it subjectively. These occasional exercises (once every week or two), usually taking no more than fifteen to twenty minutes, enliven our study and help students appreciate practices that may seem odd on first glance.

For this exercise, I bring to class a large forty-pound limestone rock from our garden. It has patches of lichen and moss growing on it. I conceal it from the class until the exercise. I tell the class we are privileged to have a guest lecturer today. Then, with some fanfare, I place the stone on a black cloth that covers the central table. My classes are usually small enough (fifteen to twenty) that students can get close to the rock. The stone has a definite presence. In the sterile environment of the classroom, the stone looks old, strange, and wild.

Instruction

I invite everyone to study/contemplate the stone for several minutes, simply observing it without thinking. Then, I invite everyone to "listen" to the stone, one of our venerable elders, and what it might say to us or teach us. Finally, students write about their observations and "conversation." I usually allow two to three minutes for simple observation and four to five minutes for listening/conversing with the stone. This is followed by five to ten minutes of writing. We then break into small groups for discussion. When we reconvene as a larger group, I usually seek a few volunteers to discuss the experience.

We then discuss how a stone might be a revelation of the sacred, and why a Shintoist might discover a *kami* in a stone. In the process, some students comment on a *numinous* quality in the stone, though they do not use that word. They discover a certain awe in its age and are surprised that this inanimate object apparently hosts numerous life forms. And, occasionally, they sense the quiet, passive wisdom in the stone. Some students will also make connections with Taoism and its concept of *pu*, the uncarved block in all its naturalness.

Course evaluations indicate that students welcome these occasional interludes for contemplative exercises and believe that they make an important contribution to their learning. In my view, they add a dimension of depth to the learning experience that is not available through discussion or lectures or media. Perhaps the closest correlate would be the natural science lab. In the lab, students confirm, by observation and experimentation, the theories/information they are learning through reading and lectures. If I did more of these exercises in class, I could imagine courses in religious studies that would have a one-hour lab associated with the course. Until then, I find that the limited, strategically planned contemplative exercises animate students and teachers, helping them to catch their breath and assimilate course content.

NOTES

Excerpts from student writing assignments in this chapter appear with the permission of the students.

1. Marcus Borg uses this language in *The Heart of Christianity: Rediscovering a Life of Faith* (San Francisco: Harper Collins, 2004), 61–66.

2. John Larrabee, "Students Look to the Skies for Inspiration," *USA Today* 7 (August 1996): 4(D).

3. The title of this section is taken from Annie Dillard, *Teaching a Stone to Talk: Expeditions and Encounters* (New York: Harper Collins, 1982). Anyone leading this contemplative exercise would probably find her chapter by that title useful. It could also be part of course readings.

24

MINDFULNESS AND CONTEMPLATIVE PRACTICE IN ART AND RELIGION

DEBORAH J. HAYNES

Teaching courses on sacred art in the great traditions of the world provides an excellent opportunity to introduce contemplative pedagogy, for it harmonizes with the sacred environment of the artist and with the culture in which the sacred art is enjoyed. For example, in the course The Dialogue of Art and Religion, students learn about Russian Orthodox icons, Himalayan Buddhist *thangkas*, and Navajo sandpaintings through studying cultural and social history, religion, formal visual analysis, and creative processes. I define this interdisciplinary teaching as a form of comparative visual studies. I normally teach this class to eighteen or twenty first-year students. Students also learn about related practices of prayer and meditation that are central to sacred traditions through practice and sustained reading and discussion.

Given the diversity of these artistic traditions, there is no single way to describe their contemplative practices. The Latin *contemplari* means to observe, consider, or gaze attentively. This definition gives clues about a way to introduce a kind of generic contemplative practice that includes four basic postures of sitting, standing, walking, and lying down. Broadly understood as methods to develop concentration, deepen understanding and insight, and to cultivate awareness and compassion, these practices can have a profound impact on a student's experience both in college and beyond. While diverse contemplative practices are rooted in the world's religious traditions, I often tell parents and students that the application of these more generic practices in a secular educational context can enhance the educational experience in unique ways. Specifically, teaching students techniques of awareness, concentration, and ways of disciplining their attention is absolutely essential in our era of fragmentation, ever-increasing speed, multitasking, and continuously interrupted attention. In my class students learn to refine their perceptual and observational skills. They are encouraged to take chances and to foster attitudes such as curiosity and wonder, rather than cynicism about the world in which we live. This chapter outlines five simple techniques that I introduce to students in this course. Each description includes notes about the relative value of introducing that particular practice.

1. The Bow. On the first day of class after all students have arrived, I introduce "the bow" before undertaking any other introductory comments.[1] I ask all of the students to sit up straight, to place their hands on their thighs and both feet on the floor, and to soften their gaze toward the center of the room. Arranging the classroom in a circle makes this exercise more meaningful, but it is possible to do it in a larger lecture-style classroom as well. After everyone has stopped moving, I simply bow my head and upper torso toward the table and invite them to do the same. I then talk about what this means in two ways: starting that first day, I ask the students to be fully present in class and to cultivate an attitude of respect for others and the material that we will be studying. We end the class with the same gesture. Over time, this collective bow becomes a profound symbol of presence and respect in the classroom.

2. Six Points of Posture. A few classes later, I suggest that the students might find it helpful to practice the "six points of posture" as they bow.[2] This exercise adds greatly to their initial concentration when they arrive in class. Many students feel self-conscious and awkward the first few times they try this, but they have repeatedly told me that over time it helps them to feel connected to the class. To establish a stable *seat*, I ask students to sit near the edge of the chair. The *legs* should be neither crossed nor stretched out, and the feet are directly under the knees. The *hands* are placed palms down on the thighs. The *torso* is relaxed, and the spine should be straight, tilting neither to the front nor back, left nor right. The *eyes* are kept open, gazing down at a spot about three to four feet in front of the student. The *lips and mouth* should be slightly open, tongue resting against the upper palate behind the teeth.

3. Mindful Breathing and Sitting Meditation. Sitting in this posture, mindful breathing and sitting meditation help to relax and focus the mind. None of us can prevent stressful situations in life, but we can begin to learn how to control our reactions to these situations. I also tell students that many religious traditions teach methods of working with the breath as part of prayer and meditation.[3]

Adopting the six points of posture, I ask students to bring attention to the breathing. Sometimes we observe the sensations of the breath moving in the abdomen, the diaphragm, or the lungs. Sometimes we focus on the light touch of air as it enters the nostrils. Sometimes we count the breath: on the exhalation, one; next exhalation, two; and all the way to ten or twenty-one. Then we start again at one. I remind students that depending upon their state of mind, their attention may wander. If so, they should name what it wanders to and come back to the breathing and counting. For instance, if a student is worried about an upcoming test, I might advise that person simply to acknowledge "I'm anxious," or "I'll think about that later"; and then to return to the breath. While every person's mind can seem impossible to tame, at moments we are able to rest in a quiet and calm state that is refreshing. If a group seems especially engaged by this kind of breath meditation, I urge them to look dispassionately at the reactions and habits of the mind. Once they have practiced focusing on the breathing, I suggest that they experiment by using sensations, sounds, or watching thoughts as the point of concentration.

4. *Beholding.* After experimenting with a series of eye exercises that help students to become aware of how they can focus their vision, students are ready to learn how to view icons, *thangkas*, and sandpaintings. I teach them how to "behold," to experience these works of art firsthand. When it is possible, I invite students to pick up a work of art, to hold it in their hands and look closely. If they cannot touch it, then we get as close as possible in order to examine the object. Sometimes this results in an experience of tremendous intimacy; at other times students are awed by what they see. Beholding is a counter both to the usual two-second walk-by experience that characterizes much museum looking and to the analytical dissection of a work of art. My own love of Buddhist *thangkas* and Islamic manuscripts and calligraphy, for example, has grown from this kind of sustained beholding. Taking students to museums and bringing actual works of art to class helps to make this a more vivid encounter for the students.

5. *Contour Portraits.* Learning to look at works of art *with regard* can be a new and profound experience for students who take so much of visual culture for granted. I teach the students blind contour drawing with their classmates as a way to learn how to observe with an attitude of deep respect.[4] Contour drawing involves trying to focus the attention, to merge touch and sight. The practice is to move the eye along with the pencil, keeping the body relaxed, and not looking at the paper. The most difficult part of the exercise for most students is to resist worrying about the outcome. Students work in pairs, where one student is the "artist," the other the "model." Then they reverse roles. Usually I start with one-minute timed portraits. Depending upon student engagement with the exercise, I may repeat it several times, with students changing partners and lengthening the amount of time for each round. Cultivating respect for one another through this exercise, I hope to awaken a greater sense of regard for the art we study.

Over the past few years my students have spoken about the way mindfulness exercises help to foster an atmosphere of respect in the classroom. They often note how these practices have effectively brought the class together as a whole, and how they help to ease general anxiety about classroom performance. When courses actively create a respectful environment, students learn to listen, write, and argue persuasively from a position of civility, which helps them to become principled community members. Perhaps most significantly, contemplative practice fosters development of what Martin Buber called "I-Thou" relationships, where other people, events, and things are treated as subjects and not merely as objects for use or enjoyment.[5] Most of us live, most of the time, in a narrow band of existence where we are surrounded by "I," "me," and "mine," and we suffer from this narrow focus. I have wondered how to help students become more present to themselves, to others, and to the greater world. As a teacher, how can I ignite passion in my students for this kind of presence in their own lives? This is precisely the work of contemplative pedagogy: it is about waking up and being present to our lives—here and now.

NOTES

1. Chögyam Trungpa wrote briefly about the bow in *Shambhala: The Sacred Path of the Warrior* (Boston: Shambhala, 1984), 138–40.

2. See Pema Chödrön, *Comfortable with Uncertainty: 108 Teachings* (Boston: Shambhala, 2002), 15–16.

3. The practical use of mindfulness outlined here is extrapolated from the teachings of Thich Nhat Hanh, *The Miracle of Mindfulness: A Manual on Meditation* (Boston: Beacon Press, 1976), and Jon Kabat-Zinn, *Full Catastrophe Living: Using the Wisdom of Your Body and Mind to Face Stress, Pain, and Illness* (New York: Delacorte Press, 1990). For a useful overview of approaches from Christian, Jewish, Sufi, Hindu, and Buddhist traditions, see Marcia Z. Nelson, *Come and Sit* (Woodstock: Skylight Paths, 2001). On working with the breath, see Richard Rosen, *The Yoga of Breath: A Step-by-Step Guide to Pranayama* (Boston: Shambhala, 2002).

4. Kimon Nicolaides, *The Natural Way to Draw: A Working Plan for Art Study* (Boston: Houghton Mifflin, 1941).

5. Martin Buber, *I and Thou*, trans. Ronald Gregor Smith (New York: Scribner, 1958).

VI

CONCLUSION

Does It Work? Evaluations from Our Students

25

EMOTIONAL LEARNING

Re-cognizing Emotion in a Buddhism Course

JUDITH SIMMER-BROWN

For the last thirty years, I have taught a text seminar for graduate students on the foundational primary texts, in translation, from Indian Buddhism. A portion of the course focuses on the tradition of the Abhidharma, the third "basket" of the Buddhist canon that systematizes the commentarial material from the early Indian tradition. These texts are notoriously opaque, appearing as books of lists that are unadorned taxonomies of mental states discovered in Buddhist meditation. Frankly, teaching these texts began as a daunting enterprise. But, as the years have passed, contemplative pedagogy has brought many opportunities for the texts to serve as gateways for students to investigate emotions.

In recent years, I have also taught a version of this course online as a Naropa University elective. My online students are less academically prepared, for the most part, than my degree-seeking students, but they come from a variety of fascinating settings—business travelers, members of the military in remote locations, European and Asian students, people caring for an elderly parent, as well as on-campus undergraduate degree-seeking students with difficult academic schedules. In the online medium, I have continued to use contemplative methods, teaching meditation practice that is a required part of course homework, and guiding contemplations on the subject matter of the course, such as the unit on emotion. Student outcomes in the narratives on guided contemplations are essentially the same as with my students in the live classroom. The student comments quoted further on are all from my online students from 2001 to the present.

There is no real Sanskrit or Tibetan word for "emotion," and the terms used are colored by their ethical and soteriological result. For example, *klesha* (*kilesa* in

229

Pali, *nyon-mongs* in Tibetan), deriving from the Sanskrit root of the word meaning "torture," leads to painful results when acted upon. Wholesome emotions,
kushala in Sanskrit (*kusala* in Pali, *mkha-pa* in Tibetan), are so-called because
they lead to temporary, pleasant experiences of well-being. Our course examines
the context of these terms and the emotional experiences associated with each,
based on the sutras of the first "basket," which suggest that the experience of suffering is the foundation of the Buddhist path.[1] The sutras assert: the primary
content of suffering is painful emotionality that fuels impulsive actions that lead
to further painful results.

The purpose of this unit of the course is to examine emotions, both positive
and negative, in a context of mindfulness practice and to see what we can learn
about them. Of course, we are also identifying the worldview and wisdom of
ancient Buddhist texts, which we explore from a third-person perspective as well,
developing historical context and philosophic view. Yet when students add their
first-person investigation to the study, the learning has an impact beyond the
narrow course content.

I invite students to investigate for themselves: What are emotions, in their
experience? How would they contrast the experience of emotions as opposed to
sense perceptions or thoughts? For additional context, we investigate the relative
paucity of emotional research in the West until the last century, compared with
twenty-five hundred years of Buddhist resources on emotion.[2] We then begin
our own research, adding first-person investigation to the third-person study of
the Buddhist texts.

In the beginning first-person investigation, I draw on a medieval Tibetan
monastic practice of noting the texture of states of mind as they arise and pass
away, using piles of dark and light dried beans.[3] Each student takes a small handful of each kind of bean, and places them on either side of their desktops, leaving
an open space directly in front of them. We begin mindfulness practice, settling
the mind by placing attention on breathing. After about four minutes of mindfulness practice, I invite the students to recall a recent experience in which they
felt strong emotion. As their memories arise in detail, I ask them to move beans
directly in front of them, one for each state of mind they witness. A dark bean
signifies a "heavy, hot, dark, sticky" emotion or mental state, while a light bean
signifies "light, bright, cool, clean" emotions. Recognizing the emotional states
arise and pass quickly (every sixtieth of a second, according to Abhidharma
texts), I invite them to move dynamically, noting the fluctuation of emotional
states. The main instructions are to observe emotional states without any
attempt to judge or change them. If judgment comes, they are to note it and
continue the observation. When a plotline develops, they are to pay attention to
the feeling-tone rather than the specific events or justifications that arise. The
determination of "light" or "heavy" is a subjective one that may come from
observing the feeling-tone of body and mind.

In class, we have a discussion about their experience. Online students journal about their experience, in response to prompts in a threaded discussion.

> The color of beans oscillated between the dark and light beans with each storyline that occurred in my thought process. A thought would arise, followed by an emotion, being either a white or dark bean, then that thought would change, [causing] my emotion to change to the opposite color bean. Eventually, the story would fall away and both emotions would cease. This is exactly what I learned from this meditation practice that emotions arise and fall with the thoughts that rise and fall. The emotions follow a curve, similar to a sine graph, equal values of hot, negative, heavy and light, cool, positive. (RF 2008)

Another student describes his experience of the practice:

> This exercise was very helpful in pointing out the moment-to-moment nature of our emotions. Quickly labeling each thought as dark or light simplified the practice. Sometimes my initial feeling of darkness or lightness would change as I was placing the bean. For example, it is a very dark and foggy day out here next to the Pacific. I caught a glimpse of the fog pouring in towards me over the ridge outside my window. My initial emotion was dread or fear and darkness, so I labeled it with a dark bean, but then that emotion evolved into a light one as I felt glad to be experiencing this foggy aspect of the world. (RG 2006)

This student reflected on the total experience of the practice, giving an overview:

> Negative emotions stirred my mind with a kind of antic energy. Impatience, for example, led to fidgeting and would probably leave me feeling worn out if it continued for too long. Negative emotions like anger can give a quick rush of alertness, but it burns up quickly. The sense of energy from a positive emotion, such as a calm feeling of patience, brought a more healthy sense of energy—relaxed, alert, and without agitation. It too was temporary, but a positive emotion seems less likely to leave me feeling depleted. The experience of a negative emotion felt sort of enclosed and obscured. It was like a temporary narrowing of vision. When I felt inattentive I would place a dark bean in front of me—it felt right to do so because inattention seemed to both take up and dull my whole mind. (PR 2006)

In the next week, I introduce a new investigation, based on the texts' depiction of "root" *kleshas* of hatred, desire, and bewilderment, and additional lists from the *Abhidharma-samuccaya*, totaling twenty-six recurring *kleshas*.[4] Each is described phenomenologically as psychological experience, and commentaries from the Tibetan tradition summarize the main points.

> What is anger? It is a vindictive attitude towards sentient beings, towards frustration, and towards that which gives rise to one's frustrations. Its function is to serve as a basis for fault-finding and for never finding even a moment of happiness.[5]

Commentaries add that anger, for example, exaggerates the negative qualities of the object while dismissing its positive qualities, dramatically distorting our perceptions. It also roughens the mind, making ordinary situations unbearable.[6]

Then we sit together in class at our desks, or in front of our computers, in mindful meditation. In my online audio instructions, I ask students to remember a recent time when they felt angry or enraged. I lead them through the contemplation: Let your memory return to the experience. Who was there? What was happening? Who said what, who did what? I encourage them to allow the memory to be as vivid as possible. What is hatred or anger? What does it feel like physically? Emotionally? Mentally? When they are finished, I ask them to describe their experiences without any judgment or plotline. I also ask them to note what happens if they try to suppress or manipulate their emotions.

The results are powerful, as students let themselves revisit painful feelings and get to know them a bit. A student describes intense anger and its aftermath.

> Yes, I experience *kleshas* or torturous emotions, but the one *klesha* that rears its ugly head the most is aggressiveness, hatred, and anger. I experience a spiraling from one moment of anger to all the past, related anger experiences and potential or future anger experiences. During this time there is no way to see clearly or experience peace of mind. The spiraling just continues, out of control. It is true that everything that happens during this escalated spiraling is filtered through the rage and can only be viewed as dangerous and threatening. Obsession with the negative, to the point of not being able to let go, I almost feel a "thriving" in my anger. It's true for me that the mind during this time cannot settle, but is restless and definitely any attempts to move away from the suffering only intensify one's torturous emotions. Dissatisfaction, disappointment, guilt, hurt, loss of self-respect, loneliness, anger with yourself, and ultimately depression are what I experience as suffering. (SS 2003)

Experiencing intense emotions within the context of meditation allows students to find an alternative to the intensity. This does not mean rejecting emotions; instead, it is possible to experience the intensity without pouring fuel on the fire. Mindfulness and awareness provide a direct way to see how intense emotions are painful, and when we can experience pain directly, it is possible to drop our habitual patterns without forcing ourselves to do so. When we experience the painfulness of a flame against our outstretched hands, we will naturally pull away, and that is what mindfulness and awareness show us. This student describes graphically the experience of being swept away by intense emotion, and then finding ground by returning to mindfulness of breathing.

> Being shaken up and smashed by a wave, being tickled with electric feathers, a burning orb of spinning screams. I experience the *kleshas* in my stomach, or in my heart, trapped in muscles, some are warm, some are icy, some are sharp others are like a mist. A shooting of racing reactions goes off, if unrecognized, I am lost, I am the *klesha*, raging, suffering, speaking harsh words, reacting impulsive and deluded. They may make absolutely no sense, they don't—nonetheless, my whole perception is transformed by them, distorted, it's like looking out of some mind goggles that create atmospheres for reality. . . . I find the breath to be KEY. Meditation allows observation, the observer disappears and awareness is the ground. . . . There is a space, a gap a flash of choice, whereby there is an opportunity to be at the eye of the spiral enjoying the arising of vibrations and experiences. This only happens to me when my practice is regular. (FA 2003)

When the emotions become very intense, I ask the students to consciously drop the plotline, the storyline. Mindfulness of breathing places them in the present moment with intense emotions, so that they can feel the emotional energy directly.

> In my experience of *kleshas*, they usually begin as something small such as an offhand comment and spiral into something large that seems to take over my world. One *klesha* leads to the next, jealousy, anger, irritation and on and on. This spiral of negative emotions is usually fueled by my internal dialog and discursiveness. When I see this start to happen it is very helpful for me to just take a deep breath and drop my storylines for a second. (KM 2001)

Sometimes, the plotline creates an important foundation for the emotional intensity, but if we can feel the emotion directly, not obsessing about the story, then the plotline changes dramatically. This student had been drawn into the emotional drama of a friend, and felt extreme anger toward her.

In doing the meditation her face came up for me. I could feel my whole body tense, my stomach especially. It was difficult to stay with this discomfort. I could feel my body get hot and kept trying to think about something else. Eventually, I don't remember exactly when, I started to laugh out loud at myself. The intensity of my anger about my friend suddenly seemed so absurd. She hasn't done anything to me. Yet, here I sit full of rage and discomfort. When the instruction was to let it go I could feel the last of the tension leave my body. Suddenly, I could let go of my desire to control her. Through humor I found the space I needed to move out of the spiral of my experience of the *kleshas*. (AS 2008)

After these guided contemplations on intense feelings, we discuss the usual ways we avoid feeling our emotions. We either suppress them or distance ourselves from them, or we indulge in them and cathartically dump them on others. The Abhidharma texts imply that direct experience of painful emotions, rather than just being swept away by them, leads to the opportunity to let them go. When we fully feel their pain, we can surrender them while honoring the curiosity of our minds. This student responds from her experience with mindfulness of intense emotions.

I found that sometimes after meditating with focus on the breath, the mind's curiosity rises, wanting to know again what it was that bothered it so much before the meditation. A few times I decided to experiment and watch to see where it went because I really couldn't remember what the *klesha* was and how awful it was. Like someone who had lost their keys, the mind methodically retraced itself back to the *klesha*—and there I was with it again! I realized how tricky that was! It's like a magnet how it wants to get back there! I could see how rather than stay in that empty moment, it wanted to return to old familiar activity. This helped me to see curiosity as a function of the mind's nature, and to understand more deeply what being with a new moment is instead of going back. (YA 2001)

My students report that this emotional learning is wonderfully empowering for them. They see that they are not alone in the experience of inner turmoil. They become skilled with contemplative tools and perspectives that allow them a full emotional life without feeling helpless before an emotional hijacking. They learn that intense emotion, when unexamined and not directly experienced, drives them to cause harm to themselves and others. They also learn that there is wisdom within the emotion, and when they learn to listen to intense emotions within the context of mindfulness, that wisdom is available to enrich their everyday lives.

NOTES

1. Dhamma-cakka-ppavattana-sutta, Rewata Dhamma, *The First Discourse of the Buddha* (Boston: Wisdom Publications, 1997), 17–21; Ariya-pariyesana Sutta, John J. Holder, ed. and trans., *The Early Buddhist Discourses* (Indianapolis: Hackett, 2006), 1–18.
2. William James, "What Is an Emotion?" *Mind* 9 (1884): 188–205; Robert Solomon, *The Passions: Emotions and the Meaning of Life* (Indianapolis: Hackett, 1993); Paul Ekman, *Emotions Revealed* (New York: Holt, 2007); Daniel Goleman, *Emotional Intelligence* (New York: Bantam Books, 1995).
3. In Tibet, black and white stones are used. I learned this practice from H. E. Shamar Rinpoche in the early 1980s. It is also described in Geshe Gyatso, *Meaningful to Behold* (London: Tharpa, 1985); Georges B. J. Dreyfus, *The Sound of Two Hands Clapping* (Berkeley: University of California Press, 2003).
4. *Abhidharma Samuccaya of Asanga*, French translation by Walpola Rahula, English translation by Sara Boin-Webb (Berkeley: Asian Humanities Press, 2001); Geshe Rabten, *Mind and Its Functions* (Mt. Pelerin: Tharpa Choeling, 1975), 74–94; Mipham, *Gateway to Knowledge* (Hong Kong: Rangjung Yeshe, 1997), Vol. I, 25–29.
5. Herbert V. Guenther and Leslie S. Kawamura, trans., *Mind in Buddhist Psychology* (Emeryville: Dharma Publishing, 1975), 66.
6. Ibid., 66–67; Geshe Rabten, *Mind and Its Functions*, 75–76.

26

MEDITATION IN THE CLASSROOM

What Do Students Say They Learn?

FRAN GRACE

Does meditation help students? How could it not?! I'm glad I have a lifetime ahead of me to fine-tune this practice.

—Carolyn Hedge, student

What do students say they learn in a contemplative classroom? Their remarks may be enthusiastic, as in the opening quote, but do their self-assessed learning outcomes match our professorial and institutional goals for a liberal arts education?

This chapter shares my discoveries and five years of qualitative data from students at the University of Redlands. Students were asked to reflect upon their learning outcomes throughout the semester, in private writing, peer groups, and anonymous formats. By taking stock of their learning in a sequenced manner, they were able to identify their progress or lack of it. Some students were asked to write extended evaluations in narrative form at the end of a course, which I did not see until the following semester. During the span of years presented in this chapter (2004–2009), I also conducted audio-recorded informal conversations with small groups of students in order to invite dialogic synergy in the assessment process. Although the data are suggestive rather than conclusive (pending longitudinal investigation), students are strongly positive about the benefits of meditation and contemplative learning. Even students who failed the courses declared the learning to be uniquely valuable.

This chapter highlights specific learning outcomes from meditation, as per student self-assessment, which match the aims of liberal education according to *College Learning for the New Global Century*, published by the Association of American Colleges and Universities in 2007:[1]

- inner fortitude, self-knowledge, and personal renewal
- disciplined habits of mind and the alleviation of impediments to academic excellence
- ethical cultivation for personal and civic responsibility

Students have given permission to quote from their written and verbal work, and in most cases, to use their real names. Although we have chosen not to identify their philosophical or religious orientations, the reader may be interested to know that the students quoted here represent the following worldviews: agnosticism, atheism, Zen Buddhism, Russian Orthodoxy, Islam, Raja yoga, Self-Realization Fellowship, Latter-day Saints, Protestantism, Catholicism, and Reform Judaism. The quotes I have included represent trends supported by many other such comments I could not incorporate. I thank these students for their willingness to share their insights and discoveries with me and the readers of this book.

INNER FORTITUDE, SELF-KNOWLEDGE, AND PERSONAL RENEWAL

> Meditation is a lot harder than it looks.
> —Kelli Mackenzie

The syllabus description for the Introduction to Meditation course opens: "This course is about what you learn in silence." Students initially dislike the silence; actually, they dislike how unruly their mind is, a fact which the silence allows them to notice immediately.

> [A month into the semester] I still feel anxiety as we meditate in silence. I find myself thinking about all the other work I have to do. [Mid-semester] Today I finally felt a breakthrough. I was able to be silently still and let my mind relax without drifting completely off. I would compare it to a wave near the beach that slowly rolls in, quiet and small and then slowly glides back out into the large ocean.
> —Olivia Elis

A single mother of two children, one with disabilities, started off her Introduction to Meditation course frustrated by stillness: "Who knew sitting still for 40 minutes could feel like *insanity*?!" Over time, however, she observed how the meditation practice taught her to "find an inner peace" she had "lost." She had been feeling "disconnected—like a robot who just gets through the day." A turning point came during one class session when I asked the students to do a contemplative exercise outside called Nature Observation. I told them, "Sit still in one place and see what nature reveals to you about a problem or question you have in your life." Observing the palm trees, this student discovered what was lacking in her life: inspiration. "I feel like the leaves on a palm tree— securely attached at the top, like my fine education I'm getting—but just blowing around, waiting for some true inspiration and direction to strike my life. When the wind stops, the leaves just hang down. I don't want that to be the metaphor for my life." Meditation helped her to reconnect to the purpose of her life.

The Nature Observation exercise, though very simple, can rouse profound existential truth. By observing the dance of sunlight through afternoon clouds, Kevin Vollmer became conscious of the ungraspable nature of his own accomplishments:

> I watched the clouds as they were covering the whole sky. I could see the sun light almost popping through the clouds. The scene was amazing, but it will be gone the next day or next moment. . . . I need to realize that good things will happen for me but to not become cocky or self centered because like the clouds, it will all be gone the next day and something new will be in the picture. I need to humble myself.

Contemplative self-knowledge is difficult for students because it leads inevitably to personal responsibility for their inner world. They see how much easier it is to blame others for their dissatisfaction than take ownership of their own responses. The highly touted goal of "critical thinking" is not actually possible without probing into the nature of one's own inner workings. Critical thinking without contemplative inner inquiry is like a blindfolded archer shooting arrows. We cannot correctly see the faulty logic in the arguments of others until we verify the clarity of our own perceptual lens. Christine Bellows, an art major, said it well: "You must cleanse your mirror in order to see yourself and others with an undistorted view." Hence, the Socratic teaching that self-examination is the philosopher's first step; such rigorous investigation of one's interior reality requires what the Association of American Colleges and Universities calls "inner fortitude":

> It takes a lot of courage to be in the Meditation course. If you view it as an opportunity to grow, then it will bring up some things that may be very difficult for you to handle and face within yourself. Things that you didn't even know were there.   —Kristi Gober

Natalie McDonald, a double major honors student in English and religious studies, remarked on the different sort of rigor required by contemplative learning:

> I've been a good student. I'm smart. I do all the reading for my classes.
> But with this class, it demands so much more. It's probably one of the
> hardest classes I've taken because it asks me to do so much that I've
> never done before—to see what needs to change inside of me—and
> then do it!

Students express deep gratitude to have the opportunity to learn methods of self-
knowledge and personal renewal, because the learning will benefit them for the
rest of their lives. As Kaleena Wakamatsu, a double major honors student in
business and religious studies, observed: "This class has endless value to me. I
will use its knowledge for the rest of my life."

Johnny Gannaw, a government major who was involved as a senator in student government, began the Meditation course with confusion and skepticism:
"I didn't know how to do it. It seemed no different than taking a nap . . . or
thinking about clubs, parties, stupid things I've done, sex, money, homework."
What was the point, he wondered? Then, when he did his first Walking Meditation, he experienced the difference between "being" and "doing," between the
way in which you get somewhere (means) and the fact that you get somewhere
(ends or outcome):

> I am always so busy on campus and always in a jet hurry to get from
> point A to point B. This meditation allowed me to step in places I've
> never been and embrace the beauty around me. What a relief to be
> placed in a situation where the outcome is not the strength but the
> steps taken that hold the power.

He was stunned to realize that he had been a student on the campus for almost
four years, walking over the exact same knoll of grass, but had "not ever really
seen it." He asked the class: "Wouldn't the world be different if our government
leaders took a few minutes every day to do walking meditation?"

Students say they must unlearn cultural programs rooted in the Protestant
ethic that links self-worth with staying busy. Students come to realize that personal
productivity is not sustainable unless it effulges from heart-mind-body wholeness.
What does it matter how much a person gets done if the doing is halfhearted or
drains health? Recent research in cognitive science suggests that multitasking is
inefficient, in fact.[2] In spite of such findings, students often have to articulate the
importance of a mindful lifestyle to parents who are reluctant to pay tuition dollars
for a contemplative course in which "you are doing nothing." Some parents, echo-
ing the dominant cultural belief, see sitting still as a "waste of time."

Amanda Ferguson, sociology major, recounted: "I remember telling my mom about the meditations in class. She was not happy about it and said, 'So I'm paying all this money for you just to sit in silence?' I told her, 'When else do I ever just sit down? I never want to miss that class because it forces me to sit down and pay attention to my body and to what my mind is actually doing.'" Through observing her mind, Amanda connected to a self-correcting capacity to hone her own humanity: "There are things that I was doing and had no idea about. Why was I doing this? Why pick fights with people? Why react this way? And as soon as I sat down and saw it, I understood the reasons and how to fix it." A few moments of stillness, she reported, saved her time in the long run because stillness expedited problem-solving. After the midterm exam for the Seminar on Compassion course, an exam that included a contemplative section on self-awareness, she wrote a letter of thanks: "I absolutely loved this exam. I've never had a class assignment challenge me so much, and I am a different person because of it. Thank you for this opportunity!"

DISCIPLINED "HABITS OF MIND" AND THE ALLEVIATION OF IMPEDIMENTS TO ACADEMIC EXCELLENCE

The documentary film *A Semester* Within: *Exploring Meditation* includes a spontaneous conversation with ten students. I happened to ask them, "You're paying a lot of money to sit in class. Would you say that there are times when you aren't present?" The students laughed quite a lot at this question, immediately acknowledging the waywardness of the mind: "Oh! My mind wanders all the time in class!" They agreed that meditation helps them "get more out of" their academic work because they learn how to "bring the mind back" when a professor is lecturing or other students are talking.[3] An award-winning student in art and mathematics, and excellent athlete in track, Rena Satre-Meloy appreciated the newfound capacity to "be present," which she learned from meditation: "I honestly never realized how I was always somewhere else, thinking about the future or the past or what was going to happen half-an-hour from then. Even though I was there in body, my mind was almost constantly somewhere else. I am so grateful for this heightened awareness." Another student noted how meditation increased his ability to concentrate on homework in spite of noisy surroundings:

> One of the skills I have picked up from meditating this semester is being able to block out interference and focus on what I need to. Previously, when I had to read, do homework or think about something, I would have to be in a completely silent room in order to concentrate. But now I am able to focus on my task even if there is outside noise.
> —Trent Cummins

Meditation appears to sharpen habits of mind as students become aware of the nature of thinking and how to harness the mind's capacities for the pursuit of truth. Students are no longer so subject to mental turmoil, because they know it is like the waves on the surface of the ocean. The students observe that they are able to enjoy mental evenness and vitality even in stressful situations, such as test anxiety and paper deadlines.

> Meditation made me feel completely revitalized. I had to write a paper after our class, and I noticed how quickly and confidently I did it. This class has impacted my ability to think with a peaceful mindset. My mind was always wandering. I am now able to focus.
> —Nathalie Olson-Studler

> I sat down to meditate today just before taking an exam. I did the breathing meditation where I concentrated on the end of my nose. I continued to do this . . . until the worries of the exam lifted away. By the time I took the exam I was calm and fairly at peace. I completed the exam fairly quickly and confidently.   —Erik Diefendorf

The case of Hafsa Ahmed, a senior accounting major, exemplifies the dramatic shift that happens for some students. When she showed up for her first contemplative course, Hafsa appeared to be scattered and fretful. Though an excellent student, she admitted that she had difficulty with attention skills and life balance. By the end of the first meditation course, she had connected to an inner stillness that allowed her to focus her attention when needed. "Meditation taught me to clear my mind. It is difficult to sit and take exams. Sitting in meditation and actually viewing my thoughts has cleared my mind so I can concentrate better." She completed four contemplative courses, a data point on her transcript that evidently impressed the business firm that hired her upon graduation, as per her report.

Students recount that meditation helps them with mental clarity. Jon Geleris, a pre-med biology major, was doubtful that meditation would have any relation to his work as a scientist. However, his first contemplative course convinced him of the power of meditation to improve him as a thinker:

> The Mystics class helped me in my biology major in a way I never could have imagined. Of all the classes I have taken so far, none has improved me as a thinker as much as that class. I realized that science is not just about identifying what others have discovered, but challenging what is believed and discovering the truth.

Another student, Carolyn Hedge, was gratified to realize the authority she now exercised over her own mental capacity: "I'm proud that I'm actually blocking out the irrelevant thoughts and actions." Sean Hansen, an outstanding student and athlete who initially found the stillness of meditation practice to be daunting in light of her proclivity for competitiveness, came to appreciate its clarifying effect: "It felt good to clear my head, even if it was just ten minutes. Focusing on deep breaths as I do homework has helped me, and I think I am calmer overall." Students notice that meditation is more mentally refreshing than taking naps or relaxing with video games or television, a learning outcome that matches the quantitative study done at the University of Kentucky.[4]

> Every time I felt overwhelmed by the stress of papers, I would sit down and meditate. After the meditation I felt re-energized and able to keep working. I only wish I had learned this earlier because when I was stressed before I used to take naps. I would have a really hard time waking up and it would take me forever to get back into the groove of a paper. But when I meditate, I can come back to reality quickly and just restart my work without any delay.   —Garth Sodetani

In addition to honing habits of mind such as focused attention, mental clarity, and inner calm in the midst of turmoil, meditation appears to be highly successful in the alleviation of factors that impede the academic success of students: stress, emotional and psychological problems (eating disorders, anger, self-hatred, depression, anxiety), sleep deprivation, and addiction. The self-assessments from my students correspond with quantitative research on the psychological and health benefits of meditation.[5] Meditation gives students the option to determine their internal responses to uncomfortable situations even though they cannot control the situations themselves.

> Through meditation, I learned that my thoughts don't have to control me. After six years of an eating disorder, I am finally winning. I don't feel like a prisoner any more.   —Ashley McQuown

> Meditation has allowed me to see the pattern of my own thoughts. I now have a greater understanding of where my anxieties come from and how to control them. This gives me confidence as a student.
>   —Kevin McNaney

Some students experience a mitigation of lifelong, self-defeating patterns for the first time. They report that meditation allowed them to take the reins of their functioning into their own hands.

> Sometimes, the rage builds up inside so much I want to explode. But I have learned now not to act. Rather, I can take a deep breath and wait until it's gone. It takes about ninety seconds for the anger to leave.

Every time I feel this way, I go by myself, close my eyes and meditate. I just watch the feelings that make me angry pass by like each thought is a cloud in the sky floating away. Before learning meditation, if I ever felt this way, I would always have to let it out in a physical way . . .
—Anonymous

Meditation has changed me. When my anxiety builds up—a lifelong problem—I know I can center myself in meditation. I don't fret over how I wish things were different any more. This helps me a great deal in all of my personal endeavors.   —Samantha Brzozowski

All of a sudden, it seemed, my life changed. I wanted to do better in school. I got up early, started talking to my parents again, bought a bike and began exercising. I even quit smoking—which I'd tried to do since fourteen. What happened? Through meditation, I began to take control of the filter through which I was seeing myself and others.
—Nathan Vonderau

ETHICAL CULTIVATION:
PERSONAL AND SOCIAL RESPONSIBILITY

Self-knowledge, paradoxically, leads to self-forgetting and thereby becomes the fulcrum to self-transcendence and service to others. Academicians are sometimes disapproving of self-knowledge because they conflate it with "personal opinion" or "personal therapy." However, the feedback from students indicates that contemplative process serves as a sharp spade that uproots personal opinion and, thereby, clears the way for a replacement of the "personal" with the "collective." Rather than self-indulgent, meditation can be self-emptying. The students in my classes report with surprise how their reactions to others become more open-minded and forgiving as a result of meditation. Sean O'Brien, who plans on becoming a police officer, disclosed how meditation helped him to be more patient with others:

Before meditation, I didn't have any patience. I was always in a rush and would be aggravated if people were not on time. Meditation has taught me to get rid of such negativities and be able to enjoy other people, instead of just focusing on myself.

Another student, Brianna Wetteland, reported that meditation helped her to be forgiving toward her family and to face hostile customers at her workplace:

I realized throughout this semester meditating that I had a lot of resentments towards a lot of people in my life, even ones I didn't know well. I was just angry in my thoughts—nice on the outside but on the inside not very kind. Through meditation, I felt myself changing on the inside, becoming more forgiving towards my peers and family. One day at work, a customer told me I "wasn't the sharpest pencil in the box." My immediate reaction was to feel hurt. But then, I wanted to feel compassion for him, so I walked away from the table and breathed in and out a few times. I told myself "This is not about me." When I went back to the table, I looked him in the eye, smiled, and it was genuine.

Paige Sumida chose a compassion practice called *tonglen* (sending and taking, on the medium of the breath) meditation as her most consistent practice outside of class. Since this practice can be done without other people knowing, she discovered it to be the perfect way of expressing compassion to a teammate of hers who was upset but unapproachable:

At tennis practice, everyone was a little sluggish and tired, and all of our bodies were sore from lifting weights the day before. One girl, in particular, was having a rough day. I noticed her posture was down, and her emotional state was negative. I knew that it was a great time to practice *tonglen*, with her obvious suffering. With every breath I took in, I told myself that I was taking in her pain, and, when I breathed out, that I was releasing some healing and positive energy. I could have sworn I saw a difference in her posture and attitude almost immediately. It was as if she realized that she had the power to turn things around, and it was amazing seeing such a change in being.

Meditation teaches students to discern subtle ethical complexities, as the inner practices illuminate the motivations behind their ethical actions. They learn to distinguish the virtue of forgiveness from the vice of resignation; the virtue of loving service from the vice of guilt; and the virtue of compassion from the vices of pitying and rescuing. In the Seminar on Compassion course, their insights often come from applying a particular contemplative practice to their service-learning work in difficult situations: autistic children, abandoned animals, older adults in nursing homes, medically fragile children in crisis care, and rehabilitation centers.

You can be a support for others but you cannot do it for them. And you can't give them the ideas of how to do it, because your idea and your path are different from what theirs would be. It's the hardest thing to be compassionate to others without rescuing them!   —Monica Ek

[Community service with autistic children in a classroom] I started out with sympathy and pity, not compassion. I focused not on the beings that existed in front of me, but rather I saw children who were suffering because of their disabilities and who were going to be facing a difficult world. It was not until we studied Mother Teresa that I realized the arrogance behind this type of compassion. I realized that for months I had been failing to love these kids exactly as they are. I was pinning them down with my sympathetic lens and pitying them for something that they are not even aware of as a burden in their life.
                                                              —Katelyn LaPine

[Community service at a nursing home] I practiced deep listening and tried to block out any self-preoccupied thoughts. At first this was difficult, but as I became more interested, I found it easy to pay attention. Mother Teresa said the poorest of the poor in our nation are the neglected and unloved.   —Caitlin Bonner

[Community service at a shelter for homeless families] I have seen a change in myself that has been evolving since the first week here. At first, I was often overcome with a sense of guilt. However this is not what Gandhi, Mother Teresa and the other exemplars taught. They did not help others out of guilt or fear. I have lost the guilt, and now I open my heart to others, genuinely having a desire to be there with them at the moment to help any way I can. I have seen that we are all trying to avoid the suffering of life.   —Lanie Dubasik

[Community service with medically fragile children in crisis care] I learned to look past the child's disability and love them for who and what they are. Not all of them are able to do the things they want, but that is why I am there. If they like to play video games but cannot use their hands, I am their hands.   —Rosanna Bustamante

Furthermore, students learn to take responsibility for their inner intention. Words and actions are, of course, ethically important. However, spiritual masters such as Mother Teresa emphasize that genuine compassion is fundamentally an *inner* reality: "It is not how much we do, but how much *love* we put into the doing. . . . Do small things with great love."[6] With meditation, students awakened to the power of their very own breath as a vehicle for cultivating compassion in their heart-mind.

[Community service work with abandoned animals] I really like the (*tonglen*) meditation we did in class when we breathed in some of the suffering of the world. So each time that I took a dog out for a walk, I would try and relieve some of its suffering by breathing it in as we were walking, and breathing out hope and healing.   —Mikayla Bruce

[Community service at animal shelter] I could not change the fact that some animals needed to be put down because of aggression or illness but I could change the way I judged those who were involved. Mother Teresa had the biggest impact on my compassion practice. Every time I walked into the shelter I realized that the animals wanted something very simple: love. I couldn't give them a home or all of my time but I could make their day a little brighter. Every second I spent with an animal was a second that they didn't sit in the cage alone.
     —Amber Hurley

[Community service at an Alzheimer's unit] There are a couple women that get very frustrated when they don't understand or when they can't express themselves. One woman, Maria, had never felt comfortable enough to speak to me before, although I could tell that she was having a hard time. As I saw her struggle with a trivia game, I sat next to her calmly and practiced breathing in her suffering. I thought about all of the frustration she must feel, as well as the heartache from recently losing her husband. Soon, I calmly pointed out how to play the game. She turned to me and, for the first time, told me "Thank you." It was the most genuine and heartfelt "Thank you" that I have ever heard.
     —Jennifer Nance

Meditation practice cultivated a reverence for all forms of life, no matter how small. Erik Diefendorf was a double major in history and religious studies whom I often witnessed rushing from one place to another with a cup of coffee in his hand. Near the end of the semester, he experienced a moment of connection with an insect during our Nature Observation exercise.

While I was writing about the grass (which I thought was important), something else happened. A small green insect landed on my finger as I wrote. Normally I would immediately crush it or brush it from my finger, but this time I did not. I looked at it, studying its light green body and the way its two wings made one when together. I didn't have it in me to kill this insect. I became aware of its existence and it of mine. I may never share such acute awareness of power between two

beings in such a way again. In a brief moment that bug was the only
thing I felt connected to.   —Erik Diefendorf

Students struggled to be kind and loving to all forms of life, and without attachment. The Nature Observation exercise instilled a reverence for life, while the
Death Meditation brought an awareness of impermanence, as these students
note:

> The meditation on the decomposition of objects really brings into view
> how impermanent things are. Nothing lasts forever, so why crave it?
> Why obsess over it? I used this meditation practice with the "perfect
> body" image, then later on the Nintendo game cube . . . I don't even
> have time to play video games and yet I crave them. I used this medita-
> tion to watch the game break, rust, decompose, and add pollution and
> junk to the earth. I see that the world is constantly changing, and so
> are we. Why get attached?   —Sarah Longwell

> Meditation has helped me to want fewer things. I am happier with
> what I have right now.   —Anastasiya Nefedova

> [Community service at animal shelter] I have had impermanence
> thrown in my face every day at the shelter. Many times I come in to see
> a dog I made friends with the week before only to find a red line
> through his kennel card—he was put down. The Dalai Lama says:
> "Even though we may not see the results consciously, we still have set
> into motion positive psychological forces."   —Chelsea Crowl

CONCLUSION

In the several years I have been teaching contemplative-based courses, I cannot
ignore the fact that many students refer to their learning of meditation as one
of the most significant assets from their college education. Why are meditation
methods so powerful? My guess is that contemplative teaching activates the
"teacher" *within* them. They learn *self*-mastery, in addition to mastery of subject matter. Self-mastery involves incisive interior practices to liberate the highest excellence from all that would impede it in oneself. Once activated, this
highest excellence becomes the student's most reliable ethical and intellectual
rudder, obviating the need to please others or default to popular opinion. The
famous Zen teacher, D. T. Suzuki: "Teaching is not difficult, listening is not
difficult, but what is truly difficult is to become conscious of what you have in
yourself and be able to use it as your own."[7] Through meditation, students

become conscious of their inner resources and how to channel those resources for the benefit of their intellectual pursuits and the world at large. They begin to embody "the habitual vision of greatness," for themselves and others.[8] By uncovering the source of peace within themselves, they become an avenue of peace to others.

> My major is peace studies. How will I ever be able to negotiate peace among nations if I am not at peace within myself? —Laura Closson

NOTES

1. *College Learning for the New Global Century* (Washington, D.C.: Association of American Colleges and Universities, 2007).
2. J. S. Rubinstein, D. E. Meyer, J. E. Evans, "Executive Control in Cognitive Processes in Task-Switching," *Journal of Experimental Psychology: Human Perception and Performance* 27, no. 4 (2001):, 763–97.
3. Fran Grace (writer, executive producer, director) and Richard Spender (director, co-producer, editor), documentary film, *A Semester* Within: *Exploring Meditation* (2008).
4. Bruce O'Hara, research presented at Society for Neuroscience, Annual Meeting, Washington, D.C., 2005, reported in Alison Motluk, "Meditation Builds Up the Brain," *New Scientist* (November 15, 2005). O'Hara's study at the University of Kentucky demonstrated that students' brain functioning is more enhanced by forty minutes of meditation than by napping, watching TV, reading, or talking.
5. This research is voluminous. Harold Roth and Tobin Hart cite many sources in their chapters for this book. For quick reference, see Sharon Begley, *Train Your Mind, Change Your Brain* (New York: Ballantine Books, 2007); B. Alan Wallace, *Attention Revolution: Unlocking the Power of the Focused Mind* (Boston: Wisdom Publications, 2006); "The Science and Clinical Applications of Meditation," Washington, D.C., 2005, hosted by the Johns Hopkins School of Medicine, Georgetown University, and the Mind and Life Institute (6-disc DVD).
6. Mother Teresa, *Love: The Words and Inspiration of Mother Teresa* (Boulder: Blue Mountain Press, 2007), 28, 61.
7. D. T. Suzuki, "Teacher and Student," *The Inner Journey: Views from the Buddhist Tradition*, ed. Philip Novak (Sandpoint: Morning Light Press, 2005), 125.
8. *The Great Conversation: The Substance of a Liberal Education*, Vol. I, Great Books of the Western World (Chicago: Encyclopedia Britannica, 1952), 2. Thanks to Gabe Valencia.

SELECTED BIBLIOGRAPHY

Abram, David. *Spell of the Sensuous: Perception and Language in a More-Than-Human World*. New York: Vintage, 1996.

Aftanas, Ljubomir, and Semen Golosheykin. "Impact of Regular Meditation Practice on EEG Activity at Rest and During Evoked Negative Emotions." *International Journal of Neuroscience* 115 (2005): 893–909.

Artress, Lauren. *Walking a Sacred Path: Rediscovering the Labyrinth as a Spiritual Practice*. New York: Riverhead Books, 2006.

Association of American Colleges and Universities. *College Learning for the New Global Century*. Washington, D.C.: Association of American Colleges and Universities, 2007.

Austin, James H. *Zen and the Brain*. Cambridge: MIT Press, 1999.

Austin, James H. *Zen-Brain Reflections*. Cambridge: MIT Press, 2006.

Bache, Christopher M. *The Living Classroom*. Albany: State University of New York Press, 2008.

Baer, Ruth A. "Mindfulness Training as a Clinical Intervention: A Conceptual Review." *Clinical Psychology: Science and Practice* 10, no. 2 (Summer 2003): 125–43.

Bartlett, Thomas. "Professors Are More Religious Than Some Might Assume, Survey Finds." *Chronicle of Higher Education* 53 (October 20, 2006): A26.

Beck, Guy. "Hearing the Sacred: Introducing Religious Chant and Music into Religious Studies Teaching." *Spotlight on Teaching/ Religious Studies News* 16, no. 2 (2001): 2.

Begley, Sharon. *Train Your Mind, Change Your Brain*. New York: Ballantine Books, 2007.

Bender, Courtney. "Religion and Spirituality: History, Discourse, Measurement." Higher Education Research Institute of UCLA (January 2007). http://www.heri.ucla.edu/index.php

Benson, Herbert. *The Relaxation Response*. New York: Harper, 2000.

Bishop, Scott, Mark Lau, Shauna Shapiro, Linda Carlson, Nicole Anderson, James Carmody, Zindel Segal, Susan Abbey, Michael Speca, Drew Velting, and Gerald Devins. "Mindfulness: A Proposed Operational Definition." *Clinical Psychology: Science and Practice* 11, no. 3 (Fall 2004): 230–41.

Blook, Howard. *Global Brain*. New York: John Wiley and Sons, 2000.

Bohm, David. *Wholeness and the Implicate Order*. New York: Routledge, 1980.

Bourdieu, Pierre. *Outline of a Theory of Practice*. Translated by Richard Nice. Cambridge and New York: Cambridge University Press, 1977.

Braskamp, Larry A. "Fostering Religious and Spiritual Development of Students during College." Higher Education Research Institute of UCLA (February 2007). http://www.heri.ucla.edu/index.php.

Brown, Sid. *A Buddhist in the Classroom*. Albany: State University of New York Press, 2008.

Burmark, Lynell, and Lou Fournier. *Enlighten Up! An Educator's Guide to Stress-Free Living*. Alexandria: Association for Supervision and Curriculum Development, 2003.

Casey, Michael. *Sacred Reading: The Ancient Art of Lectio Divina*. Liguori: Liguori Publications, 1996.

Chickering, A. W., J. C. Dalton, and L. Stamm. *Encouraging Spirituality and Authenticity in Higher Education*. San Francisco: Jossey-Bass, 2006.

Chryssavgis, John. *In the Heart of the Desert: The Spirituality of the Desert Fathers and Mothers*. Bloomington: World Wisdom, 2003.

Claxton, G. "Thinking at the Edge: Developing Soft Creativity." *Cambridge Journal of Education* 36, no. 3 (2006): 351–62.

Cullen, Lisa Takeuchi. "How to Get Smarter, One Breath at a Time." *Time* (January 16, 2006): 93.

d'Aquili, Eugene, and Andrew B. Newberg. *The Mystical Mind: Probing the Biology of Religious Experience*. Minneapolis: Fortress Press, 1999.

David, Caroline Franks. *The Evidential Force of Religious Experience*. Oxford: Clarendon Press, 1989.

Davidson, Richard, and Anne Harrington, eds. *Visions of Compassion*. New York: Oxford University Press, 2002.

de Wit, Han. *Contemplative Psychology*. Translated by Marie Louise Baird. Pittsburgh: Duquesne University Press, 1991.

Duerr, M., A. Zajonc, and D. Dana. "Survey of Transformative and Spiritual Dimensions of Higher Education." *Journal of Transformative Education* 1, no. 3 (2003): 177–211.

Dustin, Christopher A., and Joanna E. Ziegler. *Practicing Morality: Art, Philosophy, and Contemplative Seeing*. New York: Palgrave Macmillan, 2005.

Edwards, Mark U., Jr. *Religion on Our Campuses: A Professor's Guide to Communities, Conflicts, and Promising Conversations*. New York: Palgrave Macmillan, 2006.

Ekman, Paul. *Emotions Revealed*. New York: Holt Publishers, 2007.

Ekman, Paul, Richard J. Davidson, Matthieu Ricard, and B. Alan Wallace. "Buddhist and Psychological Perspectives on Emotions and Well-Being." *American Psychological Society* 14 (2005): 59–63.

Ellison, Katherine. "Mastering Your Own Mind." *Psychology Today* (Sept/Oct 2006), http://www.psychologytoday.com/articles/200608/mastering-your-own-mind.

Emory University. "Study Conducted on Use of Meditation for Depression (2005)." The Emory-Tibet Partnership. http://tibet.emory.edu/research/index.html (accessed October 2, 2007).

Finkel, David. *Teaching with Your Mouth Shut*. Portsmouth: Boynton/Cook Publishers, 2000.

Freire, Paulo. *Pedagogy of the Oppressed, Thirtieth Anniversary Edition*. New York: Continuum, 2000.

Gimello, Robert. *Mysticism and Philosophical Analysis*. Edited by Steven T. Katz. Oxford and New York: Oxford University Press, 1978.

Glazer, Steven, ed. *The Heart of Learning: Spirituality in Education*. New York: Penguin Putnam, 1999.

Goleman, Daniel. *Emotional Intelligence*. New York: Bantam Books, 1995.

Goleman, Daniel. *The Meditative Mind*. Los Angeles: J. P. Tarcher, 1988.

Goleman, Daniel. *The Varieties of Meditative Experience*. New York: E. P. Dutton, 1977.

Grace, Fran. "Pedagogy of Reverence: A Narrative Account." *Religion and Education* 36, no. 2 (2009):102–23.

Gravois, John. "Meditate on It: Can Adding Contemplation to the Classroom Lead Students to More Eureka Moments?" *Chronicle of Higher Education* (October 21, 2005).

Griffin, David Ray, ed. *Deep Religious Pluralism*. Louisville: Westminster John Knox Press, 2005.

Griffiths, Paul J. *Religious Reading*. New York: Oxford University Press, 1999.

Gunaratana, H. *Mindfulness in Plain English*. Boston: Wisdom Publications, 1993.

Hagerty, Barbara Bradley. *Fingerprints of God: The Search for the Science of Spirituality*. New York: Riverhead Books, 2009.

Haidt, Jonathan. *The Happiness Hypothesis: Finding Modern Truth in Ancient Wisdom*. New York: Basic Books, 2006.

Hall, Thelma, RSC. *Too Deep for Words: Rediscovering Lectio Divina*. Mahwah: Paulist Press, 1988.

Hanh, Thich Nhat. *Being Peace*. Berkeley: Parallax Press, 1987.

Hanh, Thich Nhat. *The Miracle of Mindfulness: A Manual on Meditation*. Boston: Beacon Press, 1976.

Harrington, Anne, and Arthur Zajonc, eds. *The Dalai Lama at M.I.T.* Cambridge: Harvard University Press, 2006.

Harris, J. Irene, Sean W. Schoneman, and Stephanie R. Carrera. "Preferred Prayer Styles and Anxiety Control." *Journal of Religion and Health* 44, no. 4 (Winter 2005): 403–12.

Hart, Tobin. "Opening the Contemplative Mind in the Classroom." *Journal of Transformative Education* 2, no. 1 (2004): 28–46.

Harward, Donald. "Engaged Learning and the Core Purposes of Liberal Education: Bringing Theory to Practice." *Liberal Education* (Winter 2007): 8–10.

Hawkins, David R. *Power vs. Force: Anatomy of Consciousness.* Sedona: Veritas, 1995.

Hawkins, David R. *Realizing the Root of Consciousness: Meditative and Contemplative Techniques* (Audio). Sedona: Veritas, 2002.

Higher Education Research Institute (HERI). *The Spiritual Life of College Students: A National Study of College Students' Search for Meaning and Purpose: Executive Summary.* Los Angeles: University of California, Los Angeles, 2005.

hooks, bell. *Teaching to Transgress: Education as the Practice of Freedom.* New York: Routledge, 1994.

hooks, bell. *Women/Writing/Teaching.* Albany: State University of New York Press, 1998.

Hunt, Valerie. *Infinite Mind: Science of the Human Vibrations of Consciousness.* Malibu: Malibu Publications, 1996.

Jacobsen, Douglas, and Rhonda Hustedt Jacobsen, eds. *The American University in a Postsecular Age.* New York: Oxford University Press, 2008.

James, William. *The Principles of Psychology.* New York: Holt, 1890.

James, William. *The Varieties of Religious Experience.* New York: The Modern Library, 1999.

Johnson, Don Hanlon. *Bone, Breath, and Gesture: Practices of Embodiment.* Berkeley: North Atlantic Books, 1995.

Kabat-Zinn, Jon. *Full Catastrophe Living.* New York: Delacorte Press, 1990.

Kabat-Zinn, Jon. "Influence of Mindfulness-Based Stress-Reduction Intervention on Rates of Skin Clearing in Patients with Moderate to Severe Psoriasis Undergoing Phototherapy UVB and Photochemotherapy PUVA." *Psychosomatic Medicine* 60 (1998): 625–32.

Kadison, Richard. *College of the Overwhelmed: The Campus Mental Health Crisis and What to Do About It.* San Francisco: Jossey-Bass, 2004.

Kaufman, Stewart. *At Home in the Universe.* New York: Oxford University Press, 1995.

Kazanjian, Victor H. Jr., and Peter L. Laurence, eds. *Education as Transformation: Religious Pluralism, Spirituality, and a New Vision for Higher Education in America.* New York: Peter Lang, 2006.

Kirkland, Russell. "Teaching Taoism in the 1990s." *Teaching Theology and Religion* 1, no. 2 (1998): 121–29.

Kumar, Satish. *You Are Therefore I Am: A Declaration of Interdependence.* Darting-ton: Green Books, 2006.

Lakoff, George. *Women, Fire, and Dangerous Things: What Categories Reveal About the Mind.* Chicago: University of Chicago Press, 1987.

Langer, Ellen J. *The Power of Mindful Learning.* Cambridge: Perseus, 1997.

Lazar, Sarah et al. "Functional Brain Mapping of the Relaxation Response and Meditation." *NeuroReport* (May 15, 2000): 1–5.

Lutz, Antoine, et al. "Long-Term Meditators Self-Induce High Amplitude Gamma Synchrony During Mental Practice." *Proceedings from the National Academy of Science* 101, no. 46 (2004): 16369–73.

Maitland, Jeffrey. *Spacious Body: Explorations in Somatic Ontology.* Berkeley: North Atlantic Books, 1995.

Makransky, John. *Awakening through Love.* Boston: Wisdom Publications, 2007.

Marini, Stephen. "Sacred Music in the Religious Studies Classroom." *Spotlight on Teaching/ Religious Studies News* 16, no. 2 (2001): 3.

Marsden, George M. *The Soul of the American University: From the Protestant Establishment to Established Nonbelief.* New York: Oxford University Press, 1994.

Marsden, George M., and Bradley J. Longfield, eds. *The Secularization of the Academy.* New York: Oxford University Press, 1992.

Maryl, Damon. "Introduction." Higher Education Research Institute of UCLA (April 2007). http://www.heri.ucla.edu/index.php.

Miller, James, and Elijah Siegler. "Of Alchemy and Authenticity: Teaching About Taoism Today." *Teaching Theology and Religion* 10, no. 2 (2007): 101–108.

Miller, John P. *Educating for Wisdom and Compassion.* Thousand Oaks: Corwin Press, 2006.

Miller, John P. *The Holistic Curriculum.* Toronto: University of Toronto Press, 2007.

Mind and Life Institute. "The Science and Clinical Applications of Meditation: Dialogues in Washington, D.C.," hosted by the Johns Hopkins School of Medicine, Georgetown University, and the Mind and Life Institute, 2005. 4-DVD set.

Murphy, Michael, and Steven Donovan. *The Physical and Psychological Effects of Meditation.* Sausalito: Institute of Noetic Sciences, 1999.

Nagatomo, Shigenori. *Attunement Through the Body.* Albany: State University of New York Press, 1992.

Nelson, Marcia Z. *Come and Sit.* Woodstock: Skylight Paths, 2001.

O'Hara, Bruce. "Meditation Is Good for the Brain." Presentation at Society for Neuroscience, Annual Meeting, Washington, D.C., 2005.

Palmer, Parker. *The Courage to Teach: Exploring the Inner Landscape of a Teacher's Life.* San Francisco: Jossey-Bass, 1998.

Palmer, Parker. *To Know as We Are Known: Education as a Spiritual Journey*. San Francisco: Harper Collins, 1993.

Palmer, Parker J. "The Violence of Our Knowledge: Toward a Spirituality of Higher Education." The Michael Keenan Memorial Lecture, Berea College, Kentucky, 1993.

Pennington, M. Basil, OCSO. *Lectio Divina: Renewing the Ancient Practice of Praying the Scriptures*. New York: Crossroads, 1998.

Proctor, James, ed. *Science, Religion, and the Human Experience*. New York and Oxford: Oxford University Press, 2005.

Radin, Dean. *Entangled Minds*. New York: Pocket Books, 2006.

Redden, Elizabeth. "Meditative Spaces." Inside Higher Ed.Com (December 3, 2007). www.insidehighered.com/news/2007/12/03/meditation (accessed March 15, 2009).

Redden, Elizabeth. "More Spiritual, But Not in Church." Inside Higher Ed.Com (December 18, 2007). http://www.insidehighered.com (accessed March 15, 2009).

Rein, Glen, Mike Atkinson, and Rollin McCraty. "The Physiological and Psychological Effects of Compassion and Anger." *Journal of Advancement in Medicine* 8, no. 2 (1995): 87–105.

Rendon, Laura. *Sentipensante (Sensing/Thinking) Pedagogy: Education for Wholeness, Social Justice and Liberation*. Sterling: Stylus, 2009.

Rosen, Richard. *The Yoga of Breath: A Step-by-Step Guide to Pranayama*. Boston: Shambhala, 2002.

Roth, Harold D. "Against Cognitive Imperialism: A Call for a Non-Ethnocentric Approach to Cognitive Science and Religious Studies." *Religion East and West* 8 (October 2008): 1–26.

Roth, Harold D. "Contemplative Studies: Prospects for a New Field." *Teachers College Record* 108, no. 9 (2006): 1787–1815.

Rubinstein, J. S., D. E. Meyer, and J. E. Evans. "Executive Control in Cognitive Processes in Task-Switching." *Journal of Experimental Psychology: Human Perception and Performance* 27, no. 4 (2001): 763–97.

Sarbacker, Stuart. "Skillful Means: What Can Buddhism Teach Us About Teaching Buddhism?" *Method and Theory in the Study of Religion* 17, no. 5 (2005): 264–73.

Saylor, Frederica. "Study: Meditation Has Place in Business." *Science and Theology News* (April 2004): 16.

Schmidt, Leigh E. "Spirituality in America." *The Wilson Quarterly* (Autumn 2005): 42–48.

Schwehn, Mark R. *Exiles from Eden: Religion and the Academic Vocation in America*. New York: Oxford University Press, 1993.

Seligman, Martin. *Authentic Happiness: Using the New Positive Psychology to Realize Your Potential for Lasting Fulfillment*. New York: The Free Press, 2004.

Senge, Peter, Otto Sharma, Joseph Jaworski, and Betty Sue Flowers. *Presence: Exploring Professional Change in People, Organizations, and Society*. Cambridge: Society for Organizational Learning, 2004.

Sharf, Robert. "Buddhist Modernism and the Rhetoric of Meditative Experience." *Numen* 42, no. 3 (1995): 228–83.

Sharf, Robert. "Experience." *Critical Terms for Religious Studies*. Edited by Mark C. Taylor. Chicago: University of Chicago Press, 1998, 94–116.

Siegel, Daniel J. *The Mindful Brain: Reflection and Attunement in the Cultivation of Well-Being*. New York: W. W. Norton & Company, 2007.

Simmer-Brown, Judith. "The Question Is the Answer: Naropa University's Contemplative Pedagogy." *Religion and Education* 36, no. 2 (2009): 89–101.

Sivasankaran, Satish. "The Effect of a Six-Week Yoga and Meditation Program on Endothelial Function." Presented at American Heart Association Scientific Sessions, New Orleans, 2004.

Smith, Huston. *Tales of Wonder: Adventures Chasing the Divine, an Autobiography*. New York: Harper Collins, 2009.

Soelle, Dorothee. *Silent Cry: Mysticism and Resistance*. Minneapolis: Fortress Press, 2001.

Solomon, Robert. *The Passions: Emotions and the Meaning of Life*. Indianapolis: Hackett, 1993.

Sommerville, C. John. *The Decline of the Secular University*. New York: Oxford University Press, 2006.

Stahl, Robert J. *Using "Think-Time" Behaviors to Promote Information Processing, Learning, and On-Task Participation: An Instructional Module*. Tempe: Arizona State University Press, 1990.

Stapp, Henry. *Mindful Universe: Quantum Mechanics and the Participating Observer*. Berlin: Springer, 2007.

Stock, Brian. "The Contemplative Life and the Teaching of the Humanities." *Teachers College Record* 108, no. 9 (September 2006): 1760–64.

Strogaz, Steve. *Sync*. New York: Hyperion Books, 2003.

Tacon, Anna M. "Meditation as a Complementary Therapy in Cancer." *Family and Community Health* 26, no. 1 (January-March 2003): 64–74.

Tannen, Deborah. *The Argument Culture*. New York: Random House, 1999.

Targ, Russell, and Jane Katra. "Close to Grace: The Physics of Silent Mind." *Spirituality and Health* (July/August 2003), http://www.spiritualityhealth. com/NMagazine/articles.php?id=3.

Taylor, Jill Bolte. *My Stroke of Insight: A Brain Scientist's Personal Journey*. New York: Viking Press, 2008.

Thompson, Eva. *Between Ourselves: Second-Person Issues in the Study of Consciousness*. Bowling Green: Imprint Academic, 2001.

Tiller, William, Walter Dibble, and Michael Kohane. *Conscious Acts of Creation: Emergence of a New Physics*. Walnut Creek: Pavior Publishing, 2001.

Tobin, Kenneth. "The Role of Wait Time in Higher Cognitive Level Learning." *Review of Educational Research* 57 (Spring 1987): 69–95.

Trungpa, Chögyam. *Shambhala: The Sacred Path of the Warrior*. Boston: Shambhala, 1984.

University of Redlands. Student Reflections from Contemplative-Based Academic Courses, 2007–2009. http://www.redlands.edu/Docs/Student_Reflections_about_Meditation_for_website_11-09%281%29.pdf (accessed February 18, 2010).

Varela, Francisco, Eleanor Rosch, and Evan Thompson. *The Embodied Mind: Cognitive Science and Human Experience*. Cambridge: MIT Press, 1993.

Varela, Francisco J. "Neurophenomenology: A Methodological Remedy for the Hard Problem." *Journal of Consciousness Studies* 3 (1996): 330–49.

Varela, Francisco, and Jonathan Shear, eds. *The View from Within: First-Person Approaches to the Study of Consciousness*. Bowling Green: Imprint Academic, 1999.

Wallace, B. Alan. *Attention Revolution: Unblocking the Power of the Focused Mind*. Boston: Wisdom Publications, 2006.

Wallace, B. Alan. *Contemplative Science: Where Buddhism and Neuroscience Converge*. New York: Columbia University Press, 2007.

Wallace, B. Alan. *Mind in the Balance: Meditation in Science, Buddhism, and Christianity*. New York: Columbia University Press, 2009.

Wallace, B. Alan. *The Taboo of Subjectivity: Toward a New Science of Consciousness*. Oxford and New York: Oxford University Press, 2000.

Wallace, B. Alan, and Shauna L. Shapiro. "Mental Balance and Well-Being: Building Bridges Between Buddhism and Western Psychology." *American Psychologist* 61 (October 2006): 690–701.

Walsh, Roger. "Phenomenological Mapping and Comparisons of Shamanic, Buddhist, Yogic, and Schizophrenic Experiences." *Journal of the American Academy of Religion* 61, no. 4 (1993): 739–69.

Walvoord, Barbara E. *Teaching and Learning in College Introductory Religion Courses*. Malden: Blackwell, 2008.

Weil, Simone. *Waiting for God*. New York: Harper Collins, 2001.

Wilber, Ken, Jack Engler, and Daniel Brown, eds. *Transformations of Consciousness*. Boston: Shambhala, 1986.

Woods, Jennifer . "Study Finds Meditation May Aid Eating Disorders." *Science and Theology News* (May 2004): 15.

Yandell, Keith E. *The Epistemology of Religious Experience*. Cambridge and New York: Cambridge University Press, 1994.

Zajonc, Arthur. "Cognitive-Affective Connections in Teaching and Learning: The Relationship Between Love and Knowledge." *Journal of Cognitive-Affective Learning* 3, no. 1 (2006): 1–9.

CONTRIBUTORS

DALE ASRAEL is Associate Professor in Religious Studies and Transpersonal Psychology at Naropa University in Boulder, Colorado. Previously, she taught music and French in the British Columbia public schools and at The Vidya School, a Buddhist-inspired elementary and high school in Boulder, Colorado. She also serves as an Acharya in the Shambhala Buddhist lineage of Tibetan Buddhism, teaches meditation programs and intensive practice retreats internationally, and trains meditation teachers.

CHRISTOPHER M. BACHE has been Professor of Religious Studies at Youngstown State University in Ohio for three decades and adjunct faculty at the California Institute of Integral Studies in San Francisco. For two years (2000–2002) he was Director of Transformative Learning at the Institute of Noetic Sciences. An award-winning professor, his areas of teaching include Eastern religions, transpersonal psychology, consciousness research, and Buddhism. He is the author of three books: *Lifecycles*; *Dark Night, Early Dawn*; and *The Living Classroom: Teaching and Collective Consciousness*.

BRIDGET BLOMFIELD is Assistant Professor of Islamic Studies at University of Nebraska at Omaha (UNO). She also serves as director of the newly funded Islamic Studies program at UNO. Her areas of expertise include women's studies in religion, Sufism, Shi'ism, and ritual studies. Her dissertation, *The Language of Tears*, is a study of Shi'a Muslim women's religious rituals, particularly those rituals performed during the month of Muharram.

RICHARD C. BROWN is Associate Professor of Contemplative Education, a department that he founded at Naropa University in 1990. He has served as a consultant with the Garrison Institute's Initiative on Contemplation and Education since 2006. As a longtime practitioner of Tibetan Buddhism, he writes and presents about Buddhist views and practices of child and adolescent spiritual development and contemplative teacher education. He is a member of Naropa's Center for the Advancement of Contemplative Education, and has directed the university's contemplative pedagogy seminars for higher education faculty. Recently, he taught contemplative education workshops in Europe and is now consulting on the kingdom of Bhutan's major project to reform public education and teacher training systems.

SID BROWN is Associate Professor of Religion and Director of Environmental Studies at Sewanee: The University of the South. After being introduced to the study of Buddhism through the Antioch Program for Buddhist Studies in Bodh Gaya, India in 1982, Sid Brown received her MA in Religion from Florida State University and her PhD in Religious Studies from the University of Virginia. Her books include *The Journey of One Buddhist Nun*, a biography of a Thai nun, and *A Buddhist in the Classroom*, an exploration of the ethical quandaries, lived experiences, and intimacy of teaching. As a Buddhist practitioner herself, she has benefited from studying under many teachers, including Sister Ayya Khema, Phillip Moffitt, Sally Clough-Armstrong, and Ajahn Thanissaro, and is currently in Spirit Rock's Dedicated Practitioners Program. She has recently won the Teacher of the Year award at Sewanee.

THOMAS B. COBURN is President Emeritus of Naropa University in Boulder, Colorado, where he established the Center for the Advancement of Contemplative Education and became a national leader in contemplative education. Previously he served as Vice President of the University/Dean of Academic Affairs and Charles A. Dana Professor of Religious Studies at St. Lawrence University in Canton, New York. His academic specialty is South and East Asia and the Islamic world. His books are *Encountering the Goddess: A Translation of the Devi-Mahatmya and a Study of Its Interpretation* and *Devi Mahatmya: The Crystallization of the Goddess Tradition*. Coburn contributed to writings about the art of teaching in *Leading from Within: Poetry That Sustains the Courage to Lead*.

JANE COMPSON is Instructor in Philosophy at the University of Central Florida. She teaches courses in Buddhism, religion and medicine, and various types of applied ethics. She was inspired to introduce contemplative techniques into her teaching after attending a retreat for academics organized by the Center for Contemplative Mind in Society, of which she is a member. She now uses contemplative practices in all of her classes and finds them integral to her teaching.

JOHN D. COPENHAVER is Professor of Religion and Philosophy at Shenandoah University. He was trained at The Catholic University of America (MA and PhD), and Fuller Theological Seminary (MDiv). Ordained in the United

Methodist Church, his key areas of academic interest are spirituality, interfaith dialogue, the contemporary dialogue between science and religion, and the philosophy of nonviolence. In 1999 he presented a paper on interfaith peacemaking to the Parliament of World Religions meeting in Capetown, South Africa. In Winchester, he serves as President of the Valley Interfaith Council. In the fall of 2009 he was the faculty leader of the Shenandoah EcoVenture, a partnership of Shenandoah University and filmmakers from The Downstream Project, to produce a documentary film while backpacking with students 150 miles on the Appalachian Trail and then kayaking back down the Shenandoah River. The EcoVenture included contemplative practices for deepening students' affinity with nature.

ANDREW O. FORT is Professor of Asian religions at Texas Christian University in Fort Worth, Texas. He has published three books, *The Self and Its States: A States of Consciousness Doctrine in Advaita Vedanta*; *Living Liberation in Hindu Thought* (ed. with Patricia Y. Mumme); and *Jivanmukti in Transformation: Embodied Liberation in Advaita and Neo-Vedanta*. At TCU, he has been chair of the faculty senate and has won a number of teaching awards, including Mortarboard's Top Prof and the Deans' Award for Teaching.

ANN GLEIG is an Advanced Doctoral Candidate at the Religious Studies Department at Rice University. Her work examines the interface between spirituality and psychoanalysis and the American assimilation of Asian contemplative traditions. She also has a strong interest in innovative pedagogies, particularly those developed within contemplative, feminist, and queer studies.

FRAN GRACE serves as Professor of Religious Studies and Steward of the Meditation Room at University of Redlands, California. Her early academic work explored the oppressive side of religion, exemplified by *Carry A. Nation: Retelling the Life*, featured on the CSPAN Booknotes Program and funded by a Pew Fellowship in Religion and American Religion from Yale. Though her early contemplative training and certification as a spiritual director were guided by Catholic nuns, her contemplative heart found a home when she encountered her spiritual teacher, David R. Hawkins, and the path of Devotional Nonduality. In 2008, she created a documentary film on contemplative teaching: *A Semester Within: Exploring Meditation*. She has been the recipient of several teaching awards and served as Co-Chair of the Teaching Religion Section of the American Academy of Religion.

TOBIN HART is Professor of Psychology at the University of West Georgia. He is co-founder and President of the ChildSpirit Institute, a nonprofit educational and research hub exploring and nurturing the spirituality of children and adults (www.childspirit.net). His work explores human consciousness, especially at the nexus of psychology, spirituality, and education. His most recent books include: *From Information to Transformation: Education for the Evolution of Consciousness* and *The Secret Spiritual World of Children*. Hart is a father, author, teacher, psychologist, and speaker.

DEBORAH J. HAYNES is Professor of Art and Art History at the University of Colorado at Boulder, and former Chair of the department from 1998–2002. In 2003 she began planning and developing a new residential academic program in the visual and performing arts, which is now in its sixth year with 275 students. Haynes is the author of four books: *Bakhtin and the Visual Arts*; *The Vocation of the Artist*; *Art Lessons: Meditations on the Creative Life*; and *Book of This Place: The Land, Art, and Spirituality*. She has also published numerous articles in a variety of scholarly and popular publications on philosophy of art and pedagogy. Her creative work includes drawing and carving words in marble.

LOUIS KOMJATHY is Assistant Professor of Theology and Religious Studies at the University of San Diego and Research Fellow in the Institute of Religion, Science, and Social Studies at Shandong University. He serves as Co-Director of the Center for Daoist Studies and as Co-Chair of the Daoist Studies Group of the American Academy of Religion. His books include: *Title Index to Daoist Collections*; *Cultivating Perfection: Mysticism and Self-Transformation in Early Quanzhen Daoism*; and *Handbooks for Daoist Practice*.

ANNE CAROLYN KLEIN is Professor of Religious Studies, focusing on Buddhism, at Rice University and a founding Director and Resident Teacher of Dawn Mountain Tibetan Temple, Community Center Research Institute in Houston (www.dawnmountain.org). Her books, spanning three of the five Tibetan traditions, include *Knowledge and Liberation*; *Meeting the Great Bliss Queen*; *Path to the Middle*; and *Unbounded Wholeness: Dzogchen, Bon and the Logic of the Nonconceptual* with Geshe Tenzin Wangyal Rinopche. All pertain to the nature of consciousness as understood from a variety of Indian and Tibetan Buddhist perspectives. Her most recent project is a chantable English translation of the Longchen Nyingthig foundational practices, begun under the auspices of an American Council of Learned Societies grant and completed through a grant from the Ford Foundation.

MICHELLE LELWICA is Associate Professor in Religion at Concordia College in Moorhead, Minnesota, where she teaches classes in the areas of religion, culture, gender, and embodiment, including a class on mindfulness practice. Her research has focused largely on the spiritual dimensions of women's troubled relationships to their bodies in the context of American culture. More recently she is exploring embodied/contemplative pedagogy as a subject of scholarly interest and classroom practice.

JOHN MAKRANSKY is Associate Professor of Buddhism and Comparative Theology at Boston College, guiding teacher of the Foundation for Active Compassion, and senior faculty advisor for the Kathmandu University Centre for Buddhist Studies in Nepal. In the American Academy of Religion, John is Co-Chair of the Buddhist Critical-Constructive Reflection Group and faculty instructor for the Luce Summer Seminars on Theologies of Religious Pluralism. His most recent book is *Awakening Through Love: Unveiling Your Deepest Goodness*.

BARBARA (BOBBI) PATTERSON is Senior Lecturer in Religion at Emory University. Her research focuses on Christian spiritual practices, particularly in relation to contemporary issues of the environment, sustainability, and place. With training in cultural studies, feminist theory, psychodynamics, and theology, her academic interests meet at the intersections of symbolism and embodied practices and personal growth and community thriving. An advocate of "scholar citizenship" for faculty and students, she facilitates regional and national workshops and programs on experiential education and community-based teaching and learning. She is an ordained Episcopal priest. Living in Decatur, Georgia, with her husband and dogs, she enjoys kayaking, swimming, and hiking.

LAURIE L. PATTON is Charles Howard Candler Professor of Early Indian Religions at Emory University. Her scholarly interests are in the interpretation of early Indian ritual and narrative, comparative mythology, literary theory in the study of religion, and women and Hinduism in contemporary India. She is the author or editor of seven books, the most recent ones being *Jewels of Authority: Women and Text in the Hindu Tradition*; *Bringing the Gods to Mind: Mantra and Ritual in Early Indian Sacrifice*; and *The Indo-Aryan Controversy: Evidence and Inference in Indian History*. Her translation of the *Bhagavad Gita* has been included in the Penguin Classics Series in the United States. At Emory, she has also served as Winship Distinguished Research Professor in the Humanities (2003–2006); Chair of the Department (2000–2007); and Head of the Religions and Human Spirit Strategic Plan, which, among other projects, created and supported the Initiative in Contemplative Studies at Emory.

HAROLD D. ROTH is Professor of Religious Studies and East Asian Studies at Brown University and is the director of the Contemplative Studies Initiative there. A pioneer in developing contemplative studies as an academic field, Roth is also a specialist in early Chinese religious thought, classical Daoism, the history of East Asian religions, and the comparative study of mysticism and the practice of meditation. His publications include four books, *The Textual History of the Huai-nan Tzu*; *"Inward Training" and the Foundations of Taoist Mysticism*; *Daoist Identity: Cosmology, Lineage, and Ritual* (with Livia Kohn); and *A Companion to Angus C. Graham's Chuang Tzu: The Inner Chapters* (Society for Asian and Comparative Philosophy, 2003) and many chapters and articles in his fields. Along with John S. Major, Sarah Queen, and Andrew S. Meyer, Roth has completed the first complete English translation of the Han dynasty Daoist philosophical compendium, Huainanzi: *The Huainanzi: A Guide to the Theory and Practice of Government in Early Han China, by Liu An, King of Huainan.*

STUART RAY SARBACKER is Assistant Professor of Indian Philosophy and Comparative Religion at Oregon State University. His research centers on the practice of yoga (both physical and contemplative disciplines) in both its historical and contemporary contexts. The author of *Samadhi: The Numinous and Cessative in Indo-Tibetan Yoga*, he has also published articles on teaching and served as Co-Chair of the Yoga in Theory and Practice Consultation of the American Academy of Religion.

JUDITH SIMMER-BROWN is Professor of Religious Studies at Naropa University in Boulder, Colorado, where she is one of the founders; she is also an Acharya in the Shambhala Buddhist lineage and Dean of the Shambhala Teachers' Academy. She specializes in Indo-Tibetan Buddhist texts and history, American Buddhism, interreligious dialogue, and contemplative education. She was a member of the Cobb-Abe Christian-Buddhist Theological Encounter for twenty years, and currently serves on the steering committee of the American Academy of Religion's Buddhist Critical-Constructive Reflection group. She has published many articles, and the book, *Dakini's Warm Breath: The Feminine Principle in Tibetan Buddhism.*

ROBERT A. F. THURMAN is the Jey Tsong Khapa Professor of Indo-Tibetan Buddhist Studies at Columbia University, and he also serves as the president of Tibet House and a teacher at Menla Mountain Retreat and Conference Center. As a former Buddhist monk closely associated with the Dalai Lama, he has been instrumental in translating Buddhism for a Western audience. Among his many publications are *The Smile of the Buddha*; *Anger*; *The Central Philosophy of Tibet*; and *Why the Dalai Lama Matters.*

KRISTINE T. UTTERBACK is Associate Professor of Religious Studies and History at the University of Wyoming, where she has taught since 1986. Her research interests include contemplative education, Jewish-Christian relations in medieval Christian Spain and world Christianity, with a special interest in Hong Kong. She is the author of *Pastoral Care and Administration in Mid-Fourteenth Century Barcelona: Exercising the 'Art of Arts'.*

SHU-CHIN WU is Assistant Professor of Asian History and Co-Director of the Asian Studies program at Agnes Scott College. She is also a board member of ASIANetwork. Her research and teaching interests include modern Chinese social and intellectual history, ancient Chinese thought, the representation of history in film and literature, the Vietnam War, and theory and practice of history.

INDEX